About the Book

Rock guitarist, composer, producer, and musical mentor: Domenic Troiano was one of the greatest Canadian musicians of his generation. Starting out in the 1960s Toronto club scene with Robbie Lane & the Disciples and Rompin' Ronnie Hawkins, Domenic made his musical mark with the Five Rogues, the Mandala, Bush, the James Gang, and the Guess Who. Along the way, he would share the stage with legends like Eric Clapton, David Foster and Carlos Santana. What remained constant was Domenic's desire to be the best that he could be: a guitarist extraordinaire, an accomplished composer and arranger, a musical explorer on a never-ending quest.

Domenic Troiano – His Life and Music, captures his career and character, from his youth to his final days and his legacy. Featuring submissions from more than 180 colleagues, friends, family and fans, Mark Doble and Frank Troiano have thoroughly chronicled Domenic's musical adventures as well as the profound influence he had on those he encountered throughout his career.

With a foreword by fellow guitarist Alex Lifeson of Rush and a complete listing of Domenic's discography and television film credits, *Domenic Troiano – His Life and Music* is an authoritative and comprehensive account—an essential reference for anyone interested in him and his work.

"There are a lot of musicians that are proficient at many different genres of music. Then there are those few who are great at many different genres. This was one of the many gifts D.T. had in abundance. From the incomparable sounds of the Mandala, to the progressive intellectual, Bush, to the high-octane sounds of the rock group The James Gang, and of course everyone's favourite the Guess Who, Donnie could cover it all with ease, grace and pure talent! I had the honour and pleasure of witnessing this talent up close when, for a brief time, we played in the same band together, though mostly I was just a fan, marvelling at this huge Canadian talent. Thank you, B. J. Cook for bringing Donnie into my life, and thank you, Donnie Troiano for gracing us with your monster talent! You made all of us Canadians very proud!"

- **David Foster, composer, arranger, record producer, and music executive**

"In the early sixties when I joined Ronnie Hawkins and the Hawks, there was one young guitar gunslinger around who impressed me. Domenic pulled guitar tricks outta me I had picked up down south that I never shared with anybody. I could tell he had the magic—and he had it in spades."

- **Robbie Robertson, guitarist, songwriter, The Band, Bob Dylan, solo artist**

"Domenic Troiano was everywhere! He was in my favourite Toronto bands from Robbie Lane and the Disciples to the Mandala (my absolute fave!) to Bush. He was all over my teenage rock landscape and was so much better than anyone else on that instrument in our town that someone, somewhere was always talking about him! Then I went from fan to maker, starting my career working at Nimbus 9 Productions with the father of Canadian production, Jack Richardson, who happened to be the producer of the Guess Who and—sure enough—Donnie showed up there too! And did I mention that I'd been a huge James Gang fan? Well, you know the rest of that story."

- **Bob Ezrin, producer—Pink Floyd, Peter Gabriel, Alice Cooper, and many others**

"He lifted the band from what was a good, well-known band to a better musically and more popular group—one of the best bands in Canada. Domenic took our band to another level. Whitey and the Roulettes knew how to rehearse, but not to the intensity that Domenic pushed us. He wanted every note precise right down to a T. It was good for us and we enjoyed his leadership. It was great."

-   **George Olliver, lead vocalist—the Mandala**

"Donnie set musical goals and he wouldn't stop until they were achieved. He, as our musical leader, made almost all the decisions as to the song layouts, breaks, etc. He was decades ahead of us in musical ability, knowledge, and foresight, and he made such a difference in our live show. Sometimes I would sit and watch him play and it was truly magical."

-   **Robbie Lane, lead vocalist—Robbie Lane and the Disciples**

"So, we're doing three or four days at the 'Whiskey,' opening for some band called the Mandala. The first night, it was all local musicians and the place was full. The second and third nights, there were lineups, because word spread really fast. That kind of R & B, nobody in , let alone , was playing that kind of stuff. And they killed it! And that's how I met the Mandala in Los Angelos, long before I ever had a clue they were from Toronto!"

-   **Bob Segarini, singer-songwriter, broadcaster, writer**

"Donnie and I worked together in the Ronnie Hawkins Band early on. In 1965, I had a hit record, but my band had broken up. But Donnie had a band and we all knew each other, so they teamed us up. All you had to do was listen to him play once and you knew—you knew that this guy was a special kind of musician. He was the first guy that I ever saw playing with all four fingers—his dexterity and his style—he was a 'schooled' guitar player. He had obviously studied it. The rest of us were just barroom, pick-it-up self-taught blues players. He had a whole lot more musicality than we did! Donnie was very special; very important. He was a great guy! He is so missed."

-   **David Clayton-Thomas, lead vocalist—Blood, Sweat & Tears, solo artist**

"I moved to Toronto in 1977 ... my producer was Gary Katz, and he asked me about Dom the great guitar player from Toronto. Gary was Steely Dan's producer and just loved Domenic's playing. I know they worked together when Gary, Donald, and Walter Becker moved back to New York from L.A. I remember calling Gary on many occasions after I moved back to Toronto in 1990 and he would answer the phone 'how are you Dom,' and I'd have to say, 'Gary, it's Marc Jordan.' 'Oh,' Gary said, 'Toronto number ... I thought it was Domenic.' Then he'd launch into a story about Domenic, the gentle man from Toronto who played his ass off and everyone knew he was the man."

- **Marc Jordan, singer-songwriter/guitarist**

"We'd met him before, in the late sixties in New York when we were doing session work for Gary Katz. He had just done a couple years with a popular 'blue-eyed' soul unit, the Mandala. We were both knocked out by his beautiful technique and the energy he brought to the session. He could do it all—startling licks, clear octave lines, driving rhythm parts—whatever the party called for. Everyone wanted to play with Dom. When we were starting up Steely Dan, he was one of the first guys we called. Dom said thanks, but he was just too busy."

- **Donald Fagen, lead vocalist/band leader—Steely Dan**

"... He had just started his new band, Bush. Donnie and I hit it off right from the get-go. We were a couple of hot, young guitar players and we ended up spending a lot of time together ... We traded ideas; we learned from each other, there was no competition but only the sharing from each other's bag of tricks ... Domenic's guitar playing was way ahead of its time. He melded radically different genres into his own unique style. He was dedicated, multifaceted, and a very gifted guitarist. He could play anything!"

- **Elliot Randall, guitarist/session musician—Steely Dan, Peter Frampton, the Doobie Brothers, and many others**

"Sometimes when you're a kid, an early teenager, in our case in west-end Toronto, the local guys that make it are bigger than life, bigger than anything you have ever heard including the Beatles, the Stones. Domenic Troiano and the Mandala were like that to us. Domenic showed us that anything was

possible if you were dedicated enough ... his style, his Tele, he was it, he was our guitar hero ... ours."

- **Tom Cochrane, singer-songwriter/guitarist/recording artist**

"Recording 'The Joke's on Me' album with Domenic was a real thrill; backed by a first-class rhythm section—it was a fusion of R & B and prog rock. Even though he had many big successes to his credit, he was still a very calm, grounded individual who played a mean guitar, was very philosophical about his success and happy to offer good advice—great memories of a true gentleman."

- **Terry Brown, producer/engineer—Rush, Blue Rodeo, Max Webster, and many others**

"Guitarists such as Tommy Tedesco (Wrecking Crew), Eric Clapton, and many others would watch Donnie play live whenever possible to try and understand his complex technique. Donnie had developed a special thumb pick with a flat pick epoxied to it, which allowed him to play multiple parts at the same time. He would be playing a lead riff, and on top of that he would play a harmonics riff one octave higher at a faster pace and coupled with his special guitar electronics—the end result was a very unique, soulful and intensely emotional sound. Most guitarists watching him would need to see his performance in slow motion in order to better understand the complexity of his technique. Donnie was a visionary, well ahead of his time, his stage performances magical. He was a guitar god and no one could come close to playing like him! People like him only come along once every hundred years."

- **Bruce Winfield Brown, musician/recording engineer**

"The Stampeders arrived in Ontario in the summer of 1966. We performed at a large venue called The Broom & Stone, opening for The Five Rogues. We opened, playing mostly cover tunes, wearing our matching black cowboy hats and denim outfits, including matching ankle style cowboy boots. We were politely accepted by the crowd who seemed to know something we didn't. We found out when the Rogues went on—with lead singer George Olliver holding court, Whitey Glan on drums, Joey Chirowski on keys, Don Elliot on bass, and the incomparable Domenic Troiano on guitars and vocals. They

were mesmerising, teasing the crowd to join their Soul Crusade with each member contributing, including a well-timed light show. Working the crowd up to a fevered pitch—I think they did several encores. At the end of the night the whole band pitched in to help the crew load their gear into the truck. We thought that was very classy, having no crew of our own."

- **Ronnie King, singer-songwriter/bassist—the Stampeders**

"Remarkably, his signature virtuoso style was as rhythmic as it was melodic! The precision of his articulation and the cadence of his rhythm playing were as tight as it gets, and he locked in with the swing of the drums like no one else. Dom's lightning fast flourishes, slow steamy grinds, and riffs of all shapes hung on every beat of every bar. His Memphis R & B roots were on full display every time he mesmerized an audience with his wizardry. The only thing more incredible than Dom's talent was his generous spirit, his humility, and the gracious respect he showed others."

- **Gil Moore, drummer—Triumph, founder/owner—**
  Metalworks Studio & Music School

"We stayed in touch, played on a couple gigs, or sessions in Toronto. He always got in touch if he was in NYC or when I was in Toronto. Donnie knew the business! Man, he was a true professional, deservedly really busy his whole career, and we didn't see that much of each other as time moved on, since we were both so active as 'studio cats' and touring, in our own spheres, but he was an unforgettable human being, all sweetness and music ... and taken from us way too soon."

- **Randy Brecker, trumpeter/composer/producer—**
  The Brecker Brothers

"Domenic was a living legend to me. When I was a teenager in the sixties, rumours circulated about Donnie's mythic Fender Telecaster being baked in his mother's oven, with a coating of floor wax, which gave it that amazing tone! We heard that Domenic Troiano actually slit a speaker in his Traynor amp with a razor blade, to give it that great sound! Of course, this is what happens, from the dynamic excitement generated by an immense *talent—apocryphal swirls and eddies form in its wake. It took us all a few more years to figure out that amazing tone and great sound come from the head, the heart, then out through the hands."*

- **Rik Emmett, guitarist/singer-songwriter—Triumph**

"Donnie was a god to us! For years, every time I ran into Dom I would sheepishly introduce myself to him. Finally, one day, I started my usual reintroduction and he stopped me by saying, 'Greg, I know who you are.'"

- **Greg Godovitz, author/bassist/singer-songwriter—Goddo**

"Donnie was a kind, gentle, and very sensitive man. He wasn't a know-it-all, nor was he narrow-minded, but in fact he was open-minded, smart, modest and inquisitive. At times he was embarrassed by the kudos he received for his talents and achievements. Musically he was unafraid, spontaneous, and I personally witnessed some unbelievable 'guitaring' during the times that we got together to jam. He was my dear, dear friend and I think of him every day."

- **Eric Mercury, singer-songwriter/recording artist**

"I realize now what an interesting bond we had. We were on the same page on so many things. Donnie liked having someone he trusted with whom he could share things, sometimes deep personal thoughts other than music. So many of our conversations seemed to commence with one of us asking rhetorically, 'Do you believe this shit?' or, 'what do you think about ...' The fact we had that kind of relationship for so long is special to me."

- **Roy Kenner, lead vocalist/songwriter—R.K. and the Associates, the Mandala, Bush, James Gang, Troiano**

Domenic was one of the finest talents, one of the greatest gentlemen, an irreplaceable original! When Domenic came into the Guess Who, we stepped up our game. It was wonderful. If you listen to some of the things that we produced on those albums, and listened to the music, and listened to the chord progressions, you have to get excited about it. And if you don't, you're not a musician! I don't know what you are. I'm sorry we didn't have more time both personally and musically.

- **Garry Peterson, drums & percussion – The Guess Who**

"I first met Donnie in 1982 at the Club Bluenote on Pears Avenue in Toronto. I was in the original house band there, Gangbuster. We hit it off instantly … Donnie was one of those guys that all the musicians liked, regardless of style of music. You could sense his constant search for new sounds, to push himself further. He was never in a rush, and took his time with everything. He never learned to read or write music, so there were no charts. He'd just play it for you."

- **Lou Pomanti, keyboard player/producer/composer—The Dexters, Blood, Sweat & Tears**

"My partner Grant and I opened a guitar specialty shop on Kingston Road in Toronto. On one occasion, I handed Donnie back his BC Rich guitar that was just set up. He was in quite a hurry on his way to a session and just quickly ripped off one of his killer licks to check it out. I was in awe. He suddenly stopped hurrying and took his time to slowly show me several times how to play that lick. He made sure I had it before he left.

Last week I was with a guitarist friend on our farm discussing music and why the good old days' music was so much more appealing, and why the modern cookie cutter stuff doesn't cut it for us. I showed my friend that lick Donnie showed me in the late seventies. It was the music that didn't get killed by the cookie cutters. Originality and soulful guitar delivered by a true master and a really nice guy."

- **Dan Charman, guitar-tech, Twelfth Fret Guitar Pro Shop**

He was a big influence on my music and I developed as a musician. Donnie was one of those guys who made everybody better! He probably turned the Guess Who into the tightest live act that we had ever been. And he was a really great guy!

- **Bill Wallace, singer, songwriter, bassist – The Guess Who, Crowcuss, Kilowatt**

To Jim
Enjoy!

FE Troiano

DOMENIC TROIANO

HIS LIFE AND MUSIC

WRITTEN BY

MARK DOBLE
FRANK TROIANO

FOREWORD BY

ALEX LIFESON

 FriesenPress

Suite 300 - 990 Fort St
Victoria, BC, V8V 3K2
Canada

www.friesenpress.com

ISBN
978-1-03-910616-1 (Hardcover)
978-1-03-910615-4 (Paperback)
978-1-03-910617-8 (eBook)

1. Biography & Autobiography, Composers & Musicians

Distributed to the trade by The Ingram Book Company

TABLE OF CONTENTS

Foreword   xiii

Chapter 0: Mellow Carmelo Palumbo   1

Chapter 1: 356 Sammon Avenue   13

Chapter 2: My Old Toronto Home   33

Chapter 3: Opportunity   57

Chapter 4: Rock and Roll Madness   79

Chapter 5: The Wear and the Tear on My Mind   97

Chapter 6: Passin' Thru   119

Chapter 7: Power in the Music   143

Chapter 8: Independence   169

Chapter 9: Changing of the Guard   189

Chapter 10: All I Need is Music   209

Chapter 11: We All Need Love   229

Chapter 12: Your Past Is a Part of You   251

Discography: Singles   269

Discography: Albums   273

Unreleased Demos and Live Recordings   279

Domenic Troiano: Scoring Credits   289

Additional Tributes   291

Photo Credits   301

Authors' Acknowledgments   303

About the Authors   307

FOREWORD

"Then one day, he bought a guitar
Lightning struck, and now he's come so far with
Fret Fever, how that boy loved his guitar
Fret Fever, everybody knew he had to be a star"
(Fret Fever; Lyrics by Domenic Troiano)

Alex Lifeson, Domenic Troiano, 2000 (Troiano Family Archives)

The first time I met Domenic (Donnie) Troiano was at Centennial Arena on June 30, 1967, the eve of Canada's centennial year. The Mandala was headlining a four-act bill in the new arena, and it was the place to be. They had a stellar year and were easily the hottest band on the Toronto scene and a must see for any music fan, especially a thirteen-year-old budding guitarist with big dreams.

At the show, I hooked up with lots of friends from school and watched all the opening bands, although I have no recollection of them—I was there to see the Mandala, but most importantly, to watch Donnie play his Telecaster and hear his amazing tones. He was the first guitarist I'd seen utilizing a distortion pedal and it blew my young mind. As I watched him play with such abandon, I remember envying his skill and confidence, characteristics that were rare at my level of experience! Yet he made it look so easy and fun.

After they finished their set, I wandered over to the stage's left wing that was barricaded by the hockey boards, and waited to catch a glimpse of Donnie and hopefully have an "opportunity" to let him know how much I admired him, like it would matter coming from some random kid, but it did matter! As I waved and didn't expect much in return, he walked over to me and accepted my compliments humbly and graciously. We chatted for a bit and I mentioned that I had just started playing guitar and how much I loved it and how it had become the central focus in my life. He said it was the best thing in the world and that I should keep practicing and learning because it wasn't easy to become a great player. He didn't speak down to me, a thirteen-year-old fan, but rather spoke to me in a way that made me feel like I actually was a guitarist, and that was so uplifting. He gave me an autograph, a guitar pick, and a Mandala button I wore for ages. He could have just ignored me, but instead spent his time lifting the spirit of a stranger who would embark on an incredible journey of his own, playing a guitar.

It wasn't until many years later that our paths crossed again. He was the musical director at an awards event in 1990 when Rush received an Artist of the Decade (1980) award. I remember seeing Donnie on the stage, and I couldn't wait to remind him of our first encounter twenty-three years earlier. We both shared a good laugh about the power of fate and its unexpected pathways. We met again a decade later when we played together at the Capitol Theatre in Toronto in an environment that was home to us both—a dressing room filled with great musicians, greater stories, and beer!

We connected again from time to time, mostly at The Orbit Room, and it was always a treat to be in his presence. Before he passed in May of 2005, I was fortunate to be able to visit with him in hospital along with Bernie LaBarge, another great guitarist and personal influence that grew up a fan of Donnie's and became a close friend of his as well. We were both drawn to Donnie's integrity, work ethic, wit, and intelligence. He was a great role model and we were so lucky he came into our lives.

And now, in these pages, he will come into yours as well.

- Alex Lifeson, founder, guitarist/composer—Rush

Domenic playing his 1963 Fender Telecaster 2004 (Photo: Gary Taylor)

MELLOW CARMELO PALUMBO

"Cross Country Man, driving your car
Sometimes driving close, sometimes driving far
Where will your travels take you today
Starting in Toronto, driving out to L.A.
What makes you keep on driving—driving your car all day,
Cross Country Man
(*Cross Country Man*, lyrics by Domenic Troiano)

Roy Kenner, Domenic Troiano, Carmelo Palumbo 1969 (Troiano Family Archives)

Everything is everything, man! (Carmelo Palumbo)

1

Through "coke-bottle" glasses, he gazes quizzically, sifting through the wreckage of scattered equipment, amps, pre-amps, cables, and guitar cases. The car's a write-off; the trailer is almost destroyed, and the cabinets are split and broken. Someone has to put all this stuff back together and make sure it works at showtime. Someone simply has to do it. That someone is the road manager, Carmelo Palumbo.

I met Carmelo through Joey Chirowski. He came to the Bluenote in 1965 and started working for us as a roadie, P.A. and "light man," and all-around Man Friday. Carmelo was a unique and very misunderstood individual. I always felt he was born in the wrong time. He was too trusting and too innocent for the twentieth century. Of course, that's part of what made him special.
-   Domenic Troiano; personal journal

He was probably more experimental with drugs than the rest of us. He was more of an exploratory kind with that, so that he could expand his mind.
-   Roy Kenner, lead vocalist; interview with Mark Doble,
    September 14, 2020

Dom had a real soft spot for Carmelo, as did I. Some say the "Chong" character of Cheech and Chong was modelled after Carmelo. Not a stretch at all—they were identical. I hired Carmelo for my band; he was the subject of the B side of the Mandala's single, Love-Itis—called *Mellow Carmello Palumbo*—a great, wacky track that Donnie absolutely nailed as the most perfect musical description of Carmelo.
-   Peter Cardinali, bassist and president of Alma Records;
    email to Frank Troiano, October, 2020

In the spring of 1970, Canadian-born Tommy Chong had a one-man comedy act that opened for Bush at the Irma Hotel in L.A., where he met Carmelo Palumbo. There are those who believe Chong's 70s stoner-dude persona made famous in films and live performances by the comedy duo Cheech and Chong is modelled after Carmelo ... both characters are strikingly similar.

His attitude was very "outside the boundaries"—but he was still likeable. Everything he said was very mellow. He was very much of a comedian, always had us laughing at his jokes. He was a great guy and we loved to have him as part of the band.
- George Olliver, lead vocalist; interview with Mark Doble, September 28, 2020

Carmelo had this kind of prescient gift. He could read people really well. Carmelo had an intuitive feel for people in a situation. It got to the point where you really paid attention to it when he would say, "Hey man, you know this guy or this situation doesn't feel right." And he'd be right pretty well every fuckin' time. He had a heightened intuitive nature.
- Roy Kenner, lead vocalist; interview with Mark Doble, September 14, 2020

"Mellow" Carmelo Palumbo was a different dude. He and "the weed" were seldom apart. The guys were nervous that he would get them into trouble. There's the sixties-psychedelic instrumental, *Mellow Carmello Palumbo* from the SOUL CRUSADE album that Domenic named after him. Domenic loved him dearly.

Carmelo was as much a part of the Mandala and Bush as anyone in the band. He was a very creative and musical "light man." He had an uncanny knack of fixing things he didn't really understand.
- Domenic Troiano; personal journal

I also heard Carmelo speaking on the phone to a University of Toronto science professor about his plan for perpetual motion. The professor kept him on the phone for over an hour, but Carmelo never followed up. Behind his look and the hippie mentality everyone loved about him, he was an extremely smart man.
- Peter Cardinali, bass guitarist – the Dexters; email to Frank Troiano, October, 2020

He had crazy eyes behind his thick-lensed spectacles. Legally blind, Carmelo used to drive the equipment van until he went through a set of traffic lights in a vicious rainstorm in Cleveland.

Well, he's a sweetheart of a guy, I can tell you that! He's got a heart as big as the great outdoors. He was very tight with Donnie. We worked together for a long time. Carmelo was, for the most part, a pretty quiet guy, but as strong as a bull. He was a really good worker, dedicated to what he was doing, and he very much loved Donnie.

- Blaine Pritchett, sound technician; interview with
  Mark Doble, September 14, 2020

Sweet. Blaine, as well as Prakash John and Roy Kenner, all used the same adjective. It was Carmelo who approached Donnie about bringing Blaine on as part of the crew, even offering to personally take a pay cut so the band could afford it. Because that's just the kind of guy he was.

How Donnie got attached to Carmelo, I don't recall the genesis of that, but the two of them were really close. He was sort of like the original "beatnik" if you will, and the 60s kind of laid back hippie. He was kind of a combination of those two things, but naturally so. That was just his disposition. He had a big fuckin' smile, I remember that. He was so laid back, it was insane, but he was also very responsible, which sounds like a contradiction.

- Roy Kenner, lead vocalist; interview with Mark Doble,
  September 14, 2020

If you were in Domenic's band in any capacity, you were "family." If you talk to the folks today who were with Domenic Troiano in the studio, on the stage, or on the road you will be hard-pressed to find someone who didn't appreciate this sense of loyalty, and in turn, loved him for it! This was true for Carmelo Palumbo, who also happened to be along for the ride in 1971 in the station wagon on that fateful road trip to Vegas.

A deafening crash! The equipment trailer jackknifed with the station wagon, sliding off the road, hurtling through the air—complete disorientation, and then … the crash. Suddenly sitting there in the station wagon, almost upside-down and sideways in the Nevada desert, it was eerily quiet. Guitarist/leader Domenic Troiano, lead vocalist Roy Kenner, bassist Prakash John, organist Hughie Sullivan, and the roadie, Carmelo Palumbo, all of them band members, each thinking three things (in no particular order): I am still alive … get out of the car … and, what's happened to our gear?

The car had not totally flipped over. The trailer and the car jackknifed. I remember that. The car ended up on its side. I remember thinking, "What the fuck happened here? Once we came to a stop, I knew that I was OK. I didn't know about anybody else. I don't recall who said, "We gotta get out of the car."
- Roy Kenner, lead vocalist; interview with Mark Doble, September 14, 2020

Bush was the group that evolved out of the Mandala in 1969. In contrast to the Mandala's dynamic and dramatic psychedelic musical persona focused on visual impact and special effects, Bush was four guys playing music really, really well, as if their backs were to the audience. After writing and rehearsing in Arizona in the summer of '69, they had settled in Los Angeles, recording a terrific album which they were now promoting through a seemingly endless North American tour.

Opening acts are not paid well. Bush was the opening act for hit record headliners like Three Dog Night and Steppenwolf, whose fans quite honestly did *not* come out to hear the guys in Bush jam for thirty minutes on songs they had never heard before. It was hard. Exhaustion and frustration from the work and lack of funds was setting in. Emotions were coming out at the seams. The signs of disintegration were there, as the guys headed for a two-week residency in Las Vegas at a club called the Pink Pussycat-a-Go-Go, where they would "headline" a gruelling graveyard shift from 2:00 a.m. through to 8:00 a.m. for two weeks straight.

We're on our way to Vegas; this would probably be May of '71. And Bush and Hughie Sullivan, who used to be in the Mandala—our organ player, he wasn't in Bush. He had come back down to the States, but he was going through a real depressing time in his life. He wanted to be in the band again, so we said, "What the hell? It's Hughie." So alright, we get him into the band. So, we're going to Vegas, ostensibly to make some money (because we were broke) and to work Hughie in. On the Monday, on the way down, we get into a car accident—wipe out the car—our

equipment is strewn all over the desert basically. Miraculously, no one got hurt, but the car was a total write-off.

- Domenic Troiano; interview with Martin Melhuish, February, 1996

Roy Kenner was driving, with Domenic riding shotgun. In the back seat behind Roy was Prakash John, the bass player of the group, who had been behind the wheel all the previous night. Hughie Sullivan was in back behind Domenic. Between Prakash and Hughie, sat Carmelo.

I was so mad at Roy. I'd just friggin' told him! I'd been driving the whole night, and I just couldn't drive further. Donnie was worried I couldn't drive any more, and of course Roy comes in and I tell him not to let the trailer get caught between these other big vehicles. But you finally relent and let Roy get behind the wheel, and where does he put you?

- Prakash John, bass guitarist—Bush; interview with
  Mark Doble, September 14, 2020

Prakash's recollection of what would turn out to be a pivotal episode in the storied history of Bush is consistent with Roy's.

We ended up in the car on our side. It was really silent. I thought what probably everyone else in the car thought: "I'm the only one alive and everyone else is dead." We came off that highway doing seventy-five with the bloody trailer hammering on the side (it was jackknifed). And when it was silent, we all thought … and then we all started talking at the same time and we had to open the side window and climb out of it. I looked up the side of the ridge we had come down and at the people looking down on us, and the next thing you know, Donnie's inspecting the trailer and he discovers his Telecaster case is smashed, but the Tele's in order, and the Gibson SG—the case was intact, but the neck had snapped off. Then of course he's chasing Roy down the rest of the hill to kill him, and I remember thinking, "Go ahead, Donnie! Don't let me stop you!"

- Prakash John, bass guitarist—Bush; interview with
  Mark Doble, September 14, 2020

For Donnie, what mattered most was his guitar. His Telecaster was an extension of his being. It was part of who he was. And if it was damaged, heaven help Roy Kenner.

I was driving the station wagon. I had just passed some trucks and got hit by a crosswind and the trailer started fishtailing and then we crashed into the desert. We climbed out of the vehicle unscathed, but the trailer was damaged and certain cabinets had split. Donnie was checking out the two guitar cases. He was not happy. The SG case looked perfect. Donnie opened up the case and the neck of the guitar had snapped off. The Telecaster case looked like a rat had been chewing on it. He started to open that case, and I started to run into the desert as Donnie yelled, "If the Tele is busted, I'm gonna kill ya!" A few minutes later, I heard, "You can stop running now, the Telecaster is OK!" Donnie just looked at me and shook his head for the umpteenth time. He did that a lot with me. He would either laugh *with* me or *at* me—most of the time *at* me! He did that so much, I'm surprised I didn't give him permanent whiplash.
-   Roy Kenner, lead vocalist; interview with Mark Doble,
    July 4, 2020

Carmelo was a big man and powerful. Prakash recalls Carmelo pounding a nail with his bare hand when he couldn't find a hammer. Kenner describes him as "uncommonly physically strong, whose tool box was full of bent screwdrivers." When he pushed something in and reefed on it, he just didn't know the torque that he was putting on stuff. There was no bolt that was going to beat him. He could lift a B3 organ by himself! He took great pride in his service to the band, as well as his loyalty to Donnie.

Carmelo's immediate concern was looking at the trailer and thinking about the equipment. I seem to recall that it was shortly after we started looking at the equipment, that the run into the desert happened. Carmelo had gotten the trailer opened for us so we could look at some of the equipment. There were a couple of things that needed

to be refastened together and jerry-rigged or something, and I think Carmelo did that with amp cords and extension cords.
- Roy Kenner, lead vocalist; interview with Mark Doble, September 14, 2020

Whitey Glan, the band's drummer, was back in Toronto resolving some issues, and would fly down to meet up with the guys in Vegas. The rest of the band was driving from Los Angeles.

Whitey was at a court date in Toronto for possession of marijuana. So, he had to get that taken care of and our management team in L.A. put up the money for the flight and everything, and not only got him through that trial, but for him to still maintain his visa and be able to get on the plane to fly after the trial—that was wild!
- Prakash John, bass guitarist—Bush; interview with Mark Doble, September 14, 2020

With nobody hurt (miraculously!), the show must go on. The band continued their journey to Las Vegas. Prakash recalls that once they got to the Pink Pussycat-a-Go-Go, unpacked their gear, dusted it off, and plugged it in, everything still worked! But that would be one of the very few positives of this trip.

So, we miss our first night in Vegas—gotta get the car towed in—we've got to get another car. On the second day, we're already in shit because we missed the first night, and we can't play there without sheriff's cards! We go to get sheriff's cards, and Hughie doesn't have the right papers. So, the reason we're going, that is, to break Hughie in—he can't play—so, "goodbye Hughie!" By the third night, Roy's got the famed "Vegas throat." We're down to a trio for two weeks! We're playing at this place called the Pink Pussycat (I think it was). So now we're down to three guys! It was a horrible experience.
- Domenic Troiano; interview with Martin Melhuish, February, 1996

Donnie was always the "den mother," making sure the guys were fed and paid; and if necessary, bailing his roadie out of jail.

Carmelo got arrested for being on the street and not having any money. Only in Vegas, do they arrest you for not having any money. I get a call from the jail. Carmelo says, "I'm in jail." So I go down and ask, "Why's he in jail?" They say, "He's a vagrant." I say, "He's not a fucking vagrant! He doesn't have any money!
- Domenic Troiano; interview with Martin Melhuish, February, 1996

It would fall to Donnie at the end of the two weeks to collect their wages from the club owner.

So this is the kind of two weeks that we're having. At the end of the two weeks, I go in for the second reason that we're in Vegas: to make some money. So, I go in and say, "I'd like to get paid now." And there's a guy with ten guys behind him going, "Paid? For what?" I say, "What do you mean 'for what?' We've been playing for two weeks!" He says, "I hired a five-piece band and I got a trio." I say, "But we've been playing for two weeks." He says, "I hired a five-piece band." I say, "OK, so pay us for a three-piece." He says, "No, I hired a five-piece band." So we went on like this. I finally ended up getting some money from the guy. I really didn't want to say too much, because there's these ten guys who'd be beating the shit out of me at any moment! And that sort of finished Bush off. It was kind of like the worst two weeks of my life. We knew we were breaking up anyway, but that did it!
- Domenic Troiano; interview with Martin Melhuish, February, 1996

It truly is inevitable. Every band comes to an end sooner or later. And whether the road trip to Vegas was simply one of many reasons, it was, in many respects, the straw that broke the camel's back.

There were a couple of things that had happened prior to that, and then that was pretty well the end. Things were not going the way they should have been. And we are all saying, 'This is not good.' There are no good omens for the future here, which is unfortunate, because the music had been progressing in the right direction. That was the only thing that was progressing in a direction where people were pretty happy about it, myself included. If anything, I was getting more excited about the music toward the end of Bush. And then all the ancillary stuff lands on

top of your fuckin' head. Sometimes the music can be brilliant, but then circumstances kick you in the ass.

- Roy Kenner, lead vocalist; interview with Mark Doble, September 14, 2020

Within a matter of weeks, Bush would call it quits. Rock and roll is a tough business and a hard life. But Donnie Troiano was not through with music. Not at all! Musical loyalties remained strong, and ultimately, even after the band breakup, Domenic would work on future projects with each of the guys. As hard as some of the experiences were, Domenic would find the positives. It would always be about the music. Nothing would stop that. Not family, not legal challenges, not personnel issues, and certainly not finances. There would be no regrets. And the music—the music would continue.

All these experiences are positives. They teach you something. You learn. I always consider myself very fortunate when I look back at it. I kinda got to see the rock and roll side in terms of being totally broke, with nine guys in a room, driving nine thousand miles to get to the next gig, and I don't mean to make it sound like a hardship, because it wasn't—it was great! I got to see it from what you would call "the worst of times" to "the best of times"—the limos picking you up, and you're staying in the best hotel rooms—and I got to see the whole thing. You know the one thing it teaches you? The essence of it all, it's still the music. A good hotel versus a cheap hotel—it's got shit to do with what you're doing.

- Domenic Troiano; interview with Martin Melhuish, 1996

BUSH

REB FOSTER ASSOCIATES, INC.
211 SOUTH BEVERLY DRIVE
BEVERLY HILLS, CALIFORNIA 90212
(213) 278-4822

Bush—Whitey Glan, Domenic Troiano, Prakash John, Roy Kenner, 1970
(Troiano Family Archives)

CHAPTER 1

356 SAMMON AVENUE

"Can you still remember—gettin' home late at night
Trying to be quiet—your mom and dad sleepin' tight
Up into your room—get yourself ready for bed
Deciding you're not tired, and turnin' on the radio instead
Just listening to the music, until your eyes shut closed
Dreaming 'bout the things you'd like to be before you get old."
(*All Night Radio Show,* lyrics by Domenic Troiano)

Troiano family-- Frank, Pasqua, Domenic, Gina and Raffaele, 1959
(*Troiano Family Archives*)

356 Sammon Avenue—when you walk in the door there's a set of stairs in front of you that take you upstairs. And just to the right is a small room where Donnie had all his albums and his turntable. And I come over one day and Donnie's upstairs and he's just coming out of the washroom to see who it was, and he's got a toothbrush in his mouth, he's got his guitar on, and he's listening to an album, and in between brushes he's playing along.

- Blaine Pritchett, sound technician; interview with
  Mark Doble, July 21, 2020

So, I had to either play piano or guitar. Piano didn't seem too cool to me and besides who could afford one. The summer before Grade 10 I saw Ronnie Hawkins at Scarborough Arena. Just before I went to school my dad took me down to Eaton's and bought me a fifty-dollar Harmony guitar. I was just ecstatic!

- Domenic Troiano; interview with Martin Melhuish, February 9, 1996

By age sixteen, Domenic Troiano had found his passion. The guitar— cradled in his arms, resting on his lap, or slung over his shoulder—he was never far from it. And he played it, playing *anything*—scales, arpeggios, rock riffs, blues patterns, the latest hits, you name it. The feeling one gets from playing music well, the thrill of manoeuvring a tricky phrase with a seemingly effortless dexterity, the elation of perfectly synchronized ensemble playing. It's like an elixir, a drug, a musical "high." And if you have never experienced it, you can't understand. He would do it for the rest of his days, as long as he could breathe, and nothing would stop him.

My dad used to play guitar, but I never saw him play. He'd already stopped by the time he was twenty-one because back then you didn't make a living playing music.

- Domenic Troiano; interview with Martin Melhuish, February 9, 1996

And as much as he loved his mom and dad, as much as he did not want to disappoint them, eighteen-year-old Domenic was determined to pursue his passion.

My dad, when I started getting a little more serious about guitar, and I wasn't doing my homework, started getting a little pissed off with me. And he talked to me several times. But my parents were always cool with me. It was never: "You can't do this." They were basically trying to explain to me that music wasn't a "career." It was fun, it was music, and we got you the guitar, but you can't be … And my dad told me a story.

One of his first jobs was as a cop with Customs and Immigration in Genoa. He worked the port, looking for illegal shipments and all that. He did it for two or three years, but realized he couldn't arrest people, so he quit. But one night on their rounds (and he told me this story several times, so I know it's true, and it's not something he told me just to scare the shit out of me!) they found a street guy, like a homeless guy, and they asked him what was he doing and how come he was there. He looked familiar to my father, and my father started talking to him. It ended up, he was a real famous guitarist that my dad thought was great, but realistically, back then in Europe, if you were in music and you weren't a gypsy, you were one step away from being a gypsy. Unless you were heading the symphony orchestra or something, but that was upscale. And that really shook him up, because my dad thought this guy was great and it was like, "How can a guy this good… and this is how he ended up?" And it always stuck with him. So listen, he was worried about me. It was like he was trying to tell me, "This is all great and fun, but there's school."

That's what kept me in school: my dad. By Grade 13, I was in bad shape. I would have quit, but I didn't have the nerve. I couldn't have told my father I was quitting school. But you know what? Having said that, they were really good with me. A lot of Italian families and a lot of Italian parents, they would have kicked you out of the house. My dad was a little chilly with me for a while, but he was really cool. They saw that I was really interested.
-   Domenic Troiano; interview with Martin Melhuish, February 9, 1996

My big heroes are my mom and my dad. What they went through to leave and pick up their roots and come here to make a better life, how much they had to give up. I don't know if I'd be able to do that.

- Domenic Troiano; "Local Heroes", Rita Zekas, Toronto Star, 1987

By the time he emigrated in 1948, Domenic Troiano's father, Raffaele Martino Troiano (November 11, 1911–September 9, 1999), was an accomplished person. Born in Modugno, Italy, Raffaele was eleven years old when his own father, Domenic Troiano, became ill, requiring him to quit school and work. From the start, Raffaele wanted more, and small-town Modugno did not suit him. And so, at age eighteen, he moved to Genoa to become a customs officer/policeman, serving in that capacity from 1930 to 1935. In Genoa, he became friends with professionals, doctors, and professors, and determined to make up for his lack of formal education by reading everything he could find. (His daughter Gina still has her dad's set of Italian language Encyclopaedia). After Genoa, Raffaele spent four years in the Italian army fighting a colonial war in Ethiopia. While in Genoa and Ethiopia, Raffaele corresponded with the love of his life, Pasqua D'Attoma (June 12, 1915–September 3, 2010), and upon his return to his hometown of Modugno (Bari/Puglia) in 1939, he fully expected to marry Pasqua.

However, when World War II broke out in 1940, Raffaele was immediately called back into service, and sent to fight in Albania, Greece, Yugoslavia, and finally in Sardinia where he became a prisoner of war and was held by the Americans in 1943.

Pasqua D'Attoma worked in the Bari Post Office in 1940 and prior to this helped run the family olive oil business on their farm on the outskirts of Modugno. In late 1944, Raffaele returned to Modugno, and on January 27, 1945, he and Pasqua were finally married. A year later, Pasqua gave birth to their first child.

Domenic Michael Anthony Troiano was born on January 17, 1946, in Modugno. Postwar Italy suffered from high unemployment and food and medical supply shortages. Life was not easy, and many of his compatriots immigrated to the Americas.

Raffaele's two sisters and brother had already left for Canada, so in 1948, after working for a couple of years as a mechanic at a cement factory in Bari, a disillusioned Raffaele decided to make the same move to see what Canada had to offer.

Being Italian in Toronto now, is like being in Italy. Everything's here that you'd want. But when my parents came, there was nothing here. Like the provolone didn't exist, you couldn't get espresso, there were no "Italian" stores. I realized as I got older everything that they'd gone through to have a better life, and the whole reason to have a better life, is for your kids.
- Domenic Troiano; "Domenic Troiano—Canadian Icon," *Persona*, TLN & Big Star Entertainment, 2001

Canada's postwar economy was booming and there were labour shortages that European immigration helped address. Still, Canadians were not quick to forget that Italians had been their enemies. "Toronto the Good" was a term coined by nineteenth-century Toronto mayor William Holmes Howland to reflect Toronto's very strict, Victorian values reflected and advanced by a white, Anglo-Saxon, protestant society which continued well into the 1960s throughout the Toronto area. Postwar prejudices still existed. European immigrants were welcomed, but expected to know their place as working class labourers.

Italians coming to Canada settled in the City of Toronto and surrounding area and often found work in construction trades. Over the course of the 1950s, the Italian Canadian population in Canada grew from 150,000 to 450,000 and represented 2.5 per cent of Canada's population.

Raffaele's experience in Italy as a mechanic helped him land a job at the Toronto Transit Commission (TTC) as a junior mechanic, becoming one of the first Italians ever to work for the TTC. It was stable work that would allow him to provide for his family. In future years, Raffaele would assist other Italian Canadians to obtain work with the TTC.

My parents moved here when I was three and a half, so for me it was fairly easy, but for my mom and dad, you know, you leave what you

know. You leave the country you know, that you were brought up in; the language that you speak, the food you eat, the coffee that you drink, everything!

- Domenic Troiano; "Domenic Troiano—Canadian Icon," *Persona*, TLN & Big Star Entertainment, 2001

A year later, in September 1949, Pasqua and Domenic came to Canada by ocean liner (the *Giulio Cesare*), arriving at Ellis Island, New York City, and coming to Toronto where Domenic's brother Frank (1950) and his sister Gina (1953) would be born. In 1950, the family purchased a home in the Toronto borough of East York, at 356 Sammon Avenue.

Any examination of the life of Domenic Troiano must begin at Sammon Avenue. The Troianos owned 356 Sammon Avenue from 1950 to 1976, after which they moved a few blocks away to a newer and larger home.

Family was first and foremost. Growing up on Sammon Avenue, they walked to school, work, or church. (The Troianos never owned a car. As Raffaele worked at the Toronto Transit Commission, he carried a TTC pass.) Domenic spent his formative years and more with his family, even bringing fellow band members home to enjoy the magnificent Italian cuisine prepared lovingly by Pasqua.

My fondest memory is having dinner at his mom's house on Sammon where it was all the guys eating and the women served and sat on the porch between when they were serving—it was just like "old Italian."

- Garry Peterson, drummer—The Guess Who; interview with Mark Doble, April, 2020

It became the stuff of legend among musicians and friends. Pasqua's cooking excellence is recalled by many. Lifelong musical comrade and neighbour Roy Kenner was one of the more frequent recipients of the Troiano hospitality, even to the point of asking Pasqua to teach him how to cook authentic Italian.

His mother adopted me most certainly in the food department, and I could not get out of 356 Sammon Avenue without eating Pasqua's cooking. She actually taught me how to make homemade lasagne. We

literally sat and made everything from scratch. I have never ever had anything like her cooking. It was so light and stunningly amazing.

- Roy Kenner, lead vocalist; interview with Mark Doble, July 4, 2020

John Donabie was a popular radio host in Toronto in the 1960s and 1970s, working for such flagship stations as CKFH, CHUM-FM, and "the Mighty Q-107." From his late-night slot (featuring a steady supply of R & B) he developed a faithful following of listeners, including Domenic. John and Donnie became friends and John often dined with the Troianos.

But Mrs. Troiano, we'd sit around the table, and it was like an old Italian home; everybody was comfortable with one another and chatting back and forth. She was unbelievable! She made the best pizza I ever had. I must admit that when she served it, my wife and I kind of looked at each other. Because she didn't make pizza like they do at pizzerias here. They don't like put fifty-five ingredients on it. It was basically like a huge pizza—but oh the crust—it was just unbelievable! She was just such a great cook!

- John Donabie, disc jockey/radio host; interview with
  Mark Doble, August 3, 2020

It would have been like travelling between different worlds: Sammon Avenue, a safe and quiet residential street, and the gritty and lively Toronto clubs on Yonge Street.

It was surreal. You'd go to school Monday to Friday, play with Ronnie on Friday and Saturday at Le Coq d'Or with eight hundred hookers, four hundred gangsters, and three million parties, and then go back to school on Monday.

- Domenic Troiano; interview with Martin Melhuish, February 9, 1996

Where many rock stars came out of abject poverty, were even kicked out by their parents and forced to "make it," Domenic Troiano was raised in a loving family environment, never estranged, and always knew that he could go home, and never miss a meal. He could *always* come home.

He was always excited and proud to speak of his Italian heritage. His home on Sammon Avenue in East York was the epicentre of his existence

and everyone knew it. It was no secret. He navigated both sides of his world beautifully and with style. Dom lived for his music and success in whatever form. He did not take anything for granted and kept his family and friends close—very close.

- Joey Cee, CEO—JCO Communications; email to Frank Troiano, April, 2020

It is hard to overstate the significance. Domenic was ever faithful to where he came from. And even after leaving for Los Angeles in 1969, Toronto was still and always would be home. The value system acquired growing up in the Troiano household on Sammon Avenue would stay with him.

My dad had always told me, "You know you should be proud of your heritage. Italy's a wonderful place, and we're Italian, but we came to Canada to be Canadians." I mean, my dad always said that! He said, "You're here, we came here to fit in here, but your heritage is Italian." And for the longest time, you know, that always stuck with me, but I was here. I was watching Donald Duck and playing hockey, and I didn't understand the other part of it …

- Domenic Troiano; "Domenic Troiano—Canadian Icon," *Persona*, TLN & Big Star Entertainment, 2001

When Domenic arrived in Canada in September of 1949, he had to learn English in a hurry. He was supposed to go to a Catholic school in 1951, but R H McGregor Public School accepted him in 1950 when he was only four. Domenic stood out as one of the only Italians in the public school and was the victim of prejudice. He was chased home during most lunch hours and after school. According to Frank Troiano, this went on until Grade 5 when Domenic summoned up the courage to stand up to the leader of the gang that chased him. A fight ensued, from which Domenic emerged triumphant and the harassment ceased. He attended a junior high school called Cosburn Junior High (Grades 7–9) in East York.

The prototypical Canadian pastime for kids in the 1950s and 1960s was hockey, and Domenic was passionate about the great Canadian game. In Grade 5, he was determined to play ice hockey. He wasn't a strong skater, so he tried out as a goalie and made the team. Domenic played goal for three years and while at Cosburn Junior High was a good, all-round athlete.

Donnie was quite a good hockey player. Donnie and Uncle Ralph were visiting one day and Donnie and I were outside in the schoolyard playing road hockey. He was playing goal and I was shooting at him. While playing we talked and he told me with great pride about playing a championship game at Maple Leaf Gardens the week before. I don't remember if he won or not, but I do remember that he was very proud of the way he played in goal for his team.
- Angelo Pesce, cousin; email to Frank Troiano, April, 2020

After school, we'd gather up for road hockey games. Donnie would join us, despite his living on Sammon Avenue. He was a Leroy Avenue kid for road hockey purposes. In those days, we used to have a travelling road hockey team, challenging other neighbourhood kids who lived on other streets. Streets like Kimbourne or Frankdale and many more. When winter came, we went to Dieppe Park, it had two hockey rinks and one pleasure skating rink. It was through these years that Donnie moved more to his guitar and music and I thought I was going to be the next Frank Mahovlich.
- Glenn Lupani, childhood friend; email to Frank Troiano, April, 2020

Domenic continued to be passionate about the game.

I don't think you decide what you like and what you don't like. It's like when you are a kid and you start liking a hockey team. You don't even know why sometimes, you know, the uniform's the right colour. I always liked Montreal! I mean, I liked the Leafs, but there was something about Montreal—Rocket Richard and Jean Beliveau, the name and the sound and the thing, the flying Frenchmen—something about that for me just—but can you figure that out. Do you even want to, I mean, who gives a shit? And music's the same thing. I don't think you decide what you like. You wake up one day and you're listening to something, and something turns in your stomach, and the blues stuff always did that to me.
- Domenic Troiano; interview with Martin Melhuish, February 9, 1996

Drew Tennant, roadie for the Domenic Troiano band from 1977 to 1980 recalled Domenic organizing road hockey games for the travelling troops.

The looks people gave us playing road hockey in some southern American hotel parking lots was interesting and stuck with me in a good way.
- Drew Tennant, roadie; email to Frank Troiano, May, 2020

Domenic loved and followed hockey his entire life. His close friend Seaton McLean recalls attending a Leafs game with him when they were older:

So, back around the early nineties I was given a very good pair of tickets to a Leafs game. They were right behind the glass, in a corner. I called Dom and asked him if he would like to join me at the game, his reply: "I'd love to." We got into our seats, joking about our good luck. We started to chat while waiting for the puck to drop. I don't recall who the Leafs were playing, nor do I remember who won. I do, however, remember Dom telling me a few days later that his mother had called him after the Leafs game and asked if he had enjoyed the game. His reply: "Yeah Ma, it was good," apparently didn't wash with his mother, who had actually watched the game. "I don't know how you could say the game was good, Domenic, when you didn't actually watch any of it! I saw you and your friend on TV and every time they showed the two of you, you were talking to each other, not watching the game at all, just looking at each other and talking, every time." Dom's mother was right of course, and she had the video to prove it.
- Seaton McLean, friend; email to Frank Troiano, April, 2020

Domenic was the older brother, always concerned about Frank and Gina, and felt a loving duty to stay close to them throughout their lives and involve them as much in his own.

Even though my brother Donnie was being pulled in many directions during his latter teenage years and throughout his twenties, he still made quality time to spend with my sister Gina and me. In the early sixties he purchased a basic Seabreeze record player, later replaced by an upgraded stereo system in the mid sixties. It was set up in our

second-floor playroom/study room. My sister and I were able to play a wide variety of 45s and LPs. He alerted us to the Beatles' first appearance on the Ed Sullivan show in February of 1964 and all of us watched it in our family's living room. The Beatles' phenomenon helped pull the Western world out of the post Kennedy assassination malaise.

Donnie took Gina and me to see the Beatles' movie *Hard Day's Night* when it debuted in 1964. The movie introduced us to Beatlemania, as Donnie saw the Beatles shortly after at Maple Leaf Gardens in 1964, and my sister and I saw the Beatles at the Gardens in both 1965 and 1966. He always made sure to purchase the latest Beatles, Rolling Stones, and many other bands' LPs so that we could hear them. We became big music fans and our appreciation of all genres of popular music was enhanced.

- Frank Troiano

Domenic would stay close to his siblings, making himself available to them regardless of where he happened to be. This included inviting Frank to visit him in Los Angeles, consoling teenaged Gina over the phone from Honolulu, and even employing them in his enterprises.

He was always available for advice during our times of personal crisis. Once he understood our problem, he would give calm and practical advice.

- Frank Troiano

Domenic had many hobbies, including collecting comic books, baseball, and hockey cards. He and Frank enjoyed playing table hockey. One of his favourite activities was building, modifying, and painting model cars. He had several kits that he worked on and he would actually make custom parts for his cars. When he was fourteen or so he tried to convince his father to buy an old sports car so that he could work on it in the driveway. Eventually, his father convinced him that buying a guitar was a better idea.

When I was a kid; twelve or thirteen, I was crazy about cars. I bought all the books and magazines and I spent most of my time customizing models. I went to all the hot rod shows. I really wanted to be George

Barris (car customizing legend). But then, I guess, it faded on me and as it turns out, I didn't get my driver's licence until I was about twenty-six. I was out in Los Angeles then and driving was the only way to get around.

- "Domenic Troiano, Living with Cars," Bill Taylor,
Toronto Star, February 7, 1987

Domenic tried different part-time jobs starting at the age of nine. His first job was delivering the *Toronto Star* until he put a newspaper through someone's front window. He ended up working for two years as a delivery boy for Sword's drugstore located at the corner of Sammon and Greenwood. He delivered prescriptions in East York by bicycle in all weather conditions, and he was very popular with his customers.

There were a few Catholic churches close to the Troiano home and the family would alternate attending mass between them. When Domenic turned eleven, he was sometimes given the responsibility of taking his younger brother, Frank, to mass. Typically, though, the two of them would keep walking west on Danforth until they arrived at Kalua Music at Broadview where Domenic would stop and stare at all the guitars in the window and daydream about owning one.

In Grades 8 and 9, music became a central focus, and Domenic was introduced to the sounds of Chuck Berry, Elvis Presley, Jerry Lee Lewis, and Little Richard and he became obsessed with early rock and roll. He was especially influenced by the R & B music emanating from Buffalo radio stations. By Grade 9, he knew that he wanted to be a guitar player and convinced his dad to buy one, an acoustic Harmony Patrician guitar from Eaton's department store for fifty dollars.

I remember when I was in public school the only time I failed was in music, in Grade 6. I didn't start playing guitar until Grade 10. I was always listening to music on the radio, but to me music on the radio and music in school just seemed so remote. Chuck Berry and school seemed like two different worlds. I never thought it would be of any help to me.

I got my first guitar around the time school started. My dad took me down to Eaton's and bought me a Harmony.

- Domenic Troiano; Guess Who—POWER IN THE MUSIC promo, Larry Leblanc, 1975

Domenic took lessons briefly from Larry Sykes at D & L Music on Danforth and for the rest of the summer he was self-taught. He practiced on his new guitar whenever he could, and on many a night he could be heard strumming away quietly into the wee hours.

I remember walking along Sammon Avenue and hearing this amazing music blasting out of number 356. It was Donnie practising his famous solos.

- Mario Misasi, family friend; email to Frank Troiano, March, 2020

He immersed himself—listening to records, practising, reading chord books, and meeting other guitarists and learning from them. A close neighbour, Glenn Lupani, recalls what it was like growing up with him.

Donnie went to R H McGregor (Coxwell and Sammon Avenue) and I attended Holy Cross (Donlands and Cosburn Avenue). At the end of the day, we got together. By the time I got to Grade 4, I was totally into ice hockey and Donnie was still into our road hockey, but was moving into music. I had a small radio and we would listen to CHUM radio in the summer of '58. We were listening to the music, always wondering what the next week would bring in terms of the number one hit or on CKEY, which played the music we both enjoyed. That summer Donnie would be in his room at night practising guitar. One song that sticks in my mind was Chuck Berry's *Johnny B. Goode*. Music became a common interest. It was the summer of '58 when Donnie really got the guitar itch. We would get together and watch Dick Clark's Saturday night show. I would come over to his house to listen to him play some Chuck Berry and imitate Berry's cradling the guitar and walking across the bedroom. We loved the music. I would hear him playing when the windows were open. I'm reminded more about what a good guy Donnie was. He never forgot the neighbourhood or the people. Donnie's dad

worked with the TTC; my dad owned a grocery store. The connection was our heritage and the music.

- Glenn Lupani, boyhood friend; email to Frank Troiano, March, 2020

Domenic attended his first rock and roll concert at age fourteen. And he would never forget.

I went out to the East York arena to see my first rock concert. Johnny Rhythm and the Suedes, which included Robbie Robertson on guitar, and were playing a lot of the old Ronnie Hawkins things. All the kids were dancing and trying to hustle chicks, but I was mesmerized. I just stood and watched the stage. It was incredible. That was ten years ago, man, and I've been into it ever since.

- Domenic Troiano; "Blazing Bush Ready to Set The World On Fire," Ritchie Yorke, *Toronto Telegram*, July 30, 1970

Robbie Robertson of course would go on to international success with The Band, and as a collaborator with Bob Dylan. His influence on Domenic was immediate, lasting, and profound.

In the early '60s when I joined Ronnie Hawkins and the Hawks, there was one young guitar gunslinger around who impressed me. Domenic pulled guitar tricks outta me I had picked up down south that I never shared with anybody. I could tell he had the magic—and he had it in spades.

- Robbie Robertson, guitarist/songwriter—The Band; e-mail to Frank Troiano, November 12, 2020

Domenic's sister Gina was eight years younger than him, but distinctly remembers Domenic's dedication to his musical craft.

He was such a good brother. I was his little sister, and he adored me. What I remember most was going to bed and listening to Donnie in his room practising his scales. He was trying to play quietly because he knew we were trying to sleep. Late at night he would be in his room, practising his scales. I just remember his guitar playing every night. But it was so nice to hear him play. Donnie picked up the guitar at fifteen years of age and by seventeen, he was a master!

- Gina Troiano; interview with Mark Doble, June 30, 2020

Carol Landry, Gina Troiano's best friend as a child, was often in the Troiano home and recalls how Donnie's interest in music impacted the family dynamics in their home.

When Donnie was a teenager, he had a Record Room. He loved different kinds of music and when he was home, music would always be playing! When Donnie wasn't home playing the guitar, Gina and I would spend time in the room playing records. I believe my love of music came from Donnie! It was not unusual for him to answer the door with his guitar strapped around him. Over the years, Donnie played with different bands and when he was playing in Toronto, Gina and I went to see him play on most weekends at the Gasworks, the Generator, Friar's Tavern, Silver Rail, El Mocambo, and many more.

- Carol Landry, family friend; email to Gina Troiano, July, 2020

Domenic graduated from Cosburn and started Grade 10 at East York Collegiate in the fall of 1960. He made several new friends who were musicians. He went in and out of informal bands, learning and absorbing as much as possible. He decided to go electric and updated his Harmony Patrician by adding a De Armond pickup, and he bought a Fender Deluxe Amp. In 1962, he joined his first real band—Bobby Ray and the Shades.

By Grade 11, his grades started to suffer as the workload of playing clubs every week became heavier and all he did was think about music. If you had examined his Grade 12 and 13 notebooks and textbooks, you would have found guitar chord progressions, ideas for lyrics, and lots of doodles and sketches of his guitar heroes. Future bandmate Roy Kenner attended school and lived in close proximity to the Troianos.

We went to the same schools and lived three doors away from each other. I didn't know too much about him until he started into the music. I remember going by his place and I could hear music coming from the upstairs window. And I would see him around. He started playing with other people, other groups. Robbie Robertson was a huge influence on him. Donnie was wood-shedding away, seemingly with every waking moment. He was getting better by the day. Donnie, in relatively short order, was establishing himself as a guitar-force to be reckoned with. In '63, we put R K and the Associates together and at that point, it seemed like Donnie had been playing forever. He was already that good!

By the time we quit school in '64 to go "full-time music biz," we were all aware of Donnie's talent (and by "all," I mean anyone and everyone in Toronto who was a musician or a fan). At this point, Donnie had joined the house band at the Club Bluenote.
- Roy Kenner, lead vocalist; interview with Mark Doble, July 4, 2020

The Troiano household became noisier, especially when the band practised in the basement with drums, bass, vocals, and guitar. One of his closest friends was Sonny Milne, a drummer who performed with him at their first public gig at the EY community centre.

Sometime in late 1962, Domenic and Sonny joined up with Robbie Lane's band and they became known as Robbie Lane and the Disciples. Domenic was sixteen years old and in Grade 12 and he was performing one or two gigs a week and was also rehearsing regularly with the band.

And here I was, like sixteen, and I had a great family, and I was identifying with song [lyrics] like "My momma died," and "My daddy did too," and "I've got nothin' but the blues," and "My woman left me, and I got shot in the head," and I'm going, "Yeah, wow, this is it!" Maybe it's because you *don't* have that, or maybe it's because you're *not* like that, maybe that's part of it, but again, I don't think you can decide what speaks to you, whether it's music or a book or a movie or emotionally— why do you like somebody or you don't like them. Something happens. Not that you don't have to work at it, it's not just all magic, but certain things trigger responses in you, and certain things don't. I mean the guy next to you could be totally different. In school, everyone liked the Kingston Trio. I used to get in arguments with people. And in retrospect, it's stupid of course, because if they like the Kingston Trio, it's

fine. But I'd go, "You gotta listen to B.B. King! What's the hell's wrong with you?" Of course, everyone thought I was crazy.
- Domenic Troiano; interview with Martin Melhuish, February 9, 1996

Late in 1963, when he was in Grade 13 and seventeen years old, he was playing at the Le Coq D'Or Tavern with Robbie Lane and Ronnie Hawkins Thursday, Friday, and Saturday nights, doing four or five sets a night. Somehow, he was able to complete both Grades 12 and 13 successfully.

It was incredible, really. Many teenagers Domenic's age simply would not have been allowed to play at clubs and taverns late at night in the seamier part of the city and come home in the early morning hours. Especially, with declining grades, one can imagine parents putting their foot down. Domenic was an exceptionally bright young man, full of potential. Raffaele Troiano came to Canada to make a better life for his family, and he wanted and reasonably expected Domenic to advance to higher education and lead a successful life. The life of a guitar player working the club circuit in Toronto certainly would not have aligned with that vision. But ultimately, Raffaele and Pasqua allowed Domenic to pursue his dream. And more than that, they supported him.

My mom and dad argued. Dad wanted him to go to university, while Donnie wanted to pursue a musical career. Dad was worried. My dad played guitar when he was younger for weddings and things, but it was a hobby. He was concerned that Domenic wouldn't be able to make a living. But Mom said, "Look, he has to follow his dream for a musical career and we have to let him do it. He is not going to go to university just because we tell him to!" My dad struggled with Donnie's decision, but ultimately, he was on board with it and supported him.
- Gina Troiano; interview with Mark Doble, June 30, 2020

The life and music of Domenic Troiano is very much a testament to the faith placed in him by his family and his friends. Seb Agnello, organist for the Lords of London and the band Nucleus relates, "I told Donnie that we were cousins and he replied, 'we're not cousins, but you are talented enough to be family.' Indeed, family and the friendships forged growing up would stay with Domenic for his entire life.

My mind is full of memories of my cousin Donnie ... I always remember him being in my life and taking the time and patience to explain "stuff" to me. I was his younger cousin and spent lots of time with his family on Sammon Avenue. He always had time. When he moved to L.A., he would visit and I was so excited to have him back and just have lunch with him. He would be on his guitar and he would tell me stories about Los Angeles! I was fascinated, and he just wanted to be back in Toronto.
-   Lucy Coviello, cousin; email to Frank Troiano, April, 2020

Although he was a family friend, Joe Vitale became popular among his peers for being "Domenic Troiano's cousin" (or at least perceived that way!).

Some of my friends saw me hanging with Frank Troiano one day (probably at a family get-together) and when they asked me about him, I said, "he's a family friend—like a cousin to me—his name is Frank Troiano," and everyone in unison said "related to Domenic Troiano?" and I said, "Yes, that's his older brother." The next thing you know I'm "Domenic Troiano's cousin"! That's how everyone was introducing me! No one ever had a reason to introduce me—ever!—until they thought I was Domenic's cousin. I realized how much of a following Domenic had amongst my friends. I would always be correcting them, saying, "Well, I'm like a cousin." I didn't feel comfortable taking undue credit for anything even as meaningless as being someone's cousin. ... However, one day I was being introduced to some hot chicks!
-   Joe Vitale, family friend; email to Frank Troiano, June, 2020

Frank Troiano recalls numerous adventures where Domenic involved him: allowing him to hang out backstage with Herman's Hermits and the Rolling Stones as a fifteen-year-old; inviting him for extended stays when he had moved to Los Angeles; travelling by limousine to attend Guess Who concerts; or to work as a road manager in the late 70s. Yes, he was paying it forward, setting an example and mentoring his little brother, but just as importantly, Domenic took great comfort and support from the close relationship he maintained with his family. This theme plays out throughout his life. Domenic seemed to continuously search for ways in which to share his success with friends and family, to involve them in the joy.

Donnie was fifteen years older than me and although I saw him mostly at family gatherings, he always took the time to ask about what was happening in my life and my various interests. He was on the road a lot, but despite that, Donnie's family remained very important to him, and it was exciting to have such a talented man to talk music with.

- Anthony Ferrara, cousin; email to Frank Troiano, May, 2020

In subsequent chapters, the reader will repeatedly notice the gratitude and appreciation Domenic held for his heritage. Whether in interviews, onstage, acts of kindness for others, or even in his song lyrics, Domenic consistently paid tribute to his family, humbly acknowledging their belief in him. It was something Domenic would never take for granted, and at every opportunity would seem to look for ways to pay it forward.

Finally, I recall one conversation with Donnie, I think, just before I left on my years of travelling around the world. He impressed on me the importance of doing what you really want to do, to listen to your heart and to follow your dreams. Certainly, Donnie did that and he inspired me to do the same.

- Mario Misasi, family friend; email to Frank Troiano, March, 2020

Domenic Troiano did indeed listen to his heart and follow his dreams, in large part through an indomitable spirit, but always drawing strength through the love and support that traced back to 356 Sammon Avenue.

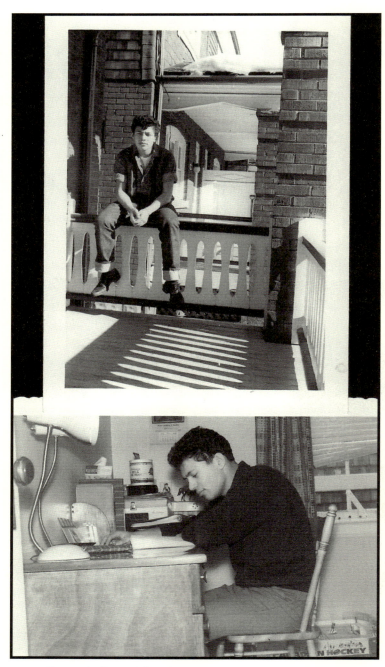

Domenic "Donnie" Troiano, 1960-1962 (Photo: Uno Igav)

CHAPTER 2

MY OLD TORONTO HOME

"Willpower—Can put you where you want to be
Willpower—can cut these chains and set you free
Willpower—is the greatest force upon the earth
Willpower—will give you strength, will give you worth."
(*Willpower*, lyrics by Domenic Troiano)

Robbie Lane and the Disciples—Back row: Bill Cudmore, Robbie, Rick Foulds,
Bert Hermiston, Front row: Gene Trach, Sonny Milne, Domenic Troiano, 1963
(Troiano Family Archives)

I want to be a musician. A lot of people still regard this as—well, what are you going to do when you grow up? I just want to be a musician. ... When I started out I was playing because I wanted to. I mean, making records was something you didn't even think about.

- "Guess What—The Guess Who's Saved. Guess How—Troiano Did It," Robert Martin, *The Globe and Mail*, 1974

Changing bandmates was never personal; it was all about becoming the best he could be. Playing in different high school groups, moving from one ensemble to the next, and never staying in the same combo for long; there was single-mindedness to it. Domenic was on a trajectory, improving every week. John Finley, who led Jon and Lee & The Checkmates and later, in 1967, joined the American band Rhinoceros, was a boyhood chum of Domenic:

I met Donnie in the early summer of 1962 at Bobby Brown's house in North Willowdale. Bobby was known professionally as Bobby Ray (his band: Bobby Ray and the Shades). We were hanging out around the front porch and adjacent front yard and that's where I was introduced to Donnie. He was there with his guitar and amp and even though he'd been playing for only six months or so, was playing John Lee Hooker licks like he grew 'em! I, being a lover of the blues of John Lee, Jimmy Reed, etc., was duly impressed and moved. We were then immediately friends.

- John Finley, singer; email to Frank Troiano, April, 2020

In the 1960s, most Toronto bands paid their dues working the bars, eateries, and nightclubs on the "Yonge Street Strip." Some would find their way out of Toronto into the Ontario hinterland playing local clubs and dances on weekends, and some would even venture into a recording studio and cut the odd record—mostly 45 rpm singles limited to one song on each side. And if you were lucky, you might even get some airplay on local Toronto radio.

The "Yonge Street Strip" stretched from Gerrard Street and south to Richmond Street, with a high density of active nightclubs and taverns featuring live bands whose purpose was to keep patrons entertained all evening as they dined and consumed alcoholic beverages.

The "Strip" was where you found venues like the Bermuda Tavern, Club Bluenote, the Zanzibar, Steele's Tavern, the Edison Hotel, Le Coq D'Or/ the Hawk's Nest, the Brown Derby, Friar's Tavern, and the Colonial. Also located at 347 Yonge Street, just north of Dundas Street, was the famous Sam the Record Man flagship store.

A few of these venues specialized in providing music of a certain type or musical genre including jazz, blues, rock and roll, rockabilly, and rhythm n' blues. In the '60s, the Colonial Tavern often featured world famous jazz artists like Miles Davis, Stan Getz, and Thelonious Monk, just to name a few.

Some of the popular local acts included Ronnie Hawkins and The Hawks, Ray Hutchinson and The Del-Tones, David Clayton-Thomas and The Shays, Little Caesar and The Consuls, Jack London and The Sparrows, The Regents, Jackie Shane, Shirley Matthews, and Shawne & Jay Jackson and The Majestics.

One of the most popular new bands was Robbie Lane and the Disciples, a group that has lasted from 1962 to the present day, still based out of Toronto for over five decades, playing bars and dances throughout Ontario. Domenic would get his start with the Disciples.

I first saw Donnie play in 1963 at the YMCA. I was fourteen years old. At that time, he was the guitar player for Robbie Lane and the Disciples. I was just starting out in music, so needless to say I was very impressed and inspired by Donnie's playing. I went on to become a founding member of Roy Kenner and the Associates and as a result I had the privilege of not only getting to know Donnie, but also playing on the same bill with both the Rogues and the Mandala on numerous occasions including opening for Wilson Pickett at Club 888. Having been a part of the Toronto music scene in the 1960s, I can say without a doubt

that Domenic Troiano was the leading influence of what we now consider the "Toronto Sound."

- Greg Carducci, bass guitarist—R. K. and the Associates; email to Frank Troiano, May, 2020

In 1963, seventeen-year-old guitarist Domenic Troiano, along with his close friend Sonny Milne would find themselves playing in the initial iteration of Robbie Lane and the Disciples.

In 1959–60, I began a band by the name of Robbie Lane and the Lincolnaires. We performed at school dances and clubs. Late in 1962 the band needed an overhaul. I met Sonny Milne through a friend and I was interested in him becoming our new drummer. He suggested that I check out Donnie Troiano. After having an audition, I was most impressed with his passion for music, his intense commitment, and the fact that he was way ahead musically than almost anyone I knew. So, Sonny and Donnie brokered a package deal including them and Bert Hermiston, a sax/flute player. Bill Cudmore (sax, harmonica), Gene Trach (bass) and Rick Foulds (piano) rounded out the rest of the band.

Donnie's passion was contagious. After a few practices, the band was much tighter and musically, Donnie became the leader. All the band members raised their game to a new, higher level. Certainly, all the band members became much more disciplined and committed.

- Robbie Lane, singer/band leader—Robbie Lane and the Disciples; interview with Frank Troiano, April 22, 2020

Before they were "the Disciples," they were originally called "Robbie Lane and the Lincolnaires".

I next remember seeing Donnie with Robbie Lane and the Lincolnaires in the summer of '63 at South Street, a hot sweaty little storefront club on Yonge Street up around the city limits, just north of Lawrence Avenue. The band was wonderful; Donnie had a Fender Telecaster guitar at this point and they played *Stormy Monday Blues*. In a marvellous band with baritone and tenor saxophones, Donnie had all the guitar chords and

licks from the Bobby Bland rendition. I was blown away and inspired; nobody I knew had that harmonically soulful command!
- John Finley, singer; email to Frank Troiano, April, 2020

The original name immediately became a point of controversy when a local band from nearby Oshawa, similarly named "The Lincolnaires," threatened legal action. And so Robbie Lane's band was promptly renamed "Robbie Lane and the Disciples."

We weren't sure as to what to do, but in the end, we decided to change our band name to Robbie Lane and the Disciples. It seemed like a big deal at the time, but we quickly forgot about it and our fans were happy with the new name.
- Robbie Lane, singer, band leader—Robbie Lane and
  the Disciples; interview with Frank Troiano, April 22, 2020

Robbie Lane and the Disciples soon became a popular band for school dances and also worked the Toronto club scene for close to a year. Domenic was still in high school, but the level of work was enough to gain confidence and for the band to develop as a performing unit, attracting the attention of some important people in the Toronto scene and landing a steady gig.

We had a very busy 1963 playing school dances, clubs, some bars, and dance halls and we kept on getting better and tighter and gelling as a band. Later in the year, Ronnie Hawkins had found out that the Hawks were intending to leave him and he developed a back-up plan. He placed us in the Le Coq D'Or Tavern dining room in the downstairs, and played with the Hawks on the main floor. He would come down a few times a night and would perform a few songs with us to keep the overflow patrons happy, as they were waiting to see the Hawks upstairs.
- Robbie Lane, singer/band leader—Robbie Lane and
  the Disciples; interview with Frank Troiano, April 22, 2020

"Rompin'" Ronnie Hawkins and the Hawks were Canada's most well-known rock and roll act. Arkansas born and raised, Hawkins relocated to Toronto in the early '60s, enjoying a six-decade career as a singer and recording artist. Hawkins would mentor an astonishing number of musicians who would later go on to greater things, most notably The Band, (formerly the Hawks) as well as later members of Janis Joplin's Full Tilt Boogie Band.

In 1964, the original "Hawks" (Robbie Robertson, Levon Helm, Richard Manuel, Garth Hudson, and Rick Danko) struck out on their own and left Hawkins' employ. Levon and the Hawks hooked up with Bob Dylan, becoming his backing ensemble during the infamous 1965–66 world tour where Dylan withstood vociferous audience rejection and criticism for "going electric" and seemingly abandoning "folk music." Following a respite in upstate New York, the Hawks would rehearse and record the majestic MUSIC FROM BIG PINK album under the new moniker: "The Band"—and almost instantly established themselves as one of the most revered and successful North American rock bands of all time.

Knowing that he was about to lose the Hawks, Ronnie Hawkins recruited Robbie Lane and the Disciples for the express purpose of turning them into his next iteration of the Hawks. Domenic recalled this period as the *real* start of his professional career.

When Levon and the other Hawks split from Ronnie to go out on their own, he asked us, that is, Robbie Lane and the Disciples, to join him. We jumped at it, but you know it wasn't for the bread. Robbie got $125 a week because he was the lead singer and I got the same because I played lead and did the arranging, but the rest of the band got $100. Ronnie was cleaning up personally, but we couldn't really beef because after all, he was the draw. His bands were always the best, and I say that because it was true, not because I was in one of them. Even though the people got off on the group, it was Ronnie they had come to see.

- Domenic Troiano; "The Wear and Tear on My Mind," Michael Sherman, *Los Angeles Free Press*, August 11, 1972

In early 1964, the Hawks left Hawkins and became Bob Dylan's back-up band. We stepped right in and moved up to the main floor of the Le Coq D'Or. We played Friday and Saturday nights and did six sets a night from eight p.m. to one a.m. Ronnie expected us to rehearse for three nights a week after closing. We would practise until three or four a.m. He would give us a list of songs to learn and occasionally he would

drop by. This was known as "Ronnie's Music Boot Camp." During this time Ronnie had asked Donnie to work for Hawk Records.

- Robbie Lane, singer/band leader—Robbie Lane and the Disciples; interview with Frank Troiano, April 22, 2020

The Hawks' standards were high, requiring discipline and dedication. Domenic thrived in this environment, developing his craft as a player, arranger, and composer, but more importantly as a professional musician. This was "paying your dues"—committing to a work ethic, being on time, daily rehearsal, which meshed perfectly with Domenic's continuous improvement focus.

I was a seventeen-year-old kid working with a high-rolling pro who was always surrounded by hookers, pimps, and gangsters. Ronnie was completely democratic. He liked everybody. And the trips he was into! See, everything he did was for a reason—usually to get strong reactions out of people.

- Domenic Troiano; "The Wear and Tear on My Mind," Michael Sherman, *Los Angeles Free Press*, August 11, 1972

Robbie Lane and the Disciples still enjoyed other engagements in the Toronto area, gaining increased exposure, experience, and also learning important lessons along the way.

Sometime during 1964, the band was asked to open for Gerry and the Pacemakers at the Eaton Auditorium (the Carlu). Freddie "Boom Boom" Cannon (*Palisades Park* and other hit singles) was to perform after us. We were opening and we were going to back Cannon and he was going to perform five songs. We met in the afternoon for a sound check and rehearsal. During the second song, Cannon shouted out to Donnie: "What the hell are you playing? That's the worst guitar playing that I have heard in my life!" We were all stunned! The promoter, the agent, the sponsors, the crew were all there and there was a moment or two of silence. Donnie was almost in tears and so hurt and he mumbled that he was playing the song as it should be. We couldn't believe what Cannon had done! He then said, "OK, let's keep going." Anyhow, the night went well and the Pacemakers were fantastic. This concert,

coupled with the Beatles concert at Maple Leaf Gardens in 1964, was the beginning of the British Invasion. The music scene would change forever in North America.

- Robbie Lane, singer/band leader—Robbie Lane and the Disciples; interview with Frank Troiano, April 22, 2020

Freddie Cannon's ill-tempered criticism did not sit well, but in the context of "paying your dues," it was probably not so bad. Domenic's astonishing ascent as "the best guitarist in the city" had earned the respect of his peers. The odd misplaced criticism wasn't going to tarnish that.

The kid who only two years previous had picked up the guitar for the first time was already leaving a lasting impression. Gene Martynec, guitarist with Bobby Kris & The Imperials at the time, would go on play in Kensington Market as well as with Bruce Cockburn in the future remembers well the impact Donnie had, even while playing with Robbie Lane.

I believe my first time seeing Donnie play may have been at the Concord Tavern on a Saturday afternoon matinee where Ronnie Hawkins and the Hawks played. It was possible for underage kids to attend the fun and where the cheapest menu items were milk and fries at thirty-five cents! It was attended by young Toronto musicians, and we loved the Hawks. We even tried to look like them and most young guitarists bought the same clothes and got their hair styled on Yonge Street. Robbie's Telecaster was the uniform for all aspiring pickers. One matinee, Donnie appeared onstage with Robbie Lane and the Disciples. I was really impressed with Donnie's playing and his presence. Those were the days when you had to have an Anglo name if you were in a band. Hence, "Donnie." His playing was an inspiration for me to work harder at the guitar. I was a member of Bobby Kris & The Imperials, and all the bands at the time were friendly and eager to befriend musicians from the other groups. Donnie was a super friendly guy and always asked what was going on in your world. That's how the friendship started. Donnie was a student of the guitar, meaning he was constantly learning and experimenting. It was my chosen instrument at the time so we would have shop talk

sessions. He was always the "maestro" and interested in all styles of music. Great inspiration for me and others.

- Gene Martynec, guitarist and composer; email to
  Frank Troiano, July, 2020

Hawkins also ran his own record label, Hawk Records, on which Robbie Lane and the Disciples recorded their first single, *Fannie Mae* b/w *The One For Me* in 1964. *Fannie Mae* is a straightforward blues/rock, composed and made famous by American R & B singer Buster Brown. However, the B side, *The One for Me*—a pretty love song featuring tasteful faux-jazz guitar and a beautiful flute solo by Hermiston—in fact, represented the first Domenic Troiano composition ever recorded.

I first saw Donnie play in the Robbie Lane band and when I saw him, I knew he had something special. When I was practicing with the Disciples, he was playing lead guitar extra good. Donnie wanted to get into music a lot heavier than just playing rockabilly. Donnie left Robbie and formed his own group and they were very successful. I believe that group was called the Mandala. I consider Donnie in the top ten with the best of them! He is greatly missed.

- Rompin' Ronnie Hawkins, singer and band leader;
  email to Frank Troiano, April, 2020

Under the moniker Ronnie Hawkins and the Hawks, the Disciples recorded a single *Got My Mojo Workin'* with Hawkins singing over a basic band accompaniment. The B side *Let the Good Times Roll* featured Domenic and saxophonist Bill Cudmore trading off solo licks.

Domenic's association with Hawk Records resulted in having his songs recorded by other artists. In 1964, Buddy Carlton and the Strato-Tones (from London, Ontario) released Domenic's *Bring Your Love* as a single.

During 1964, our first single on Hawk Records was *Fannie Mae* and the flip side was *The One for Me* written by Donnie. The band wanted to record blues and R & B and Ronnie wanted us to do pop rock and rockabilly. He won out on the second single *Ain't Love a Funny Thing*. This was the final straw for Donnie and he told Ronnie that he was

not interested in going in this musical direction and they had it out. Donnie had already been going to the Club Bluenote on Yonge Street between sets in late 1964 and was contemplating joining Whitey and the Roulettes. Terry Bush, the guitarist for the Silhouettes' Revue became our guitarist, they left the Bluenote and Donnie joined Whitey and The Roulettes and they became the house band at the Club Bluenote.

- Robbie Lane, singer/band leader—Robbie Lane and the Disciples; interview with Frank Troiano, April 22, 2020

While Ronnie Hawkins provided the vehicle, Domenic wanted more. **I wanted to be Muddy Waters and B. B. King and Ronnie wanted to be the Dave Clark Five.** Domenic wanted more than to be part of Ronnie Hawkins' backing band and was in search of a project that he could lead. After six months with Ronnie Hawkins, it was time to move on.

I started going to this club called The Bluenote, which was just up the street from us, just south of Gerrard, on Yonge, and I loved it there. They did all the R & B stuff and it was really a cool place, like an after-hours club. And I really was fascinated by that kind of music, that I gravitated toward it; and as the summer was going along with Ronnie, I was finding out more and more that I really wasn't happy with what we were doing musically. And so I kept going, "You know, I just don't like what we're doing!" And it finally ended up with me getting fired; like I got fired from Ronnie for complaining all the time, basically; and in retrospect for good reason, as I *was* complaining all the time. But I went to the Bluenote and fortunately the guitar player was leaving, and I joined. So, I started at the Bluenote, and we were the House Band, and that evolved into The Five Rogues.

- Domenic Troiano; "Domenic Troiano—Canadian Icon," *Persona*, TLN & Big Star Entertainment, 2001

At the Club Bluenote, Domenic earned nowhere near the money he made with the Hawks and Robbie Lane. And although he made efforts to leave on good terms (Domenic never stopped being good friends with Hawkins), his music came first. This would not be the last time Domenic left a good financial situation in order to be true to his own values.

Donnie set musical goals and he wouldn't stop until they were achieved. He, as our musical leader, made almost all the decisions as to the song arrangements, breaks etc. He was decades ahead of us in musical ability, knowledge, and foresight, and he made such a difference in our live show. Sometimes I would sit and watch him play and it was truly magical. Even though I was disappointed in his departure, I knew he had made the best decision for his future musical career.

- Robbie Lane, singer/band leader—Robbie Lane and the Disciples; interview with Frank Troiano, April 22, 2020

Guitarist Terry Bush replaced Domenic in Robbie Lane and the Disciples.

Back when Domenic was Donnie, I was playing in the Bluenote with Doug Riley, Steve Kennedy, Howie Glenn, and Fred Theriault (The Silhouettes), and Donnie was playing with Robbie Lane. We didn't know each other well, but we were friends. Not close, but there was a mutual respect for one another which wasn't always the case back then amongst musicians, probably 1963–64. Donnie was heavily into blues and I was more of a rock and roll player. Although the Bluenote was rhythm and blues more than rock, plus some bluesy jazz. Anyhow, Donnie left Robbie and I joined Robbie. And Donnie ended up in the Bluenote while we were playing *Forty Days* with Ronnie Hawkins. I still watched Troiano and listened. Man, did he turn into a monster player!

- Terry Bush, guitarist; email to Frank Troiano, April 7, 2020

Domenic immersed himself in the R & B he heard on Buffalo radio stations that pushed the boundaries of basic three-chord rock and roll: Chuck Berry, Ray Charles, and Albert King. R & B had an interesting complexity to it—shifting backbeats, surprising harmonic turns, almost jazzy, and great melodies. This was still pop music, but full of subtle grooves and changes. You still danced to it and it was fun to play.

I began singing at the Club Bluenote in 1960 and I stayed on until 1965. One thing that I will never forget is when the house band was changing over in mid 1964. Donnie Troiano, leaving the Disciples and joining Whitey and the Roulettes, and within weeks we had sell-out crowds and a lineup outside. The band changed their name to the Rogues and their show was full-on high energy R & B. Donnie was very gifted, and he was on a mission. Boy, could he play that Tele!

- Jayson King, vocalist—Jayson King and the Spices; interview with Frank Troiano, April, 2020

At the Club Bluenote, Donnie joined the hottest/tightest local R & B unit in town, teaming up with new mates from a group previously called Whitey and the Roulettes with Finnish-born Pentti "Whitey" Glan on drums, bassist Don Elliot, and lead vocalist/keyboard player George Olliver. They became the Rogues. Later on, when Polish-born keyboardist Joseph (Joey) Chirowski came on board, they became The Five Rogues, setting up residence as the house band at the Club Bluenote, just up the street and across from Le Coq D'Or.

Singer-songwriter Brenda Russell (who would work with Dr. Music as well as international stars Earth Wind & Fire, and Diana Ross) was in a vocal group, the Tiaras, who frequently performed at Club Bluenote recalls encountering Domenic and becoming lifelong friends with him.

Donnie was a true gentleman, always very polite and very kind and generous. He really cared for me and assisted me greatly by his encouragement and his patient musical guidance. I considered him to be like my "big brother," as he always looked out for me, protected me, and made sure nobody messed with me. I was very impressed with his bands the Rogues and the Mandala, and his guitar playing was second to none.

- Brenda Russell, singer-songwriter; interview with Frank Troiano, July 15, 2020

Mike McKenna was the person Domenic replaced at the Club Bluenote. Mike was a talented blues guitarist, well-known in Toronto music circles, who, over the course of fifty years in music played with Whitey and the Roulettes, Luke and the Apostles, the Ugly Ducklings, McKenna Mendelson Mainline, and Downchild Blues Band.

After seeing Ronnie Hawkins, Levon Helm and The Band at the Concord on Bloor, Whitey Glan and I decided to form a band called Whitey and the Roulettes, which included George Olliver and Don Elliot. Both

Domenic and Robbie Robertson were major influences on every guitar player in Toronto and it became a mandatory rule that the Fender Telecaster was the guitar of choice. Just before the Roulettes became the house band at the Club Bluenote, and shortly after Domenic had become their guitarist and the band became the Rogues, I went back to school. A year or so later we (Luke and the Apostles) were playing at the Purple Onion in Yorkville and the Rogues were playing around the corner at the Devil's Den and we would see each other between sets. Domenic was so gracious and nice and would compliment me on my playing and we jammed a few times at night's end. For me that was a real thrill. Domenic was truly a guitar legend.

- Mike McKenna, guitarist; email to Frank Troiano, April, 2020

The Rogues were one of the tightest R & B soul bands on the "Strip." George Olliver was a natural front man, and Domenic was the undisputed leader and musical director. As Whitey Glan explained, **"Things got a lot more serious after Domenic joined. Domenic had been through the Ronnie Hawkins school of rock, which meant lots of practicing"** (Whitey Glan speaking to Nicholas Jennings, *The Soul Crusade of the Mighty Mandala*— unpublished). The rhythm section of Whitey, Don Elliot, and Joey (all club circuit veterans) was superb, and under Domenic's musical leadership delivered a robust and refined rhythm and blues. George Olliver recalls:

We were stationed at the Bluenote and we were very blessed because it was the number one R & B club in Toronto at the time. The Silhouettes, who were the house band at the time decided to go out on the road. So that created an opportunity. When they decided to leave, Al Steiner, the club owner, offered me the engagement. So, we were there for about four months as Whitey and the Roulettes and apparently Domenic had heard about our show and the band and we didn't have a guitar player because Mike McKenna had decided to quit the band because he didn't like the nightclub scene. Domenic came up and immediately proposed to us that he would like to join. He had a great reputation at the time. He and Bobby Schwab were known as the best guitar players in Toronto.

- George Olliver, lead vocalist; interview with Mark Doble, July 1, 2020

I remember when I first saw him play in 1962 at Le Coq D'Or with Ronnie Hawkins on Yonge Street. We were around the corner at the Bluenote on Yonge and Gerrard. He was an impressive guitar player even then. Everyone was coming in to check him out. What I heard in his playing was raw emotion. It was very soulful music, straight from the heart. It was mindboggling to have him join our band just two weeks later. And from the minute he came in, he was the leader. He knew exactly what he wanted, and he had great ideas. He was headstrong in those days, very focused, and what he wanted always turned out to be the best thing for the band.

- George Olliver, lead vocalist; "Domenic Troiano," Greg Quill, *Toronto Star*, May, 2005

Club owner Al Steiner routinely invited visiting artists to the Bluenote after their shows. (Maple Leaf Gardens and Massey Hall were both short walks from the club.) In the course of their residency, the Rogues would end up backing Motown stars such as Martha Reeves, Edwin Starr, and others; and every night, earning the respect and admiration of these superstars along with everyone else.

Well, the year I played at the Bluenote, after I left Ronnie Hawkins, probably gave me musical direction more than anything else. It was strictly an R & B kind of club, and it was a year of backing up everybody that came into town. The Supremes played there. Stevie Wonder, the Righteous Brothers—I can't think of half the people who came through. And the Bluenote served a lot of purposes. It was really like a cult place for two or three hundred people in Toronto who loved R & B. That's where they all went. The music was great, the guy who ran the place would go to Buffalo to get all his records, things you wouldn't hear on the air, and it just taught me so much being there. It was a formative time in my life. I've always been influenced by Black music more than anything else, the blues and that whole thing. But it was at the Bluenote that I started hearing more jazz things. A lot of really good players would come down there and jam. More jazz oriented people. I still really liked blues, but I started trying to apply the things I was hearing to other things. Trying to get things that were more complicated but

still with that kind of feeling the blues gave you, and getting more into the chord thing.
- Domenic Troiano; "Domenic Troiano," Frank Emmerson, *Tempo*, July 1977

This was the Toronto Sound! This was beyond competent musicianship! The Five Rogues were blowing everyone away.

It was sometime in '65, a bunch of us guys from East York took a trip downtown to hear one of our own—Domenic Troiano at Club Bluenote. I was a "CHUM hit picker" in '63 and '64 at my school. Music was in my blood. We had a band called The Vanguards; we were just OK, playing mostly British invasion music with some R & B. What I was to experience at the Bluenote though, just blew me away. At first, we sat on the floor (it was after hours) until the band came on—The Five Rogues. Before we knew it, George Olliver comes on and the whole place was jumpin' crazy, we were all up on our feet and cheering. My eyes were on Domenic's guitar playing; being an aspiring guitar player, I had never experienced such technique and inventive playing, and this was a night I would never, ever forget!
- Evan Kozaris, guitarist and songwriter; email to Frank Troiano, June, 2020

The "Toronto Sound" refers to the unique R and B music that was being produced by Toronto bands in the 1960s. George Semkiw began his musical career as a guitarist in Ritchie Knight and the Mid-Knights and later distinguished himself as a recording engineer and producer, working with such varied acts as Duke Ellington, Stompin' Tom Connors, and Lou Reed. Prior to his passing in 2018, Semkiw described the elements that characterized the Toronto Sound:

To me the Toronto Sound was really based on the Toronto guitar players. The sound that the Toronto guitar players had was different than anything at that time. I mean nowadays you hear great guitar sounds and all of it stems from the Toronto guitar sound. Because up until then, rock and roll guitar sounds were clean regular gauge string guitar solos which were like piano strings; you couldn't bend them, you couldn't

wiggle them, you couldn't whammy them, you couldn't do much with regular strings. Toronto Sound developed using light strings – light gauge strings, so you could bend strings and sustain them. It was also the right amount of distortion that was really important in the Toronto Sound. There are a million stories around of guys that were trying to find the secret of the right distortion, and some of the pranks that were played on these poor guys to get that sound.

You go to any dance in the city at that time and you'd hear music that you'd never hear on Toronto radio ever, because they just didn't play that stuff. So, two things: guitar playing, and the fact that we all loved blues and R & B and that's what everybody got into. Check out some of these guys from Toronto like Robbie Robertson, Domenic Troiano, and Fred Keeler… It all stemmed from that Robbie Robertson type sound which was based on Howlin' Wolf and Muddy Waters.

- George Semkiw, recording engineer/producer; "Recollections and Reflections on the 40th Anniversary of the Toronto Section of the Audio Engineering Society", Youtube Video Excerpt, October 25, 2008, Toronto.

Domenic wanted to record and perform original material. As much as Domenic is deservedly recognized for his skill as a guitarist, he was first and foremost a writer and composer. It is no accident that Domenic is credited as a principle writer on all of his albums. Earl Johnson, lead guitarist for the 1970s Canadian rock group Moxy grew up watching Domenic and attests that Domenic was more of a "complete musician."

I first saw Domenic with the Rogues in the Sears Café at the Hamilton Shopping Centre circa 1965–66 when I was about sixteen years old. I remember being amazed at his technical ability, combined with great feel that he exhibited onstage. I was just getting serious about guitar and wanting to become a full-time musician back then. Probably saw Dom about five or six times back then, starting with the Rogues and then the Mandala. Saw him with Bush at the Hamilton Mountain Arena and just loved the band and the new material they were playing. I could see that Dom was an excellent songwriter as well, which just added to the aura about him in my mind. It also made me realize there was more to guitar than just playing solos and trying to become a star. Domenic was a true musician. That was very apparent.

- Earl Johnson, guitarist—Moxy; email to Frank Troiano, May, 2020

When I left Northern Ontario and arrived in Toronto as a sixteen year old, the R & B bands of the scene at that time were awe inspiring. I was a drummer but had a thing for guitarists. There were greats that shared the stage at the venue. Terry Logan...Kenny Marco...Eddy Patterson and many more. But there was one guy who seemed like he was from another planet. That of course was Donnie Troiano.

- Tony Nolasco, drummer, vocalist, McKenna Mendelson Mainline; email to Frank Troiano, March, 2021

In the spring of 1965, the Rogues left Club Bluenote. During their tenure at the club, a street-smart rounder by the name of Al Tobias became their unofficial road manager/band manager. He was helping them transition from being a house band to getting club, high school, and other bookings. He arranged for them to be signed to the Ron Scribner Agency, but gigs were sparse. They got a few high school bookings and on Sunday afternoons they occasionally got Catholic Youth Organization bookings in Catholic churches in Toronto.

After the Rogues left the Bluenote, a band led by Eric Mercury, called the Soul Searchers, became the house band.

I put together a band called the Soul Searchers and we became the house band. I became very good friends with Donnie during that year and besides his tremendous talent as a guitarist and band leader he was totally committed to music, to practicing and learning and self-improvement. He didn't care much for partying or fooling around and whenever you saw him on Yonge Street he had his guitar in one hand and sometimes a small amp in the other.

- Eric Mercury, singer-songwriter; interview with Frank Troiano, May 17, 2020

As summer approached, the management duties were gradually passed on to Mitch Markowitz, who was the band's master of ceremonies and one of their biggest fans. Duff Roman, the manager of David Clayton-Thomas and the Shays approached Mitch and the Rogues with a proposal—would the Rogues be interested in backing up David for a summer tour in Northern Ontario? The band jumped at this opportunity, as it gave them steady work and very good exposure due to David's popularity.

David Clayton-Thomas was already a giant on the Toronto music scene, having played and recorded several local hit records with his band, the Shays. David held Domenic in high regard.

I first met Donnie Troiano at the old Club Bluenote on Yonge Street in the early '60s. I knew right off that he was one helluva guitar player. He had a fire and dexterity to his playing that I had never seen before. He actually played with all four fingers, which set him apart from the rest of us two or three-fingered self-taught wannabe blues players. Once I got to know him I found him to be an open, friendly guy willing to share licks and talk guitar with any of us young Telecaster players.

At that time, Dom was forming the Rogues and I had a local hit record with the Shays, *Boom Boom*. It was very difficult for the Shays to tour, as most of them were still in high school at the time. A local agent suggested that I team up with the Rogues for some gigs. My hit record combined with the popularity of the Rogues would sell tickets and so we did a bunch of gigs together that summer … I think was about '65. Donnie and I became good friends during that time. In '66 I left for New York, and two years later Blood, Sweat & Tears took off, which kept me on the road all over the world for the next forty years.

-   David Clayton-Thomas, singer-songwriter and recording artist; email to Frank Troiano, April 1, 2020

At the time, Domenic was not entirely satisfied with how things were going with The Five Rogues and felt that David was a good match and represented just the kind of presence to boost the Rogues, if even for a short time.

Basically, when we left the Bluenote, he had just split up with the Shays. We couldn't get any work ourselves because nobody would book us playing what we were playing. All the big agents in town came down to see us and said, "The band's great, but you've got to be more like the Big Town Boys if you wanna work." They were right; we weren't getting much work. Clayton asked us to play with him for a while, which was good because he didn't have a band. We backed him up for about three months. We'd do our own set, then he'd come out and sing. He and George would do everything they could to outdo each other. That was just a part-time stop-gap until he got a new band and we got a bit more action.

- Domenic Troiano; "Black Market,"
  El Mocambo Records Inc., Press Release, 1981

David Clayton-Thomas' tenure with the Rogues was only a short-term assignment. Later in 1966, David Clayton-Thomas and the Bossmen released the sensational single *Brainwashed*, which became a hit in Canada. Following this, David would venture to New York City, achieving international success with the great jazz-rock fusion band, Blood, Sweat & Tears.

In the 1960s, Peter Taylor and Tim Notter were fans. Peter later became a promotional rep for Capitol Records, and in the 1990s, his buddy Tim Notter opened The Orbit Room, an R & B club. But in the sixties, The Five Rogues set the standard for both of them.

Jimi Hendrix wasn't the first Fender flailing guitarist we fell in love with. That was Domenic "Donnie" Troiano, though his weapon of choice was a "Tele," the immortal Telecaster. Tim and I got our nascent musical education at the feet of Domenic Troiano—literally. At Five Rogues' gigs we would weave and wind our way through the audience until we could position ourselves directly in front of him where we learned everything we needed to know about musicianship, style, chops, technique, and showmanship. Though The Five Rogues delivered up some of the hottest, tightest, jazz-influenced, rhythm and blues dance music around, you would generally find the two of us standing stock still in front of the low stage staring up in awe as we watched Donnie's fingers

wring out notes of unparalleled purity. For any musical act or artist to impress us, they had to be as good as or better than The Five Rogues.

- Peter Taylor, promotional rep—Capitol Records; email to Frank Troiano, June, 2020

After the Rogues left Club Bluenote, they experienced their share of adventures on the road:

I met Dom at Club Bluenote in '64/'65 and later, after the Rogues had left the Bluenote, they were on their way to Hamilton to play at the Flamingo Tavern across the street from where my band The Bishops were the house band. I got a call and they said that their trailer had broken down coming across the Hi level bridge just outside of Hamilton. My dad and I went and gave them a hand, fixed the trailer, and they got settled in. Domenic ended up staying at my parents' place in Hamilton. I think they (likely) would have rather had him for a son than me. He was so quiet, polite, and well-mannered.

- Russ Carter, guitarist; email to Frank Troiano, April, 2020

Outside of Toronto, the city of London, Ontario (halfway between Toronto and Windsor), became a popular haunt for the Rogues, and where Domenic would be well received throughout his career. London music executive/promoter Nick Panaseiko recalls the Rogues' first trip into town:

In 1966, New Year's Eve fell on a Friday night. I knew that the London crowd would want to party on New Year's Day… the Rogues I had never heard of … We had a packed house at the Windjammer Room. It was showtime and the stage lights went black. Then this thunderous intro, I believe by Mitch Markowitz. The band all faced the back of the stage as each individual turned around in sequence in their black pin-striped suits. London was blown away! This was the first time that they had ever witnessed a choreographed R & B act and so this was the beginning of years of friendship as London became Dom's second home.

- Nick Panaseiko, promoter; email to Frank Troiano, April, 2020

For London-based blues guitarist Bill Durst, founder of the band Thundermug, the experience of seeing Domenic with the Rogues was pivotal:

It was 1966/67 at the London Arena in London, Ontario. They came on, or should I say the drummer did, by himself! He began a fantastic beat with his bass drum tilted up in the air. Whitey Glan immediately blew away every drummer in London. Next came Don Elliott, playing a sawed-off bass guitar (unbelievably). My friend and I were both jaw-dropped. Then Joey Chirowski came on with amazing organ riffs and a tilted Hammond with his Leslie speakers painted different colours as they spun around. Each member of the band was introduced by a hidden announcer. We had never seen or heard anything like it!

The band was playing up a storm as each instrument was added, but then the guitarist was introduced. To add to the drama of the moment, the band came to a complete stop and I heard a phenomenal single ringing guitar note which was screaming and crying like a human being. It was more than a music note—it contained a primal quality and an opening of the soul of the player with all the pain, joy, and anger that was there for all to behold in that single note. I could not believe it! I did not know music could do that. I began to get a rush from the bottom of my spine to the top of my head and as the massive power of the sound and the emotion swept over me I realized I had to learn how to do that!

- Bill Durst, guitarist—Thundermug; email to Frank Troiano, April, 2020

Mitch Markowitz started hanging out with the Rogues in 1966, and tells how he came to become the band's official "announcer."

I first met Donnie and the rest of the guys in the band mid 60s, probably 1965. This was post-Bluenote and the band was gigging in around the greater Toronto area (GTA). Seeing them was a life-altering experience. SHAZAM! I was awestruck! Don, George, Whitey, and Joey were all nice guys, but Donnie was special. We hit it off immediately. Not long after my first introduction, I started hanging out with the band and getting involved. I started offering input and some direction. It was

decided that I would act as MC, introducing the band. This was one more way to set us apart from other bands.

There were also the Catholic Youth Organization (CYO) Sunday afternoon gigs in church basements. There was one dance in particular where the priest overseeing the gig walked onstage in the middle of a song, grabbed the mike from George and told the audience: "On the floor or out the door. No standing around and talking." I recall Donnie's great, warm laugh in situations like this or other situations that would have provoked a lesser leader to storm out or grab the mike back. Donnie was respectful, and kept these situations in their proper perspective. More often than not, George and the other guys followed suit, and everybody got paid ($30-$40/week).

- Mitch Markowitz, promoter; email to Frank Troiano, April, 2020

Jamaican-born Jay Douglas, who attended the same show, was mesmerized by the lead guitarist.

I couldn't take my eyes off the lead guitar player in the group, playing a white fender telecaster, who played with a whole lot of soul. He was driven—his eyes were closed so tight, his facial expression told you he was connected to the musical gods! Then he would open his eyes, I'm telling you his eyes were like an eagle's; we all know that the eagle flies higher than any other bird.

- Jay Douglas, singer; email to Frank Troiano, April, 2020

The Five Rogues were at the top of their game, and Domenic was the driving force. He was intent on writing and arranging his own material as well as playing the standard R & B playlists. The "who's who" of the music industry was consistently being blown away by the live act and especially by what Domenic was doing. Duff Roman, radio executive with CHUM Radio, greatly respected and admired Domenic's fast rise.

I became aware of Domenic Troiano during those crazy mid-60s days on Yonge Street when the Hawks had left Ronnie Hawkins and Robbie Lane and the Disciples stepped in to fill some very big shoes. Dom was part of a small but growing handful of musicians who embodied what came to be known as the "Toronto Sound," defined by rock-infused rhythm and blues led by wailing string-bending electric guitars in the hands of Robbie Robertson, Domenic Troiano, and Fred Keeler. I was able to spend some time with Domenic, who had by then moved on to The Five Rogues. Here was Dom—young, studious and so very talented—his style was rawness with musicality.

- Duff Roman, radio executive—CHUM Radio; email to
  Frank Troiano, May, 2020

Around this time, Blaine Pritchett came on the scene. A self-described tough kid from Cabbagetown, a residential neighbourhood in central Toronto, originally named in the 1840s for Macedonian and Irish immigrants said to be so poor that they grew cabbage patches in their front yards for their main food supply. Blaine would latch on with the Rogues and subsequently remain connected with Domenic throughout much of his career, and bearing witness.

I started working with the Rogues on a voluntary basis just to help out. The guys were all good guys. Donnie took me under his wing and taught me a lot. Donnie let one of the guys that was working for him go and then it was just Carmelo and me. I was doing sound and I built all Donnie's equipment. I was with Donnie through the whole time with the Rogues, about ninety percent of the Mandala, and then all of the time with The Guess Who.

- Blaine Pritchett, sound technician; interview with
  Mark Doble, July 21, 2020

By 1966, The Five Rogues were the premier performing band in the Toronto music scene and throughout Southern Ontario. But for Domenic and The Five Rogues, resting on their laurels was out of the question. It was time to take things to the next level.

Domenic "Donnie" Troiano, 1963 (Troiano Family Archives)

CHAPTER 3
OPPORTUNITY

"We came three thousand miles from Canada to L.A.
To tell you exactly how it feels
Maybe it's here we'll get our opportunity."
(*Opportunity*, lyrics by Domenic Troiano)

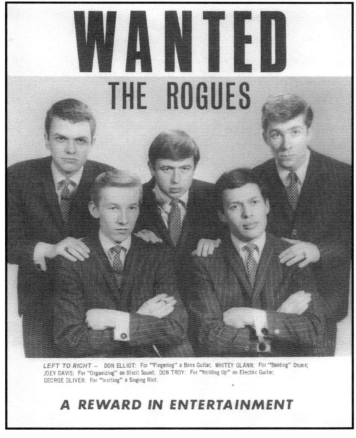

The Five Rogues—Don Elliot, Pentti "Whitey" Glan, Joey Chirowski, Domenic Troiano, George Olliver, 1965 *(Troiano Family Archives)*

Domenic was becoming a force to be reckoned with and he was revealing the discipline and talent that he would refine with the Mandala who, under the guidance of Randy Markowitz, would blow up the Toronto music scene as the Soul Crusade. Domenic drew attention and the highest regard from his fans and his fellow musicians even as the cream was rising to the top

- Duff Roman, radio executive—CHUM Radio; email to
  Frank Troiano, May, 2020

So, I took off with Terry to North Bay to see his dad and try to get some cash. I don't remember what happened to Terry's gig in Sault Ste. Marie, but I do remember that when we got to North Bay, we saw a lounge band, the Mandala, with a great guitarist named Domenic Troiano and George Olliver, a fantastic vocalist. Wow! Those guys were really cool; slick and professional R & B.

- *Waging Heavy Peace*, Neil Young, Penguin Group, Toronto, 2012

For his part, George Olliver's recollection of meeting Neil Young was somewhat different:

Actually, it was Port Arthur [later to become part of the city of Thunder Bay, Ontario] where we were playing. I remember Neil. He came up to our hotel to meet us after the show that night. He was great.

- George Olliver, lead vocalist; interview with Mark Doble,
  July 15, 2020

It was a pivotal moment in the spring of 1966 when the Rogues hired Mitch Markowitz's brother, Randy Martin (a.k.a. Riff Markowitz) to assume the full-time management of the group. Martin was host of his own children's TV program, *The Randy Dandy Show*. With a gift for promotion, Randy Martin's guidance and instinct for publicity swiftly took The Five Rogues to the next level. Mitch brought the band and his brother together.

I had my brother out to a rehearsal. He was awestruck just like everyone else who saw them. He met with Donnie and then the guys, and they were off to the races. With my brother's background in television, live theatre, and marketing, he took the band to the next level, creating the

"Soul Crusade of the Mighty Mandala" that would hypnotize audiences internationally. My brother gave them structure, discipline, timing, lighting, wardrobe, creative direction, and blood, sweat and tears. With his experience and never-ending energy he positioned the band to play with the big boys; having them booked on the same performing bills as internationally renowned rock acts. They were billed as "Canada's #1 band," with gigs at New York's top club, Steve Paul's The Scene as well as the top clubs in Los Angeles: the Whiskey-a-Go-Go, the Troubadour, and more. They had television exposure, record deals with Phil Spector and Chess Records. We gave it everything we had!

- Mitch Markowitz; email to Frank Troiano, April, 2020

Captivated by their stage presence and energy, and seeing the fevered fan reaction to Olliver's sensational soul-singer delivery, Martin set about to create a buzz that would further enhance the band's image and reputation.

Randy said about the audience, "They listen with their eyes. You don't have to be the best players in the world. You have to play well and look like you're having a good time and you know what you're doing." He taught us what show business was all about! The Mandala was the first Canadian band to use strobe lights. Randy taught the band to use theatrics. There was a lot of innovation going on at the time. Things were changing so fast. Randy took the band a long way.

- Blaine Pritchett, sound technician; interview with Mark Doble, July 21, 2020

Martin's management reaped immediate rewards with better opportunities. In the summer of 1966, they would open for Wilson Pickett at Club 888 (the Masonic Temple at Yonge Street and Davenport Road) in Toronto. The gig was notable for a number of reasons, not the least of which was the thrill of opening for an R & B legend. However, that night, as Pickett's drummer had been refused entry by Canada Customs, Whitey was asked to play drums for Pickett. After obtaining permission from the Rogues, and after playing the opening set with the Rogues, Whitey wore his distinctive Rogues striped suit as he played with Pickett's band. Pickett's band at the time also happened to include a lead guitarist by the name of Jimi

Hendrix. Following the set, Pickett even suggested that Whitey consider joining his ensemble.

That same summer, they opened for The Rolling Stones at Maple Leaf Gardens. Domenic's younger brother Frank tagged along for the concert and enjoyed a unique back-stage perspective.

June 29th was a hot, muggy night. The Ugly Ducklings opened to a great response, followed by the Rogues who had an even greater response from their loyal and passionate fans—two twenty-minute sets. They were followed by Syndicate of Sound, the Standells, and Rick Derringer and the McCoys.

In 1966, Donnie was only twenty, and what a great thrill for him to perform in front of eleven thousand fans! The air was electric; the kids were wild with anticipation and it was time for the mind-blowing main course.

The Stones were backstage, ready to go on and they were holding up Brian Jones between them as he may have been a little tipsy. They did just over an hour and a half show. I was backstage and witnessed it all. One of the fans who was seated behind the stage let herself down from above and rushed toward Jagger and was restrained. Many more jumped on the stage. It was pandemonium, especially when they performed *Satisfaction.* **After the encores, they rushed backstage and I went onto the stage and the fans had thrown all kinds of trinkets, bracelets, and film containers containing phone numbers. I waved at the fans as if I was meant to be there—I was a cocky fifteen-year-old. Donnie had gone back into the dressing room after the Rolling Stones' set and then came out. He was startled to see me onstage, but smiling at my boldness, he told me to get off, as it was time to go home. So, I did my only duty that night by carrying his '63 Tele into the car. It was the beginning of my future career as a roadie and road manager.**
- Frank Troiano

Famed DJ and radio host David Marsden was the master of ceremonies for the Stones concert.

I was the MC for the Rolling Stones concert at Maple Leaf Gardens in 1966, and the Rogues came on after the Ugly Ducklings opened and they had a large contingent of fans who really gave them a great reception. Once again, they put on a short but high-energy set and were well received. I saw the Mandala a couple of times, and I was blown away by their performance. It truly was a spectacle!

- David Marsden, radio host; interview with Frank Troiano, April, 2020

The Five Rogues became one of the first Canadian acts to utilize strobe lights. Frank Troiano recalls Randy Martin stopping by the house one evening and going up to Domenic's room to show them the new strobe light that he had just picked up in New York. Frank Troiano was fifteen years old in the mid 1960s, and saw his brother perform countless times. His recollection of two significant gigs held a year apart help illustrate the musical/professional evolution taking place within the group under Randy Martin and Domenic's direction and leadership.

The Rogues at the Pepsi Under 21 Club at the CNE, 1965 & 1966

What a difference a year makes! I attended the Rogues' August performances at the "Pepsi Under 21 Club" at the CNE in Toronto in both 1965 & 1966.

In 1965, the band members wore red "Perry Como" sweaters, chalk-striped navy dress pants, white shirts, and black shoes. I attended both an afternoon and evening performance, and the crowds numbered about 500 to 750 kids. The attendees were very enthusiastic and loud and about half of them danced during the shows. The Rogues were politely introduced by one of the CNE staff. The band played mostly R & B standards such as songs by Wilson Pickett, Sam & Dave, Billy Stewart, Tom Jones, Ray Charles, Otis Redding, Stevie Wonder, and some funky, bluesy instrumentals. Almost all the songs were cover tunes with the exception of lead guitarist Donnie Troiano's *Make It Up to You* and *I Can't Hold Out No Longer*. Lead vocalist George Olliver would occasionally sit in on keyboards while Joey Chirowski played trumpet solos. The rest of the band consisted of Don Elliot on bass, Whitey Pentti Glan on drums, and band leader Donnie Troiano on lead guitar. They were well received but did mostly cover songs.

In the spring of '66, Randy Martin (aka) "Riff" Markowitz took over the management of the Rogues and swiftly implemented wholesale changes: sound, lighting, band apparel, etc. It was truly transformational! The subsequent "Pepsi Under 21 Club" event in 1966 was a case in point. The differences in presentation and performance between '65 and '66 were like night and day.

The hall was packed with a capacity crowd of two thousand kids and many others lined up outside hoping to get in. There was a real buzz of anticipation in the air, and finally the lights were dimmed and there was a hush in the crowd. The 1966 event was called "Tempo 66, Dance," but ironically the audience was totally captivated by the performance and no one was dancing. One of the Markowitz brothers introduced the band, the lights came on full onstage, and the band went into a full-on, blistering instrumental and after a minute or two, an abrupt stop and total silence. Then a spotlight shone on the lead singer, George Olliver, as he ran onto the stage, full throttle—doing the splits, gyrating, twisting, turning, and singing the intro number. The crowd went crazy and I personally was so excited that I had goose bumps. I had never seen my brother's band have this kind of reaction before, and easily got caught up in the excitement.

The band members were wearing black, white, and grey striped suits, black shirts, white ties, grey "gangster" spats and grey suede shoes—very impressive and very different from 1965. The band's stage equipment was much improved and the sound was more powerful, crisp, and LOUD! The band's new lighting system was stunning and hypnotic.

The first set went very well and the band played more original music and a sprinkling of cover songs. The intermission between sets was badly needed as the kids came down from their high/trance and they rushed to the confectionary stands to buy soft drinks and snacks.

The second set was even more powerful. The band debuted *Opportunity*, which eventually became their first single release. The kids loved it and the guitar solo left everyone awestruck. Toward the end of the set the band did their classic routine "Soul Crusade" featuring the *Five Steps to Soul*. George Olliver whipped the crowd into mass hysteria and after offering his "soul"—he collapsed into the crowd. A pair of security guards pulled him back. The "Crusade" was so powerful that three teenaged girls fainted that night.

Later that week, the CNE asked the Rogues to tone down their show because it posed a danger to the safety of the audience. The band's manager Randy Martin declared that tempering the Rogues' act would cheat the two thousand fans, and abruptly terminated their CNE contract. This was widely covered by all the Toronto papers, including the *Toronto Star* and the *Toronto Telegram*. Indeed, the Rogues had come a long way from 1965 to 1966!

-   Frank Troiano

Toronto singer Virgil Scott provides a quasi-stream-of-consciousness account of the emotional and visual impact of the same 1966 CNE show:

1966—Saturday at the CNE, I was sixteen. We entered a room that was so very packed with teenagers, a nice-sized stage, with PA and lighting larger than we had ever seen. All of a sudden, the lights went out, a couple of girls screamed, and a voice came on the PA: "Ladies and gentlemen please welcome The Five Rogues!" Well, the lights went up huge and the band blazed into an amazing, full-tilt instrumental that featured every member. I had never heard anything like it, full, balls to the wall, take no prisoners, amazing. Terry and I were looking at each other saying, "How do they do that? Holy crap! I don't believe it!" And just when I thought everything was going to blow up, the band snapped down very soft into this weird, two-chord bluesy riff, and I looked at Terry and said, "What was that?" Then over the PA: "Ladies and gentlemen, Mr. George Olliver!" Well, that was it. The band screamed into that riff again and this guy came running out, full-on, right across the stage to the other end, and as he was running back the other way, he jumped into the air and grabbed the mike stand on his way down into the splits!

The band stopped dead—for five seconds—and then went into a very fast, full-tilt version *of I'll Go Crazy* and again Domenic went into this solo like I had never heard before and I thought, "Who is this guy and who is this band? They can't be from Toronto!" I finally took a breath and it felt like I was somewhere else in the world; somewhere fantastic, and somewhere I had never been before and I had always hoped there was somewhere like it and I remember thinking, "These guys are better than the Beatles."

- Virgil Scott, singer; email to Frank Troiano, April, 2020

With Martin, all publicity was good publicity. Stunts and controversy were the order of the day. When Toronto radio station CHUM refused to play their records, Martin arranged for two hundred teenagers to show up at the station with picket signs. When CNE officials requested that the band "tone down" their act, Martin promptly cancelled the gig and went to the press.

A rhythm and blues band, the Rogues, quit their CNE contract last night when officials asked them to tone down their act. The Rogues, performing at the Under 21 Club, said they refused to compromise their show and left a contract that had four days yet to run. "... We asked them to temper their act simply for the safety of the teenagers who were crowding in and trying to climb on the stage," said Peter Batson of the CNE staff.

- "Soul group won't tone down the act," *Toronto Telegram*, September 1, 1966

Cancelling the engagement did more to further the cause of the Rogues than it would to have gone ahead with the gig!

In the summer of '66, the legendary Bo Diddley was at Le Coq D'Or. After going upstairs to the Hawk's Nest and watching the Rogues perform, Bo was sufficiently impressed that he recommended them to his label, Chess Records. His endorsement was enough for Marshall Chess to travel from Chicago to hear for himself and sign them on the spot.

The summer of 1966 provided some terrific opportunities. Frank Troiano got to tag along again when The Five Rogues opened for Herman's Hermits at an outdoor concert.

Later in that '66 summer, on August 6th, another important concert was held in Toronto—Herman's Hermits sharing top billing with Eric Burdon and the Animals at the Maple Leaf baseball stadium. Once again CHUM 1050 AM ran a contest to choose two Toronto bands to open the evening, and the winners this time were The Five Rogues and the Spasstiks. That night, the Spasstiks came on first, followed by The Five Rogues. The Rogues caused a mini riot when George Olliver jumped off the stage and ran into the crowd and offered his tie, which he called his "soul," and dozens of long-haired girls mobbed him. He barely made it back to the stage. During the Rogues' set, the Animals arrived in two black limos and drove onto the field, causing another mini riot. Both the Animals and Herman's Hermits had tumultuous receptions from the ten thousand or so fans. I was able to go back and forth between the locker rooms and dugout, from which I watched the concert.

- Frank Troiano

Martin wanted to recreate the band's image in a way that would force fans to think differently about them. A name change was in order. So, at the end of the summer, prior to going to Chicago to record their first single, The Five Rogues would become the Mandala. In an October, 1966 press release, Martin explained:

Amid throbbing lights, frenetic motion, and immensely intense sound that "bombs the senses" and releases the mind are all apt descriptions for a new Canadian rock group that has met with phenomenal success. Recently signed by Chess Records, the world's major rhythm & blues recording company for their new KR Label, the Mandala (until recently known as the Rogues) has ignited audiences everywhere. The Mandala, a name derived from the ancient Hindu-Buddhist culture means "universe" and is symbolized by a circle-within-a-circle. It is used by the Buddhists as an aid to contemplation. The particular mandala which inspired the name symbolically portrayed five lamas who act as

bridges between the Deity and the world at large as an extension. The five members of the group see themselves as individuals trying to act as bridges in communication between people and their own emotions or souls.

The crowd seems to respond almost hypnotically. The Mandala sound, a heritage drawn from ancient India, the Orient, and liberally mixed with the rhythmic beat of the American south. Creating a wave of near-hysteria that engulfs both performers and audiences. A lighting complex especially attuned to the screaming instruments bathes all the stage and those surrounding it.

- Randy Martin; "Dazzling New Act: The Mandala," Press Release, 1966

It was, after all, the sixties. The Rolling Stones were delving into SATANIC MAJESTIES, the Beatles were on a MAGICAL MYSTERY TOUR. In 1968, the Beatles visited India to experience various aspects of Eastern mysticism. It was cool to seek a heightened mental and spiritual experience through medicinal-chemical influences or psychedelic sound. Back in Toronto, Canada, the Mandala was on a "Soul Crusade"!

For Domenic, it was about the music. Still, he respected the efforts of their new manager. Bernie Finkelstein, founder of True North Records, and at the time a manager of Toronto bands the Paupers and Kensington Market, remembered Randy introducing him to the Mandala.

One day Randy invited me to come see his band, the Mandala. This was right around the time the Paupers asked me to manage them. I was floored by the Mandala as was most of Toronto, and it was Randy who introduced me to Domenic. As the Paupers and the Mandala became more and more popular, the irony was that each band represented to some degree a separate and quite different audience. The Mandala, who played a kind of blue-eyed soul music attracted what we Villagers called a "greaser" audience and the Paupers, who were quite psychedelic had what the R & B crowd called a "hippie" audience. Both bands got US record deals at around the same time, which was quite a rarity for

66

Canadian bands during that period. The fun thing was that both bands were great and very original.

- Bernie Finkelstein, manager; email to Frank Troiano, May, 2020

Domenic's sister Gina was very young (twelve or thirteen years old) and recalled seeing the Mandala perform:

I saw them perform at the Broom and Stone. I was mesmerized by the strobe lights and the girls were screaming and going crazy over his band. It was like the Beatles!

- Gina Troiano, interview with Mark Doble, June 30, 2020

Gina's admiration for her older brother's talent extended to active promotion among her schoolmates. One of those classmates, Dave Breckels (who went on to become a professional musician), recalls the Mandala, as well as Domenic's little sister's efforts to further his cause.

I was sitting in my classroom in Grade 7, tapping on my desk with pencils as any budding thirteen-year-old drummer would and the girl in front of me turned around and firmly stated, "My brother is the greatest guitarist in the world, you know." I thought sure, sure, and asked, "What's his name?" She said, "Domenic Troiano!" This young girl knew I was trying to be a drummer and was obviously very proud of her brother and trying to impress me! I remember thinking, well unless his name is Jimi Hendrix I don't think so. The young girl was obviously Gina Troiano and we went on to be friends and classmates for a couple years at Cosburn Jr. High. The next time I heard the name Domenic Troiano I had just sneaked into a show up at Eglinton Arena to see a band everybody was talking about called The Mandala! The band and the guitarist completely blew my mind. They introduced him finally and I heard: "On guitar, Domenic Troiano!" I thought, "Holy shit! Gina was right!"

- Dave Breckels, drummer and schoolmate; email to
  Frank Troiano, June, 2020

Linda Goldman was one of those young teenagers who were mesmerized by George Olliver's showmanship.

I saw the Rogues zillions of times! The Rogues had a powerful and hypnotic show that captivated me and my girlfriends. What I loved the most was when George was in a frenzy and would take off his tie and toss it into the audience and some lucky girl would get it!
- Linda Goldman, fan/librarian; email to Frank Troiano, June, 2020

For his part, Martin very deliberately promoted the "mystique" of the extraordinary guitarist/band leader/enfant terrible:

Born in Italy, raised in Toronto, Canada, the Mandala leader on guitar— a serious-minded individualist, and master of his instrument. Since his early teens considered a guitarist of singularly extraordinary talent. No real description can be given of the electronic sounds and distortions he produces, other than to say that they create what is in effect a "sound shower" that penetrates, burns, and finally bathes the senses. Troiano's guitar, like his sight and sound unlike any other in the world, is of his own design and made entirely by hand. Its appearance is more like a violin than a guitar; it appears almost to be an extension of his body and soul.
- Randy Martin, "Dazzling New Act: The Mandala," Press Release, 1966

London, Ontario's Rick Young, rock journalist, and publisher of *Beat* magazine saw Domenic perform on many occasions in the London area and quickly became a booster.

By September 1966, the band had changed its name to the Mandala and launched its legendary Soul Crusade. I would see the Mandala at numerous venues in the London area including Wonderland Gardens, The Windjammer Room in Treasure Island, the Ivanhoe Curling Club, and Centennial Hall. Each concert was a major event and the band nurtured a loyal following in Southwestern Ontario. Local musicians watched in awe as the band performed the impossible.
- Rick Young, journalist; email to Frank Troiano, May, 2020

In October 1966, the newly named "the Mandala" travelled to Chess Studios in Chicago to record *Opportunity*, which would become the group's first hit record. (Also recorded at the same session was *From Toronto 67*, an instrumental released as the B side of their subsequent single.)

Opportunity is a slick, up-tempo rock/R & B tune. Olliver provides a soulful lead vocal that oozes righteous indignation, and Domenic renders a blistering guitar solo in the middle that is nothing short of sensational. Fellow label-mates The Dells, a successful and established R & B group in their own right (*Oh What a Night*) were enlisted to provide a full-bodied, five-part harmony to the driving rhythmic number. The lyrics are auto-biographical, describing the Mandala leaving the familiar confines of the Toronto music scene, to venture into the US, hoping for greater success in the "land of *Opportunity*."

The B side, *Lost Love*, an Olliver composition was recorded in Toronto and could not have been more opposite in tone to *Opportunity*, a slower love ballad sung with power and passion and nicely punctuated with the repeating "*Lost Love*" chorus.

Although I was the one to suggest Chess Records, Randy Markowitz did the deal and got us signed to Chess. Domenic and I really appreciated Randy. We went down to Chicago and recorded *Opportunity*. Domenic was sole writer on that tune and it had a lot of musical changes. It was an instant hit. Chess Studios was an amazing experience. We were in a studio where so many artists we had idolized had recorded. We were actually the first white group to record in their studio and get a record released. A lot of people remembered the flipside *Lost Love*, which I wrote. It was more traditional R & B. In fact, *Opportunity/Lost Love* was considered to be a double-sided hit in many provinces across Canada, where it made the top ten and in some places number one. It was a real honour for me to have the single released on Chess Records and to have recorded with Domenic.

- George Olliver, lead vocalist; interview with Mark Doble, July 1, 2020

The Mandala was taking things to the next level; increasing their fan base and popularity everywhere they went. But Martin was determined to grow the Mandala brand south of the border as well. So, the following month, in November 1966, he arranged a successful set of dates at the famed Whiskey-a-Go-Go in Hollywood.

Bob Segarini has enjoyed a remarkable career. After moving from California to Canada in the early 1970s, he recorded albums with The Wackers, The Dudes, and as a solo artist. In the '80s, Bob became a Toronto FM radio DJ, adopting the moniker "The Iceman." Today, Bob writes regular columns and music industry blogs. Originally from California, in the 1960s Bob formed a group called The Family Tree, who in 1966 happened to be the opening act for the Mandala at the Whiskey-a-Go-Go.

So, we're doing three or four days at the "Whiskey," opening for some band called the Mandala, and we go down in the afternoon to set up our gear, and we see these guys onstage in their full stage gear, and we're laughing at them because they looked so prissy in their outfits, and we're getting a kick out of it. And then they started playing, and we go "Holy fuck! These guys are amazing!" I'll never forget it. We set up our stuff and then went over to Bert Seigel's to see if they had any striped suits! The first night, it was all local musicians and the place was full. The second and third nights, there were lineups, because word spread really fast. That kind of R & B, nobody in L.A., let alone California was playing that kind of stuff. And they killed it! And that's how I met the Mandala in Los Angeles, long before I ever had a clue they were from Toronto!
-   Bob Segarini, singer-songwriter, broadcaster, writer;
    interview with Mark Doble, September 29, 2020

The sensation created through the Whiskey-a-Go-Go shows would lead to additional gigs in Los Angeles, most notably a week-long run at the "Hullaballoo," where many friends of the band were on hand to witness their debut.

The Mandala followed the opening act, on the revolving stage in their striped suits, which was a total contradiction to the hippie fashions of the day. This was the tightest band we had ever seen. They struck up with a cover of James Brown's *Think* and brought the house down. The light show, singer George Olliver's dancing, and Don Troiano's lightning

guitar licks kicked the proceedings up another notch. The final song, *Faith*, was an initiation of the whole audience into the spiritual world of "The Soul Crusade of the Mandala." With their anti-drug message and beyond psychedelic visuals, the crowd was drained. Sometime later, I heard a guy I knew made off with the Mandala's light machine. Somehow, I managed to arrange the return of the machine, and was invited to their hotel in Beverly Hills.

- Jan Alan Henderson, Los Angeles journalist; email to Frank Troiano, October, 2020

Music promoter, musician, and friend Johnny Brower was also at the Hullabaloo shows.

Dom was one of the most humble and even shy legends I ever met, and over the years I have met many who earned that station; none quite such a gentle man and soul as Dom. But it was when the Mandala stormed into Hollywood and played the Hullabaloo that I was able to thrill and beam with pride. I was gifted a backstage pass, and able to drive a couple of the boys around in my Pontiac Catalina after the show, even driving some nasty racers off Sunset Blvd and onto a lawn as we all screamed into the night at about sixty miles an hour. I think Joey said he would never get in a car with me again.

- Johnny Brower, promoter; email to Frank Troiano, April, 2020

Teri Brown, publicist, A & R Decca Records, booking agent and a friend were late-night clubbing in Los Angeles in 1966 and were curious to hear this hot Canadian band who were performing at a club called "Cyrano's."

We arrived just after midnight and witnessed one of the most power-ful musical performances that just blew us away. No music fan in L.A. had ever experienced such a high-energy and powerful music act. I befriended their manager, Randy Markowitz, that night and convinced him that I could assist the band in getting further bookings in L.A. and introducing the band to my press, radio, and television connections. I introduced them to Premier Talent Agency who subsequently assisted the band in getting bookings at the Hullabaloo, the Cheetah and the

Whiskey-a-Go-Go during this visit and their next two visits to L.A. in '68 and '69.
- Teri Brown, publicist/agent; interview with Frank Troiano, September, 2020)

Amazingly the Mandala, a band from Canada was filling Los Angeles clubs solely on the basis of their live performance and word of mouth! There were no Mandala records to buy, and nothing on the radio.

Randy Markowitz was a tremendous manager and promotional agent. He got us radio shows and got us signed to Chess Records. Randy was a pro at promoting us. In Los Angeles at the Whiskey-a-Go-Go and the Hullabaloo, we packed the places. We were noticed by important people in the industry and that was all due to Randy. We met everybody. It was amazing!
- George Olliver, lead singer; interview with Mark Doble, July 1, 2020

According to roadie/sound technician Blaine Pritchett, George Olliver also deserved credit for the sensation and stir that occurred in L.A.

They played the Hullabaloo and the Roxy and Clapton got up and played with the band one night. At one point, there was a club that the band was playing in and it was packed and Paul McCartney and a bunch of people showed up and couldn't get in.

George was a great performer. He did some things inadvertently that he shouldn't have done. But he made a lot of people sit up and take notice. Municipal regulations were such that people were not allowed to even carry their beer from one table to the next. If you wanted to do that, you had to have a waiter help you. But George had people dancing all over the club with their beer, and going out the back door of the club and in the front. The headlines back in Toronto were that the Mandala was causing a riot down on Sunset Strip! You know, he caused quite a stir!
- Blaine Pritchett, sound technician; interview with Mark Doble, July 21, 2020

That George was strong and naturally athletic helped with the stage act, but drummer Whitey Glan's experience as a competitive gymnast also contributed to George's extraordinary dance moves.

Whitey was like a national level gymnast. All those moves that George used to do in the Mandala, Whitey came up with. His dexterity and independence were amazing, he was so athletic. And he could make Donnie laugh, where Roy and I wouldn't dare try. Whitey could get away with it. Donnie deserved all of the acclaim that he received, but people need to acknowledge how brilliant Whitey was. He was a tremendous guy!

- Prakash John, bass guitarist—Bush; interview with Mark Doble, July 28, 2020

Released in January 1967, *Opportunity* immediately became the signature song and ultimately one of the most popular songs by a Toronto artist. But Toronto radio attitudes were far from supportive of their local talent.

When the record was released, CHUM wouldn't play *Opportunity*. Finally, the big radio station in Windsor was playing the shit out of it and it was getting played in the States and that forced CHUM's hand. But the record was probably out for six weeks before CHUM would even play it. But through it all, Donnie really kept his cool. He told us, "Welcome to Canada!" But he didn't get upset.

- Blaine Pritchett, sound technician; interview with Mark Doble, July 21, 2020

Although numerous other Toronto R & B artists were there and contributed, it is the Mandala and Troiano who were the acknowledged champions of the Toronto Sound. Michael Watson, promo man with CBS and Capitol Records grew up in Toronto and recalls what was happening at the time.

When I started managing my friend Bobby Dupont (the Statlers) and (with Pete Rumble) Buzz Shearman (Bo-Street Runners) in the fall of '66 and, later, Donnie Meeker (the Jax) and Virgil Scott (the Innocence) in '67/'68, my heroes were Riff Markowitz, Brian Ayres, and Tom Wilson. I was a rookie booking agent. The musicians were enthralled

with the Mandala, mesmerised by George Olliver, and the king of it all was Donnie Troiano.
- Michael Watson, promotional rep; email to Frank Troiano, May, 2020

Central to the Toronto Sound was the song *Opportunity*. Canadian songwriter, producer, and Grammy and Juno Award winner Ben Mink recalls the first time he heard the Mandala perform *Opportunity* live.

On a Sunday afternoon in the mid to late '60s my friends and I went to see a Toronto band called the Mandala at the North York "Y." They had just changed their name from the Rogues. They featured a charismatic singer, George Olliver, and an amazing guitarist, Dom Troiano, who delivered this searing, almost frightening sound from his Telecaster— his amazing finger picks and this emotional raw sound! They played a tune that they called *Opportunity* with a guitar solo that just didn't sound like a guitar solo. To me now it's an electric violin solo. It doesn't have any logic or explanation; it is just pure emotion. It was such a pivotal moment for me. It was like lightning striking when I heard that! From Toronto to L.A., *Opportunity* by the Mandala!
- Ben Mink, producer, songwriter, violinist; "My Playlist with J. J. Laborde," CBC FM Radio 1, June 21, 2020

Opportunity has remained a favourite of fans, and in 2019, over fifty years later, the song was inducted into the Canadian Songwriters Hall of Fame.

Having "conquered" Los Angeles the previous winter, the Mandala shifted to the east coast of the United States, spending much of the spring of 1967 in New York City appearing at Steve Paul's "the Scene" for an extended run. In his online biography of the Mandala, Jeremy Frey writes the following about this time:

While in the city, the Mandala took part in "Murray the K's" famous "Music in the Fifth Dimension" held at the RKO Theatre from 25 March to 2 April. The show featured a number of artists, including Wilson Pickett and the Blues Project as well as British bands Cream and The

Who, both making their debut US appearances. The group returned to Steve Paul's the Scene for a second run from 25 April through to 4 May.

- Jeremy Frey; Troianomusic.com, 2005

The other positive from the extended New York City residency was the opportunity to share playing bills with such greats as the Who, Cream (Eric Clapton), and Wilson Pickett. Pete Townshend and Eric Clapton would get together with Domenic in their hotel rooms to compare licks and jam together. For his part, fifty-three years after the fact, although his recollection is not as crystal clear, Townshend recalled the following:

I do now remember who he is, but I'm afraid I really don't have any reminiscences at all. I'm so sorry. Those were exciting times, but it was a whirlwind.

- Pete Townshend, lead guitarist, songwriter—The Who; email to Frank Troiano, October 7, 2020

Every time and everywhere they played, the Mandala and Domenic were earning substantial street cred for their high-energy show and awesome musicianship.

While in New York, the Mandala recorded their follow-up single at New York City's A & R Studios. *Give and Take* by Victor Chambers was a classic hit by Jimmy Cliff.

However, it is the B side that catches our attention, perhaps with fifty years for introspection. Looking back, this number seems to totally outclass the A side. *From Toronto-67*, this instrumental—credited to all of the Mandala members—is a fabulous blend of blues-funk-rock-psychedelia.

Released in March 1967, *Give and Take/From Toronto-67* charted in Toronto at a respectable top thirty, reaching number twenty-one, but less successful than *Opportunity,* released two months earlier.

Although both Mandala singles had charted respectably in Canada, Domenic was disappointed with the lack of promotion in the United States. In the early summer, the Mandala left Chess Records to sign with Decca records. Accordingly, the band would go into Toronto's RCA and

Sound Studios during breaks between engagements to record songs for their first full-length album.

The Mandala would spend the "summer of love" pivoting between New York City, Montreal, and Toronto (including a return trip to Los Angeles for another week at the Hullabaloo). Sadly, however, cracks were starting to show. Resentments were coming to the surface over leadership, musical direction, and even how money was being spent. This happens with most groups. There was a natural tension and competitiveness between Domenic, the acknowledged leader, and George, the flamboyant showman and lead singer.

Initially, George bought into the concept of Domenic's leadership. Over time however, George attempted to assert more of his own ideas. George was, after all, the lead singer, the guy in the spotlight, and certainly the main character in any appearance of the Mandala. In truth, it seems inevitable that the two talented and headstrong musicians would clash. On top of that, Randy Martin had rules where band members were penalized financially if they were late for sound check or rehearsal. This may have been the final straw for Olliver, who was already frustrated with his meagre forty dollars a week salary. (The Mandala was now billing up to two thousand dollars per engagement. A good portion of these proceeds went toward travel and accommodation costs, and Martin and Troiano were also investing in better equipment, stage presentation, and promotion). Finally, after a gig in New York at the end of September, the exhausted lead singer George Olliver resigned from the Mandala.

There is nothing more devastating to a successful group than the loss of the lead singer. The fans identify with the guy who sings the songs. Even more so, the loss of someone as talented and dynamic as George Olliver was potentially insurmountable. This was the leader/band maestro, who captivated and commandeered the audiences through *The Five Steps of Soul*.

I wanted more say and more of my own material on the records. At that point, I had been in the band for four years and was one of the co-founders, and I decided I wanted to develop my own solo career. I was

getting all the press and I thought that it was time for me to strike out on my own. And I was happy with my decision.

- George Olliver, lead singer; interview with Mark Doble, July 1, 2020

After a short break of a few weeks, Olliver would put together his own band, George Olliver and the Soul Children. Over five decades, George Olliver has continued to perform and record with different groups in the Toronto area and has enjoyed a great deal of success. Throughout the 1980s and 1990s, Domenic would frequently make guest appearances with George.

Soon after Olliver left, keyboardist Josef Chirowski departed as well. Chirowski would soon join the Canadian band Crowbar, and then go on to great things with Alice Cooper, Peter Gabriel, and others. He and Domenic would continue to connect for different projects years later as well.

Despite these departures, the Mandala would survive. The subsequent personnel changes would lead to an exciting next chapter.

Mandala—Joey Chirowski, Domenic Troiano, Whitey Glan, George Olliver, Don Elliot, 1967 (Troiano Family Archives)

CHAPTER 4

ROCK AND ROLL MADNESS

"Destination stardom, our intentions good
What we want, we can't see
Would we want it if we could
Rock and Roll Madness has got its grip on me."
(*Rock and Roll Madness,* lyrics by Domenic Troiano)

CRUSADE OF THE MIGHTY **Mandala**
DIRECTION: MARKOWITZ

Mandala—Roy Kenner, Domenic Troiano, Whitey Glan, Don Elliot,
Hughie Sullivan, 1968 (Troiano Family Archives)

Like that last time we were in the Bronx! We were halfway through a concert when a gunshot went off in the crowd. And suddenly there's this little guy coming up, less than five feet tall I swear, waving a .45 in his hand. The question of course was: Whose side is he on? "This is Karate Joe," some guy announced. "He's a very big man." Karate said, "If youse guys come back to da Bronx again, youse guys'll be dead guys, see?" Well, the dance was definitely over, but we had a contract for the next night as well. We took a vote and decided to go back. We went back, and the Bronx boys were waiting at the entrance. "That's it," we said, "Death Valley." But Karate said, "Youse guys got a lotta guts." And you know they were quiet as hell during the show and afterwards took us for drinks.

- "The Mandala: 5 Characters In Search of Fame," Paul King, *The Globe & Mail*, June 26, 1968

Our agent called us sometime in the later '60s and informed us that we were opening for the Mandala at a gig at the Milton arena. All the band members said in solemn unison, "Donnie!" Donnie Troiano would be on that stage over there in the cool shade of Milton Arena about ten this evening. We didn't have to be told to be early for this one. Tonight we play our first arena gig and we get to do it with the Mandala. Randy "Dandy" Markowitz, their manager, was checking out the venue. "Concrete floor ... shit acoustics ... smells bad ... small-town hockey rink."

- *Travels with My Amp*, Greg Godovitz, Abbeyfield Publishers, Toronto, 2001

In early '67, Donnie called and informed me that at some point in the near future, George and Joey were going to be leaving the band. He asked if Henry and I would consider joining the Mandala.

- Roy Kenner, lead vocalist; interview with Mark Doble, July 4, 2020

R. K. and the Associates were a local Toronto R & B unit (in 1965, they recorded and released a single, *Without My Sweet Baby/Baby You're What I Need*), playing local high schools and dance clubs. Glenn Lupani was a childhood acquaintance of both Domenic and Roy Kenner.

When Roy Kenner joined in (I think that was '67), I thought to myself, "How the hell do two guys who lived on Sammon Avenue, literally doors apart, team up and make some fantastic music?" Roy and I went to preschool together!
- Glenn Lupani, childhood friend; email to Frank Troiano, May, 2020

Roy Kenner was a charismatic presence with a powerful voice that wowed the dance crowds with his quasi-James Brown dance moves.

I came into the Mandala in the middle of the recording process for the SOUL CRUSADE album. The material was already set and my creative input was simply to learn the songs and to sing them to the best of my ability. The guys kept referring to me as "the new kid." Here I am being asked to join a band which was like a force of nature in the Canadian music industry. It was hard work; whatever they wanted me to do, I did it, and it still remains my favourite band experience.
- Roy Kenner, lead vocalist; interview with Mark Doble, July 2, 2020

Looking for someone who not only could sing but also replicate George Olliver's dynamism, Kenner was recruited along with organist Henry Babraj to join the Mandala in the fall of 1967. Babraj's tenure was short-lived, and Hugh Sullivan soon took over the keyboard responsibilities.

Hughie Sullivan was amazing. Hughie Sullivan could play piano great, but he was an organ player; in fact, the best organ player that the Mandala ever had. He understood what Donnie was doing. Like on *Give and Take*, because of the structure of what Donnie and Hughie played together, you'd swear it was a horn section onstage. Hughie's nickname was "Spud," and THE JOKE'S ON ME has a tune on it called *Spud*, named after him.
- Blaine Pritchett, sound technician; interview with Mark Doble, July 21, 2020

Other bands would have imploded, but not the Mandala. One of Kenner's first performances with the Mandala was in October at the Hullabaloo. It was the band's fourth appearance there that year, and the fans, fully invested in George Olliver, were far from receptive to the new singer strutting and leaping around the stage.

My taking over the lead vocal duties went over OK for the most part in Canada. Where it became an issue was when we went to L.A. There was very little beforehand knowledge, and here were two new kids doing SOUL CRUSADE. Hitting the stage was a disaster. The fans didn't want to be surprised and they let us know. I didn't know how to react to that. Donnie recognized that I was in trouble right away and stepped up to explain to the audience. He did the "preaching" to try to win the fans over—kind of ran interference—which helped. But I understood. What you are used to is what you like. And in this case, the fans were used to George.

- Roy Kenner, lead vocalist; interview with Mark Doble, July 2, 2020

But it would bear out, regardless of the theatrics or even the magnetic dynamism of a lead singer, the *true* leader of the Mandala was Domenic Troiano. Oshawa-born John Donabie was just starting out as a DJ for a local Oshawa radio station in 1966.

I first encountered Domenic Troiano in 1966 at the Whitby arena, and the Mandala were playing there, and I went out there with my little Phillip's tape recorder and decided I was going to interview them and I got to talk to their manager, Randy, and set it up. When the show was over, I immediately gravitated to George Olliver and we started to chat for a couple of minutes, and then all of a sudden, Domenic came up to me, and said, "Hi, I'm Domenic Troiano." He was extremely bright and knew how to organize situations very well, and he kind of walked me down the line of how the Mandala formed, going back to the Rogues, and how they all got together, the song writing, and talked about each individual member. He knew if I wanted the right answers, and I wanted the real deal, that he could give it to me. And he did it very gently when he called me over.

- John Donabie, radio host; interview with Mark Doble, August 3, 2020

John and Domenic became fast friends, and over the years he would note that Domenic's leadership style was a consistent factor, if not a common theme, in every ensemble unit he played.

He was the boss, the organizer, the brains; I mean, you can call it many things. He really did have control and that was good, because everybody needs a leader. He was like the head surgeon or the general. "You have to follow me because I know it's going to make this popular, I know it's going to make this right, just follow me!" It was the same within Bush—Prakash and Whitey—they knew he was in charge. It wasn't malicious. Donnie just had a game plan. He would look right over your head pretty much because he knew what he wanted to accomplish and he knew what he wanted to do. And he needed you to fall in line. It was never meant to intimidate or make you feel bad. He just wanted you to follow his plan.

-   John Donabie, radio host; interview with Mark Doble, August 3, 2020

Gregory Lee Fitzpatrick, bass guitarist with the Lords of London frequently shared venues with Domenic and the Mandala.

It was never about "look at me, look at my solos." If you listened closely and watched his guitar playing you would observe that the whole band arrangement was all there. Not only could Domenic squeeze other-worldly sounds through his trusted Tele at the precise time, but his underappreciated rhythm guitar playing set the table for the rest of the band. Domenic was a pioneer, an innovator, a significant influence, and a wonderful, classy, fellow musician both on and off the stage and with his fans.

-   Gregory Lee Fitzpatrick, bass guitarist—Lords of London/Nucleus; email to Frank Troiano, November, 2020

The musical maturity at such a young age was astonishing. Domenic's sense of formal conception, essential to his creative instinct, seemed to be fully developed from day one. The respect of his peers went beyond the pure musicianship. Donnie's willingness to extend a helping hand or simple guidance and encouragement did not go unnoticed. One such peer included singer-songwriter Neil Merryweather of the Toronto bands The Mynah Birds and The Tripp:

I first saw Donnie play at the Blue Note jazz/blues club in Toronto when I was a young musician and starting out as a singer in my first band. He blew me away. So many early Toronto bands looked up to Donnie's first band, the Rogues. He set the bar as a band leader. The last band I had in Toronto, The Tripp, was signed by the Mandala manager, Riff Markowitz. We had opened a show for the Mandala and it was Donnie that recognized our potential and it was he that told Riff to sign us. When a compliment was warranted, or when a suggestion would help me or my band, it was Donnie that generously gave it. I learned a lot from him both as a musician and as a person. I saw him in L.A. a few times over the years and he was always the same guy, full of love and a constant passion for music.

- Neil Merryweather, singer and bass guitarist—The Mynah Birds/The Tripp; email to Frank Troiano, January, 2021

In early 1968, things started to look up when Randy Martin was able to get the attention of producer Phil Spector, who in turn recommended the Mandala to Ahmet Ertegun, co-owner of Atlantic Records. Atlantic records liked what they heard and immediately bought out the Mandala's contract with Decca, who had by this time soured on the Mandala's musical direction. Roy Kenner's vocals would be recorded and added to the earlier recordings. The band would travel to New York to record one new track, *Love-itis* by R & B singer Harvey Scales. Although Domenic chafed at the notion of recording non-original material, he recognized the hit-potential of the song and was ecstatic to be recording for the same record company as Ray Charles and Aretha Franklin!

Arthur Thomas Woofenden was a booking agent who worked in both the Detroit and Windsor markets, and was thrilled when the Mandala agreed to rehearse at his club in Windsor for pre-production of their first album.

Rumour had it the Mandala were coming to Detroit to record and were in Windsor looking for a rehearsal hall. I drove over to their motel and boldly knocked on the door to their room. When I offered them

my club, The Intersection, in exchange for one night performing, they accepted immediately. My teenage dance hall was now the rehearsal hall for the mighty Mandala and I was on cloud nine. I would go down and watch them tighten up the songs that would later become their first album, SOUL CRUSADE. I was especially excited when Domenic Troiano informed me that Ahmet Ertegun was flying in from Atlanta to oversee the pre-production of their first album. I could hardly contain my feelings. Here I was with the Mandala rehearsing in my club, and the man responsible for so many great acts was coming to my club. When he walked into the room there was a calm that said "listen to the man" and we did. He talked with a slow, methodical confidence that left us all in awe. The song he brought and worked on with them that would be a feature on their album was *Love-itis* that was penned by Harvey Scales and Albert Vance out of Chicago. At the end of one rehearsal Domenic asked me if there were any Black churches in Windsor he could visit and listen to their rousing gospel music. Domenic said he got many of his ideas in writing R & B songs from them.

- Arthur Thomas Woofenden, promoter; email to Frank Troiano, April, 2020

SOUL CRUSADE remains a valuable and historical musical artefact for 1960s Canadian rock music. It would also be the only full-length album released by the Mandala.

World of Love is a full throated and uptempo rock song propelled by a primal percussion and a rollicking bass ostinato line that serves as a sensational album opener.

One Short Year is introduced with a short drum roll followed by Mexican trumpet lines to usher in what turns into a smooth toe tapper with focused brass interjections throughout. Quoting the original album liner notes: *"Their music is a catalytic agent, a bridge between man and his fellow. Their lyric speaks of life: 'One Short Year,' a parallel between life and the bull ring, both with their moment of truth."*

Produced and arranged by Arif Mardin and Jerry Greenberg, and recorded in New York in early 1968, *Love-itis* was a slick vehicle to showcase the new version of the Mandala with a terrific vocal and tasteful fuzz guitar lines overtop a solid horn and string accompaniment. Almost predictably, the song attracted radio attention, at least in Canada, rising to number nine on the CHUM chart. (CHUM, at 1050 on the AM dial, was the rock and roll radio authority in Toronto, Ontario, throughout the 1960s and early 1970s.) However, the song failed to have much of an impact south of the border.

Come on Home has a slower groove, opening with just electric organ playing a liturgical-churchy intro that rolls slowly into a solid blues funk in 6/8 time supported throughout by a blanket of organ punctuated by neat and bluesy guitar licks.

Every Single Day, co-written by Troiano and fellow Torontonian Keith McKie (The Vendettas/Kensington Market) is a funk-filled rhythm and blues number characterized by a seemingly disjointed riff pattern set up by the organ and decorated by some amazingly fluid guitar soloing.

Mellow Carmello Palumbo (named after Carmelo Palumbo, the band's road manager) is a psychedelic jam credited to Troiano, Don Elliot, and Whitey Glan. Starting off with a high-speed rock blues featuring great guitar and organ soloing by Troiano and Babraj respectively, the nifty tune suddenly shifts tempo and character as it disintegrates into an atonal stew of sound effects and soloing.

Can't Hold Out is another Domenic Troiano composition; more of a pop rhythm and blues tune. Roy Kenner shines in the softer-toned ballad *Don't Make Me Cry*.

Troiano's *Stop Crying on My Shoulder* is a pleasing midtempo late sixties style pop love song totally suited to Kenner's vocal style.

"Faith: of the power with which we are invested to confront the horns." (from the original album liner notes)

The last song of SOUL CRUSADE takes us back to church with the rock-funk R & B number *Faith*, in which Donnie Troiano shines as the "preacher-singer" channelling his inner James Brown and encouraging the devoted listeners with what can only be considered a fitting benediction to the musical proceedings.

SOUL CRUSADE, the only full album released by the Mandala, is a more than credible collection of songs. The Canadian music scene of the mid-1960s barely existed. The Mandala represented some of Canada's best rock musicians in Canada. Composer of nine out of ten songs, Domenic was totally involved in the musical arrangements and conception. The resultant rich and mature effort represented one of the most important records in Canadian recording history. And for many fans from that era, the music has certainly stood the test of time.

At the tender age of fifteen, I got my first taste of Toronto Soul by hearing *Opportunity* on CHUM AM. Until that fateful day, I had been saving every cent of allowance and grass cutter pay to purchase classics by James Brown, Otis Redding, Booker T and other soul greats. I found out that the Mandala was a Toronto band and I was hooked. The Christmas of '68 my parents got me a little portable battery powered record player and the SOUL CRUSADE album was bought soon afterward. I was totally blown away from the first drop of the needle and hearing the opening to *World of Love*. That album was replaced three or four times over the years until the digital age when even as recently as last month a new digital copy was purchased for my newest iPod. The SOUL CRUSADE album has stayed relevant to this day and is still an outstanding soul album from start to finish!
-    Peter Vickery, family friend; email to Frank Troiano, November, 2020

In 2008, Peter Vickery would write the liner notes to WE ALL NEED LOVE, the commemorative tribute CD to the legacy of Domenic Troiano.

Veteran radio disc jockey, Brian Master (Jewell 88.5 FM, CHUM FM, Q107) reflected on the Mandala's success in Southern Ontario at the time.

In the mid to late sixties, I started out as a DJ in the St. Catharines area and I also worked as an MC at Ron Metcalfe's teen club, The Castle in St. Kitts. The Mandala played there one weekend and I remember their striped suits and their explosive stage show ... exciting and almost

frightening! The kids loved it! On air, I played cuts from the Mandala album and got a lot of response to *Mellow Carmello Palumbo*. Our station played a lot of their music.

- Brian Master, radio host; email to Frank Troiano, May, 2020

In 1968, after releasing SOUL CRUSADE, and with *Love-itis* on the hit parade, the Mandala continued to tour Canada, the US, and even a couple of weeks in the Bahamas at the Jokers Wild nightclub in Freeport. Jim Norris, publisher of *Canadian Musician* magazine was a guitarist with the Sudbury group "The Taxi" and recalled opening for one of Kenner's first engagements with the Mandala.

In 1966 I moved from Sudbury, Ontario to attend the Music Faculty at the University of Toronto, and saw the Mandala any time I could. I was amazed at the musicianship, the stage performance, the lighting, and particularly the guitar wizardry of Domenic Troiano. In the summer of 1967, I reunited with my bandmates in Sudbury with the intention of moving to Toronto and becoming full-time musicians. Our first gig as the Taxi was opening for the Mandala, then with front man Roy Kenner, at the Club Drumbeat in Collingwood on December 2nd.

- Jim Norris, publisher; email to Frank Troiano, June, 2020

It was the Taxi's first live gig and was one of the Mandala's first gigs with Roy Kenner. After the first set, Jim saw Roy lying on the floor in the dressing room in agony as apparently Roy was not used to all the dance moves!

They had me exercising and working out to be in shape to do the dance moves. They wanted me to be able to project a similar physical presence to that of George. (Oh fuck!)

- Roy Kenner, lead vocalist; interview with Mark Doble, July 4, 2020

Intent on having Roy able to duplicate George Olliver's dextrous dance moves, the band had the road crew supervise Roy's training regime.

Roland Paquin and I used to sit in the van and run Kenner; we had him jogging beside the van! We had to get him into much better physical condition to do a lot of the stuff that George used to do. I mean, George was a bull. He had brute strength, but Roy wasn't quite as athletic.

Roland and I whipped him into shape pretty quick. But ultimately Roy did as much as George did, just a little bit differently!

- Blaine Pritchett, sound technician; interview with Mark Doble, July 21, 2020

In his eagerness, Roy was anxious to impress with his willingness to sacrifice his body for the cause of the Mandala through ever more dangerous musical acrobatics.

They would goad me into attempting things and I would never say no. They kept asking me to try more and more insane shit, waiting for me to tell them to fuck off. But I would never say no!

We were rehearsing at the Cheetah in L.A. and I was working on a microphone trick which involved throwing it up in the air. The mike comes down and hits me on the head and there's blood everywhere. And Donnie says, "What the hell happened?" So, off to the hospital; a bunch of stitches; back to rehearsal; and Donnie is just shaking his head.

Another time, in New Jersey, I dove off the amp and literally went through the stage and ripped my wrist. More blood; more stitches; and Donnie just shaking his head again.

I was never much of an athlete and I was constantly pulling hamstrings. This sometimes resulted in shots of pain killer enabling me to do those splits. And after the show, the pain became very interesting. And there would be Donnie, looking at me and just shaking his head.

- Roy Kenner, lead vocalist; interview with Mark Doble, July 4, 2020

Kenner continued to win over audiences with his dramatic and acrobatic stage antics. Guitarist and close friend of Domenic, Bernie LaBarge recounted a particularly memorable engagement where Roy's commitment to his performance craft went above and beyond.

I went to see the Mandala play at a church called St. Nick's in Hamilton, Ontario, in 1968. George Olliver had left the group and Roy Kenner had joined as lead vocalist and front man. He had huge shoes to fill, seeing that George was a stellar front man with incredible athletic ability. So here was Roy Kenner, Hugh Sullivan on Hammond B-3,

Donnie Troiano on guitar, Whitey Glan on drums, and Don Elliott on bass. I had made my way to the front of the stage, as usual. The curtain opens, and there's Roy, standing on top of Donnie's stack of Traynor amps, six feet above the stage floor. As the band launches into the first power chord, Roy jumps off the amp, leaping into the air, performs the splits on the stage floor, and lets out a blood-curdling scream, landing squarely on his "family jewels." Two roadies carry him off the stage, and the band plays on. I love Roy with all my heart, but in an instant, I'm watching the band play instrumentally, stretching the songs out as Donnie and the boys launch into some amazing playing, blowing our minds with their virtuosity. After the set, I nervously knocked on the dressing room door to see if Roy was okay. (At this point, I had never met my heroes.) The door opens, and there's Roy, covered in sweat, with an ice pack gently placed on his crotch. Whitey smiled at me and told me that Roy was okay. They played their last set without Roy, and they were stellar. I heard later that Roy was incommunicado for a few days after that.

- Bernie LaBarge, guitarist; interview with Mark Doble,
  November, 2020

Kenner was a fearless front man, even risking electrocution in the pouring rain at an outdoor festival in Philadelphia when lightning reportedly struck his microphone stand. Despite the goading and the head-shaking, Roy truly looked up to Domenic and he readily acknowledges that Domenic took him under his wing. Roy also credits him for teaching him about the non-music aspects of the "business" as well.

I believe Domenic was born an old soul. When he was eighteen, he had the maturity and wisdom of someone twice his age. He had learned quickly from mistakes he made when he was younger—the legal end of things—Donnie made sure that he read and understood everything from a legal point of view, and he made sure that I did the same. He insisted. I got that from him. It stunned me, the number of musicians in those days who had no clue about royalties and music-biz shenani- gans. He was always on top of that and made sure I got the message.

- Roy Kenner, lead vocalist; interview with Mark Doble, July 4, 2020

The Mandala appeared at a number of prestigious engagements in the summer of 1968, sharing bills with world-class acts like The Who, the Troggs, Procol Harum, and Pink Floyd, and returned in August with the intention of touring Canada when bassist Don Elliott was seriously injured in an automobile accident. Touring plans were shelved for a couple of months. When they finally started playing again, the bass duties were covered off by Hugh Sullivan on keys as they toured eastern and western Canada.

Halifax based singer/actor Terry Hatty saw this version of the Mandala, (without a bass player) during their East Coast swing.

Got in my first band in 1966. I was at St. F.X. University. Our drummer, who was from Ontario, played *Opportunity* for me, and I was shaken to the core. In '69 I saw the band in Fredericton at University of New Brunswick—Roy Kenner was singing and there was no electric bass player. I had never heard such musicianship, and I played SOUL CRUSADE until the grooves melted. Domenic had an outrageous band playing his beautiful tunes and I went to listen any time they were in town. I was totally thrilled by his guitar playing and how his writing continued to expand and deepen—I couldn't get enough of this man Domenic and his often-mesmerising band.

- Terry Hatty, vocalist and actor; email to Frank Troiano, June, 2020

Sound engineer Doug McClement remembers Domenic playing a gig in Kingston.

At the Mandala gig at QECVI in Kingston, the band started into *Love-itis*, and Domenic broke a string during the opening riff. No guitar techs in those days, so while the band was playing, he walked to the side of the stage, opened his case, pulled out a string, and changed it while the song was in progress, standing at his vocal mic and singing the harmony parts on the choruses. He managed to get it changed and tuned in time for the solo. I've seen thousands of shows, and that's the only time I've ever seen anyone do that.

- Doug McClement, engineer; email to Frank Troiano, April, 2020

By now, Domenic's guitar artistry was such that fans came to the Mandala shows simply to watch him play and marvel at the sound he produced on his Telecaster guitar. Mike Levine (bassist for Triumph in the 1970s) recalls how he and his friends approached Domenic during a break at a Mandala show.

He said hi and was very friendly. Our guitarist asked him how he got those amazing "sounds" out of his Telecaster guitar. He motioned for us to go to a quiet corner of the room and whispered, "Put your guitar in your oven at home with the temperature set at 280 degrees for two hours and baste it with butter and let it cool." On the way home, all that our guitarist talked about was Donnie and his instructions, and his intention to follow through. When he was about to do it, he realized that Donnie was pulling his leg and we all started laughing about it.

-    Mike Levine, bass guitarist; interview with Frank Troiano, June 5, 2020

Also released in the fall of 1968 was the Mandala's final single, a Kenner-Troiano collaboration, *You Got Me*. The tune was fresh and compelling with a dreamy-psychedelic lead vocal line that is sung masterfully. While the material on SOUL CRUSADE was essentially set (and recorded) before Roy joined the band, one gets the sense that with *You Got Me/Help Me*, Roy is more comfortable in his own skin. The B side, *Help Me*, was a funkier number that still rocked out with Domenic trading lead guitar licks against Kenner's vocals.

The first thing that I wrote with Donnie that I can recall was *Help Me*. We wrote a lot together, but I don't know how much I would have done without Donnie's encouragement. He knew I loved reading and had always enjoyed creative literature in school. He prodded me to try my hand at writing. First, he got me into putting lyrics together, and then using my voice to convey melody lines. But I wasn't as focused as Donnie. Donnie was focused all the time. The good part of his obsessive nature meant that he was never off. He had the ability to stay focused on writing. I was constantly jotting down song ideas or full sets of lyrics. Donnie took what I gave him and either turned it into a song or

suggested changes or additions that would only add value to complete the piece.
- Roy Kenner, lead vocalist; interview with Mark Doble, July 7, 2020

The writing partnership between Roy and Domenic would be particularly prolific over the subsequent five years, largely due to Domenic's encouragement and belief in the creative abilities of his new bandmate.

Unfortunately, *You Got Me/Help Me*, had a limited release in Toronto, and received very little radio airplay. The lack of interest in this single would in part signal the end of the Mandala. Domenic summed up the frustration of the band:

We were desperately keen to do our number as a Canadian thing. But you got tired of that when everybody in the media was trying to screw you. We couldn't get any space in any of the papers except with sensational stuff, like girls ripping off their clothes or fainting at our gigs. Nobody would write about our music—they refuse to believe that a Canadian band could actually make music.
- *Axes, Chops & Hot Licks*, Ritchie Yorke, M. G. Hurtig Ltd., 1971

In October 1968, Coca-Cola produced a promotional album called THE CANADIAN INVASION. The single-sided LP included eleven separate tracks, each lasting approximately sixty seconds, performed by five different Canadian bands: Toronto's Nucleus (formerly Lords of London), the Magic Cycle, Winnipeg's The Guess Who, Ottawa's Five Man Electrical Band, and Toronto's the Mandala. The album was specifically targeted to Canada's "youth market" by showcasing Canadian rock acts. One writer has referred to the project as "eleven cuts of cool Coke rock."

The single *You Got Me (that had recently been recorded)* is the musical basis for the two Mandala tracks (*Relief Is What I'm Wishing* and *Rehearsal*) are classic Mandala. Although none of the tunes are longer than one minute, the band certainly didn't just mail it in. THE CANADIAN INVASION was released to Canadian radio stations. Today, this rarity can fetch prices exceeding three hundred dollars at rock and roll record shows.

Domenic's Beret

Around this time, Domenic started wearing a beret, which would become a signature feature of Domenic's onstage persona. At age eighteen, Domenic's hair started to thin. He experimented with various head coverings including bandanas, Panama hats, Stetsons, and flat caps. Rumour has it that at one of Lenny Breau's concerts Domenic noticed that he was wearing a beret and thought it looked sharp and different and he decided to give it a try.

His all-time favourite guitar player was Lenny Breau. I mean, Lenny Breau was God to Donnie. We used to go to the House of Hamburg when Lenny Breau was playing there all the time, listening to him till 4:30 in the morning. Donnie would watch him and learn tricks and different things. Like Lenny would chord with his left hand but then he would take another note with one of his fingers and play another note on the neck and stroke with his thumb. Lenny was definitely Donnie's favourite guitar player. That's where the beret came from. Lenny used to wear this beret all the time and Donnie thought it was cool.

- Blaine Pritchett, sound technician; interview with Mark Doble, July 21, 2020

Over the years, both Frank and Gina continued to purchase berets for their balding brother, preferring black coloured berets manufactured in the Basque region of France.

It is a shame that SOUL CRUSADE wasn't released a year earlier. The personnel changes in 1967 made this impossible, pop music was evolving. The "Age of Aquarius" was giving way to a less psychedelic, harder power-chord rock. (Goodbye Fifth Dimension; hello Led Zeppelin!) Instead of dancing to another "soul revival," fans wanted to rock. The glorified image of the Mandala, so skilfully promoted by Randy Martin, was a less relevant construct.

In early 1969, the Mandala made several trips to the states, including the Detroit Pop Festival and the Grand Rapids Pop Festival in April. They also made one more tour through western Canada, but the Mandala was coming to an end, making their final gig on June 1, 1969, at the Hawk's Nest. Citing the previous year's car accident that sidelined Don Elliot and Whitey Glan as the beginning of the end, Domenic was coming to the realization that the Mandala had run its course.

At the end of the summer of '68 we had a bad accident and Donny Elliot got hurt and Whitey got hurt. Donny left and Whitey couldn't play for a while. As a result, the whole makeup of the band started to change. We gave it one more stab and moved to Detroit to rehearse. A number of things were going wrong. Ahmet liked the band. He didn't like Roy. Ahmet did all our demos with us but he wanted me to sing and to take off Roy's vocals. I didn't want to sing. Up to that time, everything had been fairly clear sailing, but it started getting negative.
- Domenic Troiano; "Black Market," El Mocambo Records Inc., Press Release, 1981

We realized toward the end of the Mandala that we had run this concept to death and there wasn't much further to go with it. Things had changed enough that it wasn't viable for any of us anymore. Donnie wanted to concentrate more on music rather than showbiz. That all sounded fine, well, and good, and the two guys who promoted our last US dates had talked to Donnie and offered to set us up at a ranch in Phoenix no less, so we could woodshed new material.
- Roy Kenner, lead vocalist; interview with Mark Doble, July 2, 2020

The Mandala was over, but the nucleus of Troiano, Kenner, and Glan would stay together with the addition of a local bass guitarist named Prakash John (who had been practicing with the Mandala as a potential replacement for Don Elliot). The Canadian experiment was a spent force. It was time to move south and regroup.

Mandala—Domenic Troiano, Hughie Sullivan, Whitey Glan, Roy Kenner 1969
(Troiano Family Archives)

CHAPTER 5

THE WEAR AND THE
TEAR ON MY MIND

"Lord it's the wear and the tear on my mind
It's the wear and the tear on my mind, on my mind
Why is this world so unkind?"
(*The Wear and the Tear on My Mind*, lyrics by Domenic Troiano)

BUSH

REB FOSTER ASSOCIATES, INC.
211 SOUTH BEVERLY DRIVE
BEVERLY HILLS, CALIFORNIA 90212
(213) 278-4822

Bush—Roy Kenner, Whitey Glan, Domenic Troiano, Prakash John, 1970
(Troiano Family Archives)

Randy Martin, as usual, was one step ahead of everyone else, and said, "Guys, this is going nowhere. Put together something new or quit the business, but don't continue the Mandala. Don't end up in that dead-end situation. Start fresh and move to the US. Don't keep throwing out the time and become a self-parody."

- Domenic Troiano; "Black Market," El Mocambo Records Inc., Press Release, 1981

After taking a few weeks off after the end of the Mandala, Domenic wanted to get back to work. With fellow Mandalas Roy Kenner and Whitey Glan and the addition of the gifted Toronto rhythm and blues bass player Prakash John, they were ready to try something new. With the invitation to stay at a friend's ranch in the Arizona desert, the fellows had an opportunity to get away from the music scene, relax, play, and write. It would be a recipe for success.

The Mandala had been going strong till early '69 and collectively we just started feeling that the Mandala had become a bit of a trap, so that when people heard the Mandala, you had to do a certain thing and our heads weren't there anymore. So, we started thinking of other things to do, and we decided most of us still wanted to play with each other, but we wanted to do something in a different context, and that's how Bush developed. And in the summer of '69 we went down to Arizona. A friend of mine had a little ranch there, which he loaned us for the summer. We stayed there over the summer and rehearsed and practiced, learned a lot of songs, did a lot of writing—and that's what developed into Bush.

- Domenic Troiano; interview with Howard Mandshein, 92 CITI-FM, January 2005

Bass guitarist Prakash John was born in 1947 in Mumbai, India, where at a young age his father insisted on music lessons—violin, piano, and singing focused on Indian and classical music. In 1960, he immigrated to Toronto where he encountered R & B music for the first time. Soon thereafter he took up the bass guitar and formed his first R & B band, the Trikq (which also included future the Mandala/Bush organist, Hugh Sullivan). When George Olliver left the Mandala in 1967, he formed a new group, George

Olliver & the Children, and Prakash was the bass player for this ensemble. In the space of a few years, Prakash became one of the premier bass players in Toronto's R & B scene. Prakash followed the Mandala closely and greatly admired Whitey Glan's percussion technique, which ended up being a key factor in drawing him to Bush.

It was in the spring of 1969. Whitey Glan and I were already friends and he knew I was a fan of The Five Rogues and had been inspired by that very band to become a bass player. I latched onto Whitey when I first saw the Rogues. He was a very charismatic person. He could make people laugh. He invited me one day just to come to jam at the Hawk's Nest, and I was playing with George Olliver and the Soul Children, and Whitey sort of knew that I wouldn't come to an audition. He knew that about me. I guess I was a coward. I have never actually "auditioned." It's not something that I would do, to put myself up there for rejection. But Whitey thought I would come over for a jam and told me that the Mandala was doing other things and they didn't have a bass player. "We want to go back to having a bass player." The jam lasted about fifteen minutes and then they asked me if I would join their band and they would be travelling to L.A.

-   Prakash John, bass guitarist; interview with Mark Doble, July 28, 2020

Prakash fondly remembers spending his time in practice and preparation at "Happy Landing Ranch" In Arizona.

We had a benevolent sponsor who loved the Mandala and he paid for the accommodation, which was phenomenal! It was the grandest old palatial estate that neighboured Barry Goldwater's daughter's ranch. I thought it was strange that his granddaughter used to come to the fence and was curious about who these long-haired hippies were. The ranch was called the Happy Landing Ranch. It was beautiful and quite spacious. But it was so hot and the place had no air conditioning. We were there about three months, but I have no sense of time, because I was practicing all the time both on my own and with the band. We had

two meals a day (which was a luxury for a musician). Carmelo (road manager) was also the chef, which was wonderful.

-   Prakash John, bass guitarist; interview with Mark Doble, July 28, 2020

Remarkably, even after the numerous personnel changes incurred through different band and solo ensembles stretching back to Robbie Lane, but continuing right up to the end, Domenic rarely became bad friends with any of his departed colleagues. Whether it was Ronnie Hawkins, David Clayton-Thomas, George Olliver, or Burton Cummings, invariably there would be future musical encounters perhaps years or decades later with Domenic guesting or producing, or just even offering moral support and encouragement. Domenic was faithful to his own. Songwriter B. J. Cook recalled first meeting Domenic while he was still in the Mandala, and spending time with him and Bush in Arizona in 1969.

I met Donnie in Vancouver sometime around 1967. Our guitar player was out because of carpel tunnel, so we were down to a trio. This quiet guy with a beret came in, sat over in the corner and didn't say anything until we were on our last break, and that's when he approached me and asked if he could sit in. Well, needless to say, he blew the roof off the joint. It was Domenic Troiano for God's sake, and we all knew he was not just another guitar player. As it turns out, the Mandala were in town for a few days, so he jammed with us every night until they left. A few years later, I was living in L.A., now Donnie had a new group, Bush, and they were rehearsing in Arizona. It was my twenty-seventh birthday and Kenner suggested I come to hang out with them. Donnie always stayed in touch, and when I moved to Toronto, it was he who took a chance on me as a writer.

-   B. J. Cook, singer-songwriter; email to Frank Troiano, April, 2020

B. J. Cook, with her spouse/partner (famed producer) David Foster would form the band Skylark and even record one of Domenic's songs. But over fifteen years later, in the mid-1980s, Domenic would enlist her to pen the lyrics to his television theme *Night Heat*.

Emerging from this desert hiatus, the newly formed Bush was motivated. Leaving Arizona for Los Angeles, the band signed with ABC Dunhill Records.

In the fall of '69 we went to L.A. We got lucky; we got signed to Reb Foster and Associates (who managed Three Dog Night and Steppenwolf) and they got us a deal with ABC Dunhill.
- Domenic Troiano; interview with Howard Mandshein, 92 CITI-FM, January 2005

Recording engineer and musician Bruce Winfield Brown was eighteen years old and still at home with his parents in Los Angeles when Bush was looking for a place to stay in L.A.

Bush needed a place to crash for a few weeks. My mother, Marj, only had one request: for Donnie to perform two or three great jazz standards every night after dinner. Our garage had a stage, drum kit, mikes, etc., as I played guitar and drums in different bands, and so Donnie performed for my parents in the garage. They loved it and it became a nightly ritual. I had never seen the Mandala. Having these top-notch musicians at the house was very special for an eighteen-year-old aspiring musician. Donnie mentored me for the entire month and he taught me so much. He was clearly the leader of the band and way ahead of his time.

Once the band got settled in, signed their management deal, etc., they moved to the Sportsmen's Lodge in Studio City. They started playing at the Irma Hotel and Teri and I went to see them once or twice a week. The band was absolutely amazing and they were getting better and better as the weeks went by. Everything was falling into place for them as they had signed with ABC Dunhill and their management, Reb Foster and Associates, managed both Three Dog Night and Steppenwolf.
- Bruce Winfield Brown, engineer and musician; interview with Frank Troiano, July 18, 2020

The band would tour in the United States, opening for Steppenwolf and Three Dog Night, who were arguably the best-selling American band of 1971. Three Dog Night acknowledged the writing talent of Domenic Troiano by recording *Writings on The Wall* and *I Can Hear You Calling,* which happened to be the B side of their monster 1971 single, *Joy To The World*. Despite their collapse in 1969, the Mandala had made an impact during their forays into the US. A compelling live act, Domenic Troiano's stock was high. And he was routinely invited to join major performing acts. One such invitation came just as Bush was about to release their first album and start touring.

We had started Bush, we had left Arizona, we were now living in L.A., and we had a house out in Thousand Oaks where we were staying. One day I got a phone call, and it was Ahmet (Ertegun) who had tracked me down through my parents, and he said, "I've got something I'd like you to do, and I think it'd be good for you. I'm not sure you're going to like it, but I think it would be good for you. So before you out and out say no, think about it." And that's when he said to me, "Would you like to be in Iron Butterfly?" At the time, it really wasn't too much of a dilemma for me, because I knew I wanted to be in Bush, and we had been rehearsing hard and practising and we really felt good about the group. And that's just one of those little footnotes in history, because it really didn't go beyond that, really.

- Domenic Troiano; interview with Howard Mandshein, 92 CITI-FM, January 2005

Domenic of course knew Ahmet Ertegun from his involvement signing the Mandala to Atlantic Records in 1968. Ahmet was one of the most respected record executives in the world, having made a name for himself by discovering Led Zeppelin and immediately signing them on the spot. Ertegun would have made a compelling case that would have been hard to decline. But Domenic was committed to Bush, and abandoning fellow band mates at this time was out of the question.

In Los Angeles, Bush was attracting attention performing in the local club scene, and Domenic's playing was having an impact. Legendary guitarist and session musician Elliott Randall is one of those who was influenced through meeting and hearing Domenic in person.

In L.A. we performed at the Whiskey-a-Go-Go and that is where I met Donnie. Donnie and I hit it off right from the get-go. We were a couple of hot, young guitar players and we ended up spending a lot of time together during the week that Eric Mercury played at the Whiskey. We traded ideas. We learned from each other; there was no competition, but only the sharing from each other's bag of tricks. There was a sense of generosity and a duty to pass along guitar knowledge to each other and to others. Domenic's guitar playing was way ahead of its time. He melded radically different genres into his own unique style. He was dedicated, multi-faceted, and a very gifted guitarist. He could play anything. That week he became one of my guitar heroes!

- Elliott Randall, guitarist; interview with Frank Troiano, May 16, 2020

Guitarist Elliot Randall is world renowned, having played with Carly Simon, the Doobie Brothers, Peter Frampton, and a host of other great jazz, rock, and R & B artists. He is most famous for the guitar solo in Steely Dan's 1972 hit record *Reelin' In the Years* (none other than Led Zeppelin's Jimmy Page has referred to this solo as his favourite guitar solo of all time!). Two years after seeing Domenic, Elliot was quick to acknowledge his influence, even as he recalled the now famous solo.

Two years later I was in the studio with Steely Dan recording their first LP, CAN'T BUY A THRILL. I did an opening solo on *Reelin' in the Years,* which is considered the fortieth best guitar solo of all time, and I give a lot of credit to the guitar upgrades that I had done in L.A. with Donnie's guidance and assistance.

- Elliot Randall, guitarist; interview with Frank Troiano, May 16, 2020

At the time of first meeting Domenic, Randall was in the employ of Canadian singer-songwriter Eric Mercury, who had just recorded his album ELECTRIC BLACK MAN. Mercury certainly knew about Domenic from his days at Toronto's Club Bluenote in the 1960s, but it was in L.A. that he would spend time and become close friends with Domenic and the rest of Bush.

In 1969, I recorded my first LP called ELECTRIC BLACK MAN. It was produced by Gary Katz and featured Elliot Randall on lead guitar.

Once the LP was completed we began a cross-country tour, and in early 1970 we were performing at the Whiskey-a-Go-Go in L.A. Donnie and his band Bush came out to see us on opening night and he hit it off with Elliot. For the rest of the week Elliot and I would visit Donnie, Whitey, Roy and Prakash and jam and sing at their communal house in the Hollywood Hills during the afternoons. We had an absolutely great time. Donnie and Elliot became fast friends. In my opinion, the best rock guitarists in 1970 were Clapton, Beck, Hendrix, and I consider Randall and Troiano to be in that select group.

- Eric Mercury, singer-songwriter; interview with Frank Troiano, May 17, 2020

Bush was a compelling live act with a dynamic lead singer in Kenner; and with Prakash and Whitey, they also boasted one of the tightest rhythm sections in North American rock. Of course, Domenic's virtuosity was well known—the ease and fluidity in which he delivered impossibly complex guitar trills and lead lines was by now astonishing.

In late February 1970, nineteen-year-old Frank Troiano flew down to L.A. to visit his brother. Domenic and the rest of Bush were staying at the Sportsmen's Lodge in Studio City.

I hadn't seen the guys since the fall of 1969 and it was great to see Whitey, Roy, Carmelo, Prakash, and of course my brother, Donnie. The band was playing at the Irma Hotel six nights a week and three sets a night. I stayed in L.A. for about four weeks and watched Bush's live show improve week after week. Their appearances at the club were in fact dress rehearsals. I was a huge fan of the Mandala, but Bush was something new and the band offered a higher calibre of very diverse music and their new music really grew on me.

The crowd was generally a hippie crowd, and many interesting people came through. I met the three lead singers of Three Dog Night and two of Frank Zappa's bandmates dropped by on several nights to watch and sometimes sit in with the band. Bush's management dropped by as well as some record company execs from Dunhill. I had use of one of the band cars and I would run errands while the band rehearsed in the afternoon. I delivered Donnie's guitar and amp to Neal Moser, the guitar tech, for repair and electronics work and picked it up a week later.

On one of Donnie's days off, he and I went to Disneyland in Anaheim and we had so much fun. It reminded me of the times we went to the CNE in Toronto. Another visitor was Mitch Markowitz. He showed up in a red Ford Mustang convertible and really looked like a tourist. He spent a few hours at our hotel and came to see us a few nights at the club. The four weeks went by fairly quickly and it was soon time to go back home. Donnie was very kind and generous with me and included me in all his activities while I was there.

- Frank Troiano; June, 2020

The self-titled BUSH album is stripped down and focused. Domenic is the undisputed leader, co-writing on all eleven tracks. Bush is considered by many to be an extension of the Mandala. But BUSH is a more "guitar-centric" album. While there are obvious R & B and funk references, BUSH is edgier than the music on SOUL CRUSADE.

A big reason for this is undoubtedly the influence of Prakash John, who delightfully matches Troiano note for note in numerous instances throughout the album, delivering rapid unison bass and lead lines that are so in sync as to sound like one person playing. At other times, there is almost a back-and-forth conversation between the instruments, and occasionally the musical dialogue verges on being "contrapuntal." Indeed, the various examples of bass and guitar interplay throughout the album help define the Bush sound. One can only imagine Domenic revelling in the experience. For his part, Prakash credits Domenic for the intense practice/rehearsal regime that he imposed on the band.

We came into the studio to record in great shape. We were completely and utterly rehearsed. Donnie and I were both into that hard, ruthless rehearsing. He found his match when it came to uninterrupted rehearsing from dawn till dusk. I was right into it. Donnie was very strict and confining in many ways, and I just did what I was told and I have no regrets at all. I came from a background of discipline and I loved rehearsing. I knew I could keep up with Donnie for every minute, for every hour he wanted to practice, I was right there. I never failed him. I learned from my experience with Bush and that's how I run my rehearsals now with the Lincolns. I loved that discipline. The great blessings I received from Donnie were remarkable!

- Prakash John, bass guitarist; interview with Mark Doble, July 28, 2020

Domenic described the first two numbers on the album:

Back Stage Girl was written by myself and Roy Kenner. It's a straight-ahead funky track, with a nice drum thing in the middle. Might be a single. *Yonge Street Patty* was a coloured dancer who used to work at Le Coq D'Or. She was really into music, much more than most chicks. I wrote the lyrics and music. There's some nice harmony things happening. Like most of the songs, it was developed in Phoenix last summer.

- Domenic Troiano; "Blazing Bush Ready to Set the World on Fire," Ritchie Yorke, *Toronto Telegram*, July 30, 1970

An upbeat funk returns to yet another biographical tune, *Got to Leave the City*, in which the singer bemoans the need to uproot and get out of town in order to survive. Suddenly, midway through the number we get the first extended soloing by Domenic, which starts out slowly before building to an intense and blistering conclusion.

Cross Country Man again abounds with biographical references in the lyrics about leaving Toronto for Los Angeles. Blaine Pritchett claims the song was about Domenic's road crew.

Cross Country Man is about Rollie, Carmelo and me—because we drove across Canada at least a dozen times from Vancouver to Newfoundland—the line, "drive, drive, drive your car" we thought was pretty cool!

- Blaine Pritchett, sound technician; interview with Mark Doble, July 21, 2020

I Can Hear You Calling is credited to all four band members, and seems like the most commercial-sounding song on the album and was covered by labelmates Three Dog Night.

Domenic handles the lead vocal on the shuffle-beat *Turn Down,* which begins with a pleasant, lilting groove leading into some serious guitar soloing that alternates between languid and frenetic and then closes with a three-part vocal harmonized scat-sing.

We're all doing some singing now, Whitey included, and we're heavily into the harmony thing. We approach the vocals like a horn section. We don't use an organ anymore, which feels strange.
- Domenic Troiano; "Blazing Bush Ready to Set the World on Fire," Ritchie Yorke, *Toronto Telegram*, July 30, 1970

Kenner returns to the lead vocal responsibilities in the album closer *Drink Your Wine.* The solid rocker begins with two choruses then shifts into the longest instrumental break on the album highlighted by the interplay between Troiano and Prakash.

It would end up being the only album Bush ever recorded, but it was an important release. Even today, the LP is a favourite among record collectors. Peter Taylor, long-time fan of Domenic's music in The Five Rogues, the Mandala, and Bush, had this to say:

The Rogues would become the Mandala and later morph into one of music's greatest, yet relatively unsung combos, Bush, a bona fide Toronto supergroup led by Troiano and fronted by Roy Kenner with the dynamite rhythm section of Whitey Glan on drums and Prakash John on bass. The Bush album is one of those "desert island discs." The band only released one, and it's a treasure. Years ago, I liquidated a huge vinyl record collection, but I kept the Bush LP.
- Peter Taylor, promotional rep; email to Frank Troiano, June, 2020

Roy Kenner was more circumspect about his own vocals, but certainly approved of the songs and the musical direction.

Although I liked what we were doing tunewise, I wasn't that satisfied with my vocals on the Bush album. Once we started playing live, I had to be a much more restrained lead singer, which was a bit of a transition

for me. But we quickly progressed and I really thought we were starting to hit our stride before it ended far too quickly.

- Roy Kenner, lead vocalist; interview with Mark Doble, July 2, 2020

In 1995, BUSH was reissued on compact disc (CD) by Magada Heritage International and included four bonus tracks taken from their final live performances on June 5 and 6, 1971, at the Bitter End in Los Angeles. Not surprisingly, the playing is stellar. The first song, *Try,* would appear on Domenic's subsequent self-titled solo album. The bluesy *Lookin'* features Kenner singing a solid lead vocal overtop Domenic's fast-moving melodic guitar accompaniment. *Wicked Woman* is a rock song containing a driving guitar riff with shifting rhythm that would later appear almost exactly intact five years later on the Cummings-Troiano song *Rich World Poor World* (included on The Guess Who's POWER IN THE MUSIC album). The last bonus song is a magnificent 20:21 minute rendition of *Cross Country Man,* which becomes an extended jam tour de force replete with soloing by everyone in the band.

One of the very first live acts that I went to see shortly after my arrival was Bush (RCA) and needless to say I was blown away by their musicianship and their powerful sound and performance. The combination of Dom and those other wonderful players in the group was undeniable, and I loved their only album too. I was disappointed the BUSH album didn't do better, and outside of the devoted following all the individuals in the band have experienced in their careers since, it still amazes me how under the radar that album was, and remains.

- Frank Davies, Daffodil Records; email to Frank Troiano, April, 2020

York University professor of music and writer Rob Bowman first witnessed Domenic performing with Bush in Hamilton, Ontario, where they were the opening act to Sly and the Family Stone.

Domenic, of course, had been a larger-than-life presence on the Toronto scene since forming The Five Rogues in the mid 1960s. While I had bought the Mandala's SOUL CRUSADE album, I was too young to see them play live. Consequently, the first time I got to see Domenic onstage was when his next group, Bush, opened up for Sly and the Family Stone

in Hamilton at the Wentworth Curling Club August 2, 1970. Sly was "über" disappointing, but Bush, led by Domenic's funky rhythm and electrifying liquid lead lines, stole the night.

- Rob Bowman, writer/professor; email to Frank Troiano, May, 2020

Another notable Canadian engagement took place that winter in Winnipeg. Winnipeg musician/author/rock musicologist John Einarson was at the Winnipeg show held at Tache Hall, which was the dormitory at the University of Manitoba. It had a small hall with a stage, and the place was packed to see Bush.

Everyone who was anyone in the Winnipeg music scene was there, including all five members of The Guess Who, who may have watched the show from the side of the stage. Bush played every song on their brilliant album that night, stretching several of them out. Bush had such a unique sound. No one else sounded like them. And the level of playing was so high. They epitomized the term "musician's musician," which is probably why so many of the audience came from the music community and were musicians themselves.

- John Einarson, author/musicologist; interview with Mark Doble, July 31, 2020

Randy Bachman postponed a business trip in order to be in the 'Peg and see Bush.

Bush in the US is a very popular group, and up here in Canada we have only got their album to go by, which I'd have to say is a little subdued and sophisticated compared to what they are capable of doing onstage. They are a musician's group, and although I had plans to be on a business trip in the US, when I heard they would be here I cancelled the trip.

- Randy Bachman; "Music by Bush At the U of M," Ann Stark, *Winnipeg Free Press*, January 18, 1971

Prakash John remembers the evening well even to this day, for several notable reasons, including a memorable transaction at the home of Guess Who bass guitarist, Jim Kale:

People still talk about that show. All The Guess Who guys sitting there with their mouths wide open. The sound in that auditorium was fabulous and the audience was with us. My bass never sounded as good. It was a tremendous gig!

After the gig we went to Jim Kale's house, in the middle of winter in snowbound Winnipeg—it was snowing and everything. I had this fabulous pair of leather boots that came right up to my kneecaps and I had this custom-made coat by North Beach and I looked like one of the members of Sly and the Family Stone. Jim Kale had to have those boots. He insisted that he was going to take my boots. Jim says, "Here." He hands me a '58 vintage bass with a maple neck and a Telecaster body. He says, "I'm giving you this bass and I'm not giving you back your boots." Now these guys are falling all over the place; they're out of it, and the road manager says we have to get going. There is snow up to your hips and I have no boots. I'm now riding on the back of my road manager, he's carrying me with the 1958 bass. And that is how I entered the hotel with no boots and the '58 bass in my hand with no case.

- Prakash John, bass guitarist; interview with Mark Doble, July 28, 2020

Expectations were high around the release of the much anticipated BUSH; however, the sequence of events (a veritable comedy of errors) that followed doomed the musical unit to a speedy and merciless demise. Two weeks prior to release, labelmates Three Dog Night and Steppenwolf sued ABC Dunhill and Bush became collateral damage in this dispute, resulting in no money being spent on promotion or to support the band while they toured. Canadian keyboardist Hugh Sullivan had come to L.A. to join the band, but was going through a personal crisis at the same time (that would only be exacerbated by the subsequent events). An ill-fated trip to Las Vegas served to confirm the sense of doom enveloping the Bush experience.

Prakash vividly recalls this seemingly pivotal episode in the history of Bush as a touring ensemble.

I had been driving all night and I just couldn't do it any more. We were coming into Death Valley, so I told Kenner to take over and please don't drive over sixty-five. But he takes off—he is already up to seventy-five or eighty. I'm sure he's thinking, "What does this guy from Bombay know about driving?" But you can feel these tremendous wind gusts and I can feel the trailer do that little shudder, and I am thinking, "This is it—we're going to die!" The trailer is now sweeping across the highway from right to left, out of control, and he's trying to hold on and all I can see is the speedometer at seventy-five miles per hour. We are now cascading off the shoulder, we start to roll, and luckily the trailer dislodged and we continued to roll down the hill. The people watching thought we were dead. We came to a halt upside down and it is dead silent. And I know I'm alive, but I don't know if anyone else is. We are in a daze. We busted out the window and crawled out and we could see the people on the highway up on the hill looking down at us in sheer astonishment that we were still alive. We were coming out of the vehicle. The engine was on fire, but we didn't care. We were just happy we were alive.

Then we started looking at the trailer. We didn't care about ourselves, but our instruments. And all I could see was Donnie chasing Kenner down the hill. Roy's lucky Donnie didn't end up killing him. And I'm thinking, "Let him kill him." To be fair to Roy, the Gibson guitar necks often and easily snap off. And the Telecaster case is smashed, but the guitar is untouched. But then we realize, "Oh no! We have to do the gig!" But—and this is a tribute to Peter Traynor who built all of our equipment back in Toronto—we had that trailer towed to the gig. We had to dust every thing off and then we plugged it all in, and it worked!
-   Prakash John, bass guitarist; interview with Mark Doble, July 28, 2020

Returning to Los Angeles with nothing to show, the band performed its final performances at the appropriately named club, "the Bitter End" on June 5 and 6, 1971. Sadly, continuing as a musical unit was deemed legally and practically impossible. Very suddenly and strangely, a promising musical entity ceased to be. Roy Kenner is succinct in describing the end of Bush.

Had we been able to get through the trials and tribulations, it would have been different, because it was evolving the right way musically. It was unfortunate that we had the political and personal stuff going on.

Once Reb Foster started suing ABC Dunhill we were a political football. And for Bush, the bitter end came at the Bitter End West.
-    Roy Kenner, lead vocalist; interview with Mark Doble, July 4, 2020

Almost twenty-five years after the fact, Domenic was able to look back and offer a more philosophical perspective on Bush's short career trajectory.

A lot of things kind of went wrong, but looking at it in retrospect, this is all part of the big picture; there's not much you can do with it. A lot of things went wrong in that band, but by the same token you could say that a lot of things went right—we got a record deal, we got a record out, we toured—I guess it wasn't just meant to be much beyond that.
-    Domenic Troiano; interview with Howard Mandshein, 92 CITI-FM, January 2005

Regardless of the astonishingly quick flameout of Bush, Domenic's reputation as a virtuoso guitarist/musician's musician was firmly established, and consequently he seemed to be in demand for session work in L.A. Domenic was eager to participate on different music projects. In 1970, the James Cotton Blues Band released their album TAKING CARE OF BUSINESS, which was produced by Todd Rundgren and featured Domenic playing on *Goodbye My Lady* and *Can't Live Without Love*.

Right around the same time as the BUSH album was recorded, Domenic was invited to participate on Randy Bachman's solo album. The resulting recording, AXE, consisted entirely of guitar instrumentals and was recorded over the course of a weekend in March, 1970, at RCA Studios in Chicago. Randy and Domenic performed all of the guitar parts (Randy also dubbed the bass parts), Garry Peterson was on drums, and Winnipegger Wes Dakus guested on steel guitar.

Dom is one of the finest guitar players around today. Even for as much as the past ten years, Dom had the reputation of being the best in the industry. I met him in Los Angeles last year and asked him if he would record AXE with me. He was everything they had said he was. He

plays some really frantic and freaky music as well as being an excellent jazz guitarist.

- Randy Bachman; "Music by Bush at the U of M," Ann Stark, *Winnipeg Free Press*, January 18, 1971

Domenic plays on five of the instrumental tracks; trading solos in *Pookie's Skuffle*, delivering a jazzed-up Lenny Breau-like solo in *Tally's Tune*, some stylish acoustic licks in the country-folk *Take The Long Way Home*, and ripping off some lightning-speed ascending/descending arpeggios in *Tin Lizzie*. Saving the best for last is the extended guitar-orchestra feast, *Noah*, that shifts back and forth between hard rock and jazz. The middle jazz section features some amazing playing between Randy and Domenic.

Randy and I had met a few times and when they were out in L.A. one time. We were putting Bush together at that point, late 1969 I believe, we had rented a house out in Thousand Oaks and Garry and Randy had come over to see us there. I had also met them in Winnipeg a year earlier because their management had promoted a Mandala concert. We had met and talked a few times, but when he called me it was quite out of the blue so I was a little surprised. What I remember most was that the sessions were in Chicago, so it gave me an opportunity to go back home and make some money. I was broke back then, but had a little money from the session so I went from Chicago to Toronto to see my mom after the sessions. It covered everything so it was great.

- Domenic Troiano; interview with John Einarson, 1999

AXE represents a meeting of the musical minds of two of the most gifted rock guitarists in North America. An interesting side note: four years after the recording of AXE, Domenic would follow in Randy's footsteps and become the lead guitarist/lead writer with the legendary Guess Who.

Shortly after Bush disbanded in June 1971, Domenic was invited to record with a California band, Rockin' Foo. Lester Brown Jr., son of the famous big band leader Les Brown, was helping produce the band.

Universal Records decided to use both me and Chip Taylor to produce the second Rockin' Foo LP and I was the drummer on some tracks and

played trumpet as well. The band leader, lyricist, and guitarist Wayne Irwin had also seen Bush, and as they had broken up by June of 1971 we decided to bring in Donnie Troiano as lead guitarist and he suggested bringing in a chorus of singers including Shawne Jackson and Smitty, Tess, and a few others. Donnie was head and shoulders above our skill level. He was invaluable in the recording process—exhibiting great insight, great instincts, and excellent guitar playing—he truly was a musical giant and at the same time he was so low key and quiet. We all learned a lot during the process.

- Lester Brown Jr., musician; email to Frank Troiano, May, 2020

The result was Rockin' Foo's second and last album. Domenic played guitar on most of the tracks and also supplied some background vocals with Shawne Jackson. Brown had seen Domenic play at the Hullabaloo with the Mandala in 1968 and Bush in 1970. Released in 1971, Rockin' Foo's self-titled second album is relatively hard to find.

With the demise of Bush, for the first time in his career, Domenic Troiano was no longer part of a band, and was living in Los Angeles with little money. But he was not without friends in the music business. Recording engineer Keith Olsen invited Domenic to come into Sound City Studios in Los Angeles to record during studio downtime; Keith introduced him to studio owner Joe Gottfried, who agreed to allow Domenic to record. This was the lifeline Domenic needed.

I never could have afforded to do it without the help I got from of a lot of old friends. Joe Gottfried, who owns Sound City Studios, offered me all the free time I needed—when he wasn't booked up, of course—in return for a small percentage, if and only if I managed to swing a label deal for the album.

- Domenic Troiano; "The Wear and Tear on My Mind," Michael Sherman, *Los Angeles Free Press*, August 11, 1972

Joe really helped me out at that point, and the studio virtually became my home. I was broke, and going to Sound City really was like going home. There was coffee to drink and a phone to use. What else does a struggling musician need?

- Domenic Troiano; interview with Martin Melhuish,
  The Toronto Sound, Liner Notes, 1998

Recorded at Sound City Studios in the summer of 1971, Domenic's self-titled solo album was just the therapy he needed. Domenic has repeatedly stated that this album was really what the follow-up to BUSH would have been had they not been compelled to disband. This is borne up by the inclusion of all the former Bush band members who sing and play on the record. For obvious reasons, it sounds just like Bush. Also, tunes like *Try, The Writings on The Wall, Let Me Go Back, I Just Lost a Friend*, and *Repossession Blues* were all part of the set lists of the last Bush shows just a few months earlier.

For this album, Domenic handled all of the lead vocal responsibilities, which was another first. Most of the songs had existed well before the album was recorded, and this, along with the proven ability of all of the players, resulted in a strong and mature collection of songs. Lyrically, there is plenty of autobiographical reference: *Let Me Go Back* recalls Domenic's time playing at the Bluenote with The Five Rogues. *Repossession Blues* alludes to an episode with the Mandala after playing a gig in Miami, Florida, where they discovered their equipment vehicle had been repossessed. *Repossession Blues* is a great B. B. King-like extended guitar blues with a terrific backing horn arrangement.

Writings on the Wall and *The Wear and the Tear on my Mind* were attempts at socio-political commentary. Living in the US, Domenic was not oblivious to the impact of the US's involvement in Vietnam and its impact on the American psyche.

In a 2005 interview, reflecting on his favourite songs from his back catalogue, Domenic cited *The Answer* (the second song on the album) as one of those special numbers.

But there was one song on that album, on the DOMENIC TROIANO record, called *The Answer* that if I do say so myself, I thought I played

**some pretty excellent guitar on, and it was sort of one of the first (I
would say)** *fusiony* **sort of guitar solos that incorporated rock, jazz,
blues—a lot of different things, that when I haven't heard it in a long
time and I hear that track, it still kind of hits me like that, I go, "Wow!"**

- Domenic Troiano; interview with Howard Mandshein, 92 Citi-FM,
  January 2005

I Just Lost a Friend features poignant lyrics about how one can learn so much
about someone even if you never meet, just by listening to their music. In
fact, the great American jazz guitarist Wes Montgomery had passed away
in 1968. Domenic had a great respect for Montgomery, and although they
had never met, *I Just Lost a Friend* was a way of paying tribute.

One of the most musically inventive tunes is *Hi Again*. Written by Troiano
and Kenner, the song includes an extended orchestral coda with a subtle
but underlying string section. This is immediately contrasted with the
minimalist fifty-five-second solo electric guitar jazz-like *356 Sammon
Avenue* (named after his parents' home address in Toronto). Although, he
was living in L.A., Domenic's roots were still back in Toronto. The very
title serves to affirm Domenic's longing for his childhood home. *Sammon
Avenue* transitions immediately into the robust brassy and bluesy afore-
mentioned *Repossession Blues*, which serves as a satisfying and appropriate
album closer.

**Troiano is also pleased with the way his solo album turned out. "Making
the album was one of those rare special projects where the flow is totally
positive throughout. None of the usual crap went down. All the guys
from Bush are on it, other friends like Shawne Jackson, Bunk Gardner,
Jay Centrelli, and Red Rhodes pitched in and it was fun, because everybody involved wanted to do it. It wasn't just another gig.**

- "The Wear and Tear on My Mind," Michael Sherman, *Los Angeles Free
  Press*, August 11, 1972

The positivity around the making of this album, that all the ex-Bush
members were not only willing, but eager to play a meaningful role in its
creation, the support of everyone who played, and the studio, speaks to the

fact that the music was more than worthy, but also that even though Bush did not end well, Domenic was still loved and held in high regard.

Our audience was mainly musicians. It's always the most gratifying thing when other musicians dig what you're into.
- Domenic Troiano; "Blazing Bush Ready to Set the World on Fire," Ritchie Yorke, *Toronto Telegram*, July 30, 1970

Danny Weis, an original guitarist in Iron Butterfly, would later record and/or perform with Burton Cummings, Bette Midler, Lou Reed, Rhinoceros, the Rascals, and the Lincolns recalled meeting Domenic in L.A., and reflected on Domenic's influence on fellow band mates even after they had moved on to other projects.

I met Domenic in the early '70s in L.A. I believe that Prakash John introduced us. Neal Moser, a guitar tech genius, had rewired Domenic's Tele in 1970 and in the early '70s Dom let me play it when I met him and it could put out some amazing sounds. I immediately had Neal rewire my Fender Tele a few weeks later. Another thing we had in common: we both took guitar lessons in L.A. from Ted Greene, a well-respected jazz musician and an amazing guitar teacher. In 1972, I went on to perform with the Rascals, Lou Reed, and finally Alice Cooper. Several of the musicians in these bands were Domenic's ex-bandmates: Joey Chirowski, Fred Mandel, Whitey Glan, and Prakash John. I could see a common thread with all of them—they had been through Domenic's musician's boot camp, which meant lots and lots of practice and rehearsals. They were all ready and eager for musical combat.
- Danny Weis, guitarist; interview with Frank Troiano, May, 2020

Domenic obtained a contract with Mercury Records to release DOMENIC TROIANO in the spring of 1972. Mentally, he was in a good space, enjoying the freedom and creative control of a solo artist, and in no hurry to become part of a band. So, surprisingly, even before his first solo album was released, Domenic was part of a group again.

Bush—Prakash John, John Donabie, Domenic Troiano, Roy Kenner 1970
(Troiano Family Archives)

CHAPTER 6

PASSIN' THRU

"Some people look outside themselves for their peace of mind
I hear things inside me, I wish you all could find
Now I know it may sound crazy, just like another line
But all I need is music, it makes me feel so fine."
(*All I Need Is Music*, lyrics by Domenic Troiano)

James Gang—Dale Peters, Jim Fox, Roy Kenner, Domenic Troiano, 1972
(*Troiano Family Archives*)

Bush broke up in 1971. My brother was struggling to make ends meet in L.A. when he received calls from the Belkin brothers and from Jimmy Fox and Dale Peters about their interest in hiring him to replace Joe. He wasn't sure if he wanted to go in that direction, but when he told me about the offer I was stunned. Of course, I told him to please accept this great opportunity as I was already a fan of the band and it was financially a no-brainer considering his situation. He went on to join the band and enjoyed two successful years with them.

- Frank Troiano; email to Bob Lefsetz (music industry analyst), November 2017

The James Gang was an internationally successful rock trio from Ohio, consisting of Jim Fox (drums, organ, vocals), Dale Peters (bass and background vocals), and Joe Walsh (guitar and lead vocals). By 1971, they had recorded four successful albums and enjoyed two hit singles (*Funk #49,* and *Walk Away*). Their second and third albums, JAMES GANG RIDES AGAIN and THIRDS both certified gold. In addition to his duties as chief writer/composer, singer, and lead guitarist, Joe Walsh had achieved international acclaim from such superstars as Eric Clapton, Jimmy Page, and Pete Townshend. The James Gang toured extensively in the US as well as the UK, opening for Three Dog Night, The Who, and Led Zeppelin.

In March 1971, the James Gang recorded their Carnegie Hall debut for their highly successful fourth album, JAMES GANG LIVE IN CONCERT. Walsh was the star. He was the lead guitarist and the voice of the James Gang, and would go on to a successful solo career punctuated by numerous hit records and ultimately join the country-rock supergroup of the '70s, the Eagles. By the fall of 1971, he had tired of and had outgrown the James Gang, advising Fox and Peters that he would be leaving the band at the end of the year. Jim Fox and Dale Peters immediately started considering potential replacements.

Dale and I first heard Domenic at a club called La Cave in Cleveland, Ohio, in about 1967 or 1968, when he was a member of the Mandala. We were blown away by the band, and especially by Donnie's playing. It

was the kind of performance that a fellow musician stores away in the back of his mind, just in case.

The "just in case" came crashing back to the front of my mind in 1971, when our current guitarist and vocalist in James Gang, Joe Walsh, let us know that he intended to move on at the end of the year. Dale and I immediately began to make a (short) list of guitar players who might have the ability and charisma to fill Joe's formidable shoes. The list was longer at first, but as we began to explore candidates, it became self-limiting as we analyzed the attributes of each, and discovered potential weaknesses, availabilities, suitability, intangibles, etc. One name that was placed high on that list from the very beginning was Domenic Troiano.

-   Jim Fox; email to Frank Troiano, April 2020

Although he wasn't getting rich, the demand for Domenic's guitar services for session work was sufficient. He had even rejected an offer to replace guitarist Rick Derringer in the Edgar Winter Group. He liked being a solo artist and was in the process of shopping around for his first solo album. And then, out of the blue, he received a call.

When the James Gang called me up a couple of years later (after Bush), they mentioned to me that they'd like to talk to me about joining the band, and could I come out to Cleveland and have a meeting. And I said sure, and we went out and talked, and at some point in the evening (I don't know when) I asked, I said, "Guys, why did you call me out of a million guys you've seen?" And so they said they'd seen Bush— we'd done a date together with the James Gang (in Texas, actually), but what I didn't realize, they said that a couple of years earlier in 1968, the Mandala had played in Cleveland, and the night that we played, Cream was doing a concert in town, and after the Cream show, Eric Clapton came down and sat in with us at the club we were playing at, and they happened to be in the crowd—Jimmy and Dale, the bass player and drummer—they happened to be in the audience that night, and it was a lot of fun. A big jam session went on till all hours of the morning, and it

really stuck with them; and that was really the main reason—that's what they remembered, and that's why they called me up.

- Domenic Troiano; interview with Howard Mandshein, 92 CITI-FM, January 2005

It remained that after leaving Ronnie Hawkins in 1964 (where he earned the princely sum of $125/week), joining the Rogues, even with the Mandala, Domenic had never earned as much as he did with Hawkins, until now.

I came back to Toronto to visit my mom. And while I was in Toronto, the James Gang called. Frankly, I was tired of being broke, and I didn't know what I was doing. And I said, "Shit, why not try it." They said they'd give me a thousand dollars a week. And I said, "A thousand dollars a week, like, OK! This time, I'm going to take some money, because I'm broke!"

- Domenic Troiano; interview with Martin Melhuish, 1997

Later that year, we began calling the various candidates from the list to come to Cleveland for some face-to-face meetings, jam sessions, and eventually for auditions. And after Donnie came in and played at length for us, two things became clear: first, he was a brilliant guitarist, more than capable of playing anything that the Gang required (as well as being a super-nice guy), and second, Donnie was not going to be our vocalist replacement for Joe. We were completely up-front with Donnie about our thoughts, and surprisingly (to us), Donnie wholly agreed. We would need a singer! But we did not expect Donnie to follow up with a suggestion we had not considered: he had a singer in mind from his days with the band Bush. His name was Roy Kenner, and he was available. Very soon after, we had Donnie back, along with Roy, for a full-blown audition and decided that we would become a quartet with the addition of both Donnie and Roy.

- Jim Fox; email to Frank Troiano, April, 2020

Roy Kenner would prove to be a life-long musical companion, from knowing him in high school, joining the Mandala, playing in Bush, the James Gang, almost all of his solo albums and beyond, Domenic was comfortable with Roy, and happy to play and write with him.

122

In a 1972 article in *Circus* magazine, Kenner is matter-of-fact:

We added two people, which makes us a completely different group; so, the sound is similar in some ways but different in a lot of others.
- Roy Kenner; "Did Walsh Shoot Down the James Gang?" *Circus*, 1972

In the same article, bassist Dale Peters expresses their original intent in replacing Walsh with Troiano and Kenner:

We've changed, I think for the better. We didn't tell Roy to sing like Joe (Walsh) and Dom to play like Joe 'cause that's kind of stupid … that defeats the purpose of playing if you just try to copy what you did before. We do half new stuff and half old stuff though.
- (Dale Peters; "Did Walsh Shoot Down the James Gang?" *Circus*, 1972

On the plus side, the James Gang were established, not a new band starting out with something to prove. They had an existing recording contract with ABC Dunhill Records, and they were experienced professionals with a rigorous touring schedule.

Replacing the lead guitarist and lead singer with two new guys was a bold move. In fact, they *would* have to prove themselves; and regardless of whether Domenic was a better guitarist and Kenner was a stronger singer than Joe (they most certainly were!), the question would be whether or not the fans would warm to such profound personnel changes.

The reaction to Donnie and me not being Joe was even bigger than it had been to the Mandala when I replaced George. The James Gang had achieved a lot more success than the Mandala so there was a larger group of fans used to a formula, and the fans get upset when you mess with the formula.
- Roy Kenner; interview with Mark Doble, July 2, 2020

There was also the question of work regimen. Domenic Troiano was a task-mastering band leader, holding his musical partners to high standards for performance as well as preparation.

Donnie had a much different approach to recording and creating. He didn't want to spend costly studio time. He would rather be well-rehearsed prior to going into the studio. Donnie would literally have figured out where everything fit on the different tracks before we started recording. There was no way that we weren't prepared.

- Roy Kenner; interview with Mark Doble, July 4, 2020

Around this same time, even though Domenic had signed on, he was still in demand to perform with other artists. One keenly interested group that tried repeatedly to obtain Domenic's services was Steely Dan.

Gary Katz, producer of all the Steely Dan records, had called me several times over the years to ask me to play—he actually asked me to be in the original group, and I had just joined the James Gang. Every time he would ask me to play, I was on tour. To make a long story short, I never got to play on one of their records. Finally, in 1982, I was in New York, doing something for Gary—another album project—and Donald (Fagen) was doing his solo record and he asked me to play on some cuts on that, so anyways I finally got to play on something after all those years.

- Domenic Troiano; interview with Howard Mandshein, 92 CITI-FM, January 2005)

Katz and Steely Dan's interest in recruiting Domenic was more than casual. Katz had visited Toronto in 1969–70 in order to expose himself to the Toronto Sound that he had been told about while producing Toronto singer Eric Mercury's ELECTRIC BLACK MAN album.

Eric told me that Domenic was one of the top guitarists in Toronto and that he had started a new band called Bush and they were on their way to L.A. via Arizona. About a year later, Elliot Randall told me about his experience in Los Angeles meeting Domenic and about his musical ability and that he was a very nice, down-to-earth guy. When Steely Dan was recording their first LP in 1972, Donald Fagen mentioned that he had seen Domenic performing in the late '60s with the Mandala in New York City. When they were preparing for their first tour in '72/'73, they

had reached out to Domenic to join the band, but he had just committed to replacing Joe Walsh in the James Gang.

- Gary Katz, producer; interview with Frank Troiano, May 18, 2020

Domenic would have been a wonderful musical fit with Steely Dan's jazz-rock-R & B sensibilities. Donald Fagen and Walter Becker's body of work is unparalleled in popular music. But as much as Fagen and Becker admired and respected the guitar artistry of Domenic Troiano, one wonders if clashes over creative control would have been anything but inevitable with such strong musical wills. Musically, it would have been terrific. However, Domenic was already committed to the James Gang, and similar to his response to Ahmet Ertegun a year earlier, he was loyal to his word.

Within days of Troiano and Kenner joining, the James Gang went into Quadraphonic Sound Studios in Nashville, Tennessee, to record nine songs for the album STRAIGHT SHOOTER. As usual, Domenic assumed the leadership, writing, or co-writing of every song on the record. And the first two songs, *Madness* and *Kick Back Man* were co-written with Roy Kenner before they joined the James Gang are an immediate signal that this James Gang was different—funkier, and with just enough of an R & B lilt.

Get Her Back Again is a quieter, melodic number that showcases Kenner's vocal range and expressiveness. *Looking for My Lady* is a straight-up rocker. Domenic takes the lead vocal on the acoustic *Getting Old* that is supported by an effective lush string arrangement by Glen Spreen. The album closes with a driving stomper, *My Door is Open.*

The album begs the question: "Did Troiano and Kenner join the James Gang, or did Fox and Peters join Bush?" One can imagine confused James Gang fans used to Joe Walsh and *Funk #49* and *Walk Away*. Overall, STRAIGHT SHOOTER, produced by Troiano ally Keith Olsen, was a worthy effort with well-written songs and was skilfully delivered. The question remained. How would this fresh funky sound be received?

This is the James Gang's fourth album, their first since the departure of Joe Walsh, and it has all the strength of their previous efforts. Roy Kenner's vocal stylings exceed the common degree of musicianship.

Instrumentally they have sustained their former level of excitement. Recommended cuts are *Get Her Back Again, Hairy Hypochondriac*, and *Getting Old*.

-   "James Gang—Straight Shooter," *Billboard Magazine*, January 8, 1972

In May 1972, the James Gang made a return appearance at Carnegie Hall. Domenic invited his brother Frank to attend.

Donnie joined the James Gang in late 1971, and after completing the first LP they went out on the road. He informed me that the band was to perform at Carnegie Hall in NYC in late May of 1972. He sent me a round trip airplane ticket to NYC and I was to spend the weekend there, as the concert was on Saturday night. It was my first time in NYC and it was very exciting to be there.

I met Jimmy Fox and Dale Peters for the first time. I chatted with Roy Kenner briefly and then Donnie and I went out and did some shopping in Manhattan. We went to Manny's Music for guitar supplies, bought a pair of shoes and some clothing, and walked for a few hours.

Showtime was 8:00 p.m. and we all got ready to head out to Carnegie Hall, a national historic landmark built in 1891. It is an iconic and treasured venue in midtown Manhattan. There were just over two thousand James Gang fans at the venue and some of them were not aware of the changeover from Joe Walsh to Domenic Troiano. After a slow and tentative start, the band played three older James Gang songs and the audience responded well and became more engaged. The guys played several songs from the new LP STRAIGHT SHOOTER and as well all the James Gang standard hits. By the end of the night most of the fans had been won over.

-   Frank Troiano; July 2020

Billboard Magazine reviewer Joe Radcliffe wrote a similarly positive review of the concert.

The several personnel changes which the James Gang has undergone within the last few months may have been the best thing to have

happened to this ABC Records act. The group, once a trio, is now a quartet of players with new faces, Domenic Troiano on lead guitar, and Roy Kenner on lead vocals.

The addition of these two young, progressive artists, has injected new life, new credibility, into the group's performance. The new sound is "heavy." A raw funk that is loud without having to recourse to loudness to communicate with its followers.

- "James Gang Elephant's Memory," Joe Radcliffe, *Billboard Magazine*, May 1972

The new material was favourably received by the rock press, and Roy and Domenic were acknowledged as more than capable replacements. However, the fan reception was not always so great.

For awhile after the new James Gang hit the road, people still called out, "Where's Joe Walsh?" Some fans even demanded their money back when they found out Joe was no longer with the band.

- "Did Walsh Shoot Down the James Gang?" *Circus*, 1972)

Making their local debut after a couple of personnel changes without warning the audience brought the James Gang a less-than-warm reception that they really didn't deserve. The fact is, though, that when leader/singer/guitarist/writer Joe Walsh dropped out of the group and was replaced by a singer and a guitarist, the group's sound was bound to change quite a bit. Particularly when the singer comes out like a Vegas lounge performer, complete with fringed jacket and dance steps. He has a good, strong voice and is cute and peppy as all-get-out, but the image of the Gang has got to change quite a bit. The new guitarist is quite good, and a little bit closer to the old James Gang identity. Much material from an upcoming ABC/Dunhill album was performed; it sounded pretty good. When the new group has had a bit of a chance to establish themselves in their new identity, the audience is bound to be more appreciative of their ability.

- "James Gang Bloodrock," *Cashbox*, February 1972

The band toured relentlessly throughout the states during the spring and summer. And while most reviewers were quick to point out that Joe Walsh was no longer part of the group, they typically acknowledged the new guys and the new music was just as good. Canadian musician Paul Hoffert, founder of the rock-orchestra Lighthouse, shares his memories of encountering Domenic with the James Gang on the North American touring circuit.

We first crossed paths when he was in the James Gang (1971–1973). Canadian musicians knew about Dom's great guitar playing and musicianship and we were always happy when one of us was able to break through into the international music scene. In that same time period my band Lighthouse was touring extensively in the US, and so it wasn't surprising that Lighthouse and the James Gang played at many of the same concerts. We would chat in those moments of intersection and I recall asking him about his interest in Black-influenced pop music—blues, R & B, soul, funk, and rock. Dom was a master of these forms and played them with authority—you might guess he was from Memphis rather than Italy via Toronto. Our conversations widened to discuss civil rights and discrimination and I was impressed by his broad interests, keen insights, and strong support for social justice.

- Paul Hoffert, band leader, composer, keyboards—Lighthouse; email to Frank Troiano, April, 2020

One of their tourmates that summer was Steely Dan, who had tried earlier to recruit Domenic, and a popular rock-jazz unit with a couple of hits (*Reelin' in the Years*, and *Do it Again*). In 2005, after Dom's passing, band leader Donald Fagen recalled:

Dom was a tourmate of ours in the mid '70s when he was with the James Gang. Walter and I used to stand in the wings after our set and watch as he played the long, psychedelic solos required of him. It was the sort of gig where he'd end up under a followspot on his knees sending these sustained, creamy lines heavenward, or at least out into the crowd of

worshipful, wine- and Quaalude-addled young men. Nevertheless, Dom always added a very personal elegance to everything he played.
- Donald Fagen; Steely Dan website, 2005

A rare audience recording of the James Gang performing at the August 12, 1972, Festival of Hope at Roosevelt Raceway in Westbury, New York, reveals a band that could rock. Kenner effectively engages the audience, Domenic takes the opportunity for extended soloing in *Lost Woman* that is certainly as satisfying as Walsh's version contained on JAMES GANG LIVE IN CONCERT. Other Walsh era gems like *Funk #49, Walk Away,* and *Stop You're Gonna Need Me*, are faithfully delivered.

Buddy Whittington, American guitarist, singer, and songwriter with John Mayall and the Bluesbreakers, and Peter Green recalled the lasting impact of seeing Domenic playing live.

Domenic was a monster guitar player and I was well aware of his music. Domenic served up tasty chops with soul. I sure remember the first time I saw him playin' that Tele with humbuckers in the James Gang. I stole a lick from him that I still use (one out of a possible two LOL). Later, I started noticing his name in the credits of TV cop shows like "Night Heat." He was a great player and he did make quite an impression on me!
- Buddy Whittington, guitarist via Ken Koekstat; email to Frank Troiano, July 2020

The next Troiano-led James Gang album, PASSIN' THRU was recorded in the summer of 1972 in Nashville and released in October. Once again, Domenic is the chief writer, having credits on all but one of the nine tunes. PASSIN' THRU is a solid collection that still stands up to this day.

The opener, *Ain't Seen Nothing Yet*, is a happy southern rocker dominated by the barrelhouse piano of David Briggs. *One Way Street* shifts gears slightly into a funkier feel with jangling guitar accompaniment, and Roy Kenner's *Had Enough* continues with the funk vibe with Jim Fox on organ. *Up to Yourself* is a stylish, straight-up rocker reminiscent of the Walsh-led

James Gang. *Everybody Needs a Hero* is keyboard dominated, featuring William Smith playing clavinet and piano.

PASSIN' THRU, in contrast to STRAIGHT SHOOTER, seems to be a clearer attempt to replicate some of the old James Gang sound and this is reflected in many of the arrangements.

This latest James Gang LP is a warm and honest musical statement. There is a mellowness and lightness of touch evident here that is most pleasing. The arrangements are precise, and provide excellent under-scoring for Roy Kenner's largely subdued vocals. Particularly welcome are *Things I Want to Say to You, Everybody Needs a Hero,* and *One Way Street.*
- *Billboard Magazine*, 1972

Television and radio personality Michael Williams recalls seeing the James Gang in Cleveland that same year.

Joe Walsh had left the James Gang to go solo. The new James Gang had regrouped, adding Roy Kenner on vocals and Bush/the Mandala guitar-ist Domenic Troiano. I remember the 1972 concert because I went with a blind friend, Debbie. The only Canadian music we knew was New Year's Eve favourite, Guy Lombardo and his Royal Canadians. I loved Joni Mitchell, Gordon Lightfoot, Buffy Sainte-Marie, Steppenwolf, Neil Young, and Rush, who were discovered in Cleveland. The festival head-liner, Buffy Sainte-Marie, was Canadian. It just was not promoted in any way. As the new James Gang climbed to the stage, the rain instantly started, the wind came off Lake Erie and blew the stage apart, and the speakers collapsed the stage thirty seconds into the first song.
- Michael Williams, Much Music VJ; email to Frank Troiano, September, 2020

In September 1972, the James Gang embarked on a short Japan tour and then returned to the US to continue touring and planning the next album, to be called JAMES GANG BANG. They had even prepared the LP cover with Domenic's picture on it. At about this time, the legal side of the music business reared its ugly head once again. The James Gang were between recording contracts, and lawsuits were filed.

Jimmy and Dale were understandably fed up with Dunhill anyways. We could all commiserate about that. There was a technical legal screwup where an option was failed to be picked up on time for Dunhill to exercise their option, so the assumption immediately was that we were out of contract. It didn't matter to Dunhill, because they basically said, "Fuck you. We'll drag it through court for so long that … you might win the battle, but you'll lose the war." And lo, it was thus.
- Roy Kenner, vocalist; interview with Mark Doble, November, 27, 2020

For Domenic, this was simply too much déjà vu. Despite the growing success of the new iteration of the James Gang, Domenic had no desire to have his career stalled and burned out by legal hassles. And when it came right down to it, the James Gang gig was no longer satisfying.

The time with the James Gang was positive in a way, but it was restricting musically. I wouldn't have been in that band longer than nine or ten months if it hadn't been for Roy. He helped me keep my sanity. Dale Peters and Jim Fox were really locked into being the "James Gang."
- Domenic Troiano; "The Outer Limits of a Guitarist Extraordinaire," John Lamont, *Stage Life*, September 1977

In a December 1972 telephone conversation with his younger brother Frank Troiano, Domenic explained his frustration and his desire to simply make music, play, and record. He had decided to leave the security of the James Gang.

Our time with Donnie was rewarding, both personally and musically. I have great memories of him with his nose often stuck in the latest copy of the *Sporting News*, exchanging complex chord formations with Jeff Beck on the single neck of one guitar, extolling the virtues of his favourite guitarist, Lenny Breau, and on and on. But most of all … those "chops."
- Jim Fox; email to Frank Troiano, April, 2020

The historical narrative around Domenic's short time in the James Gang suggests that the shadow of Joe Walsh hovered over the band in such a way that regardless of the quality musicianship or the energy of the new lead singer, the audience just would not accept the James Gang in the way that they had embraced the Joe Walsh led trio. And as time has passed, and as Domenic had a subsequently similar short tenure in The Guess Who, the pervading notion is that Domenic was simply a less-than-adequate replacement, at least in view of the fans.

The facts contradict this narrative. Leaving the band was completely Domenic's choice. The James Gang was still a force, and in demand. (Labels were competing for them.) Additionally, and for the record, Domenic did not leave until a capable replacement (Tommy Bolin, recommended by Joe Walsh) had been recruited. Not wanting to abandon the guys, Domenic did not "officially" resign from the James Gang until the legal issues were settled (in the band's favour) in the summer of 1973. Kenner would stay in the James Gang for two more years and the band would release four more albums.

Donnie and I knew that we were going to be the creative force in this version of the band. We tried to steer them in our particular musical direction, and consequently, that version of the James Gang sounded like an extension of Bush. In hindsight, perhaps what we should have done was not to have been so eager—we should have been more circumspect. We were not going to be Joe Walsh, but we could have made it a bit more palatable to James Gang fans.
- Roy Kenner; interview with Mark Doble, July 4, 2020

One funny side note: The LP cover (JAMES GANG BANG) had already been completed with Domenic on it, so when the LP was going to be released they superimposed Tommy Bolin's head on Dom's body even though he had already left!

Domenic's first solo album released almost simultaneously with his two James Gang records in 1972 was successful enough that Mercury Records were interested in a second solo project. So, Domenic started to think about recording his fourth album of original material in the short space of eighteen months. With confrere Keith Olsen at the controls at Sound City Studios in L.A., Domenic was once again in complete control.

At about this time, Frank Troiano made his second trip to L.A. to visit his brother. Domenic had now lived in the US for almost four years, but he continued to remain close to his family.

In the spring of 1973, my brother Donnie informed me that he had just purchased a house on Blix Street in North Hollywood, CA, and it was going to close sometime in the early summer. He was going to have some renovations done before moving in. He was still in the James Gang, but because of their legal issues and ongoing litigation with their record label, their career was on hold. I had already been planning on a long driving trip through Canada and the US, so I agreed to go there first and help out with the reno. It took about three days to get to my brother's house by car. I dropped off my precious cargo of three large bags of our mother's homemade *taralli* (Italian pretzels/breadsticks). My brother noticed that one of the bags seemed lighter that the other two bags and I confessed that I had dipped into the bag during the long drive, as my personal stash was finished. He forgave me.

The contractor had already started the renos. The house had several repairs to be done. It needed to be painted, a new fence to be erected, new appliances were needed, and some landscaping needed to be done. I worked for about a week and then I visited San Diego, northern Mexico, Palm Springs, and Las Vegas before heading back to Donnie's new home.

When I arrived at the house, Donnie was rehearsing with David Foster on keyboards, Willy Weeks on bass, and Kenneth "Spider" Rice on drums and they were working on some "fusion" tunes. Donnie was considering putting a new band together and going in this new direction. He had already given notice to the James Gang members and management that he would be leaving as soon as their lawsuit was settled and as soon as they had chosen a replacement guitarist.

The house renos had been completed and Donnie's home looked smashing! The backyard landscaping had three or four lemon trees added, a

couple of orange trees, and birds of paradise flowers throughout. The house itself was a Spanish colonial style home finished with stucco walls and a red clay tile roof. Donnie was so proud of his new home. He really wanted the family to see it, but my parents and sister never made it down. All we could do was to send photos back home.

Donnie took me to my first live auction the next day and we bought some Persian rugs and other accent pieces for the house. There were tennis and basketball courts nearby, and we played both sports over the next week.

We watched basketball on TV at night, and he took me to my first basketball game to watch the L.A. Lakers. Their star players were Wilt Chamberlain, Jerry West, and Connie Hawkins. Connie was good friends with Shawne Jackson, and Connie and Shawne invited us to have dinner at Ernie's Mexican Restaurant in N. Hollywood. The four of us drank three or four bottles of Blue Nun wine during dinner and we told funny stories and we laughed and laughed. I reluctantly left my brother's house and drove north on the Pacific Coast Highway to go to San Francisco and later on to British Columbia to visit friends on Vancouver Island and in the interior of B.C. before heading back home to Toronto.

-   Frank Troiano; June, 2020

Living in L.A., Domenic was in regular contact with some great talent such as Willie Weeks, one of the most renowned bass players, having played with countless greats including the Rolling Stones, Eric Clapton, Stevie Wonder, and B. B. King (just to name a few). Motown session drummer Kenneth (Spider) Rice and keyboardist William Smith (who had played on Domenic's earlier albums) filled out the rhythm section. "Spider" knew Domenic from after-hour jam sessions in Toronto back in the sixties, and recalls reconnecting with Domenic in Los Angeles.

In 1972, I relocated to Los Angeles. I was hired to do a session where I got reconnected with "Smitty" and he connected me with all the Canadian artists in L.A. namely Kenny Marco, Brenda Russell, David Clayton-Thomas, Steve Kennedy, David Foster, and Donnie Troiano. I immediately took a liking to Donnie. I loved his innovative and progressive guitar technique and he was a very stylish dresser. We would jam with Smitty and others and he invited me to play drums on his second Mercury LP that was to be called TRICKY. By then I had purchased a house in L.A. and Donnie and Smitty dropped by and we rehearsed in my garage. Donnie loved it so much that he suggested that we do the pre-production for TRICKY in my garage. Donnie hired a crew of carpenters and drywallers, and within a few days had completely converted my garage into a rehearsal space by putting up soundproofing, drywall, and carpeting, all at his expense. By the following week, we were rehearsing to record TRICKY. Smitty brought in Willie Weeks on bass and it was just the four of us and we really grooved. It was some of the best playing that I had ever been involved with. Donnie was truly a "soul brother."

We went on to record TRICKY at the Sound City Studio in early 1973 and I was very proud to be involved in this special project. We had the right combination of players and we were all on the same page. We finished in less than two weeks—it was a wonderful and enjoyable experience for all of us. I was very impressed with Donnie's songwriting.

I have great memories of Donnie. When we met, it was "love at first beat!" He was a kind, sweet man and a wonderful human being. He was an incredible guitar player, far ahead of his time. I would say he was a guitar genius. There was something very special and very creative about his playing. People like him come around very rarely.
- Kenneth "Spider Webb" Rice, drummer; interview with
  Frank Troiano, July 1, 2020

Shawne Jackson and Roy Kenner returned to join Patrice Holloway on backing vocals, and this time Domenic engaged some excellent horn players, including Tom Scott, Marion Childers, John Kelson, Doug Richardson, Ernie Watts, and William Green. John Weider played violin, Tessie Coen played additional percussion, Monty Stark was on synthesizer and Gale Levant played harp. Veteran arranger Gene Page orchestrated and arranged string and horn parts.

The recording of TRICKY occurred in late 1972 to early 1973. Retreating into the studio with the best players L.A. had to offer, and more importantly, who were more than capable of making the kind of music Domenic wanted to play, would have been therapeutic and probably reinforced his decision to leave the James Gang.

There is a sense of positivity throughout TRICKY. Making it was fun, and the record repeatedly references Domenic's formative teenage years listening to and playing music. In 2001, Domenic and I had a conversation over dessert and coffee (Domenic had herbal tea), where he emphasized that regardless of how one's musical tastes evolve, it's the music you grew up with, that you invariably return to; the songs you were enjoying when you were sixteen years old. TRICKY is exactly that kind of album. But if there is a background of past references, there is also a bold newness in the exploration of jazz elements, especially on the second side of the LP.

All Night Radio Show is pop-flavoured and nostalgic, recalling late nights tuning in radio stations from Buffalo and Nashville, listening to rock, jazz, and R & B.

All Night Radio Show; looking at that reminds me of a few people. When I was a kid, I used to be able on some nights to get Nashville, listening to John R. at night. And I would listen to WUFO in Buffalo at night. And a little later I'd listen to guys like John Donabie in Toronto, who used to have an all-night show and he used to play a lot of great R & B stuff, so it's kind of about that stuff.
    -   Domenic Troiano; interview with Martin Melhuish, 1997

Long-time Toronto FM DJ and close friend John Donabie was one of the subjects of the song.

All Night Radio Show, that's a song that he wrote, and much later he told me that he'd written it about myself and the famous "Hound" out of Buffalo, NY, because in those days, artists, after they had played a gig, it might be 1:00 in the morning or 12:00 midnight, and they might be fifty to one hundred miles outside of Toronto, and they'd be driving back in. And of course I was on from 1:00 a.m. to 6:00 a.m. on CKFH on

a show called "Where it's at." It was the only rhythm and blues show in Toronto, so he was tuned right in. We played songs that CHUM refused to play. We played every R & B thing that came out. He'd be sitting there in the car, listening to me. And then he got the idea to write *All Night Radio Show*.

- John Donabie, radio host; interview with Mark Doble, August 3, 2020

Domenic pays tribute to his hometown in *My Old Toronto Home*, where Domenic longs for the familiar surroundings of his youth. The song is built over a majestic, full-on horn arrangement.

My Old Toronto Home; I guess the home sickness kind of comes out. I was thinking about my mom and my stuff. Actually, that's a song I wish more people had heard, because I think it says a lot about Toronto in its own way.

- Domenic Troiano; interview with Martin Melhuish, 1997

The title track, *Tricky*, is an eighteen-minute jazz-blues suite taking up the entirety of side two. The suite starts with the familiar old rocker, *Fannie Mae* (that Domenic played regularly and recorded with Ronnie Hawkins in 1964). William Smith provides a barrelhouse piano solo, which is followed by a harmonica break that transitions to a full brassy accompaniment over which Domenic comes out flying with a triumphant solo guitar benediction. The instrumental *Blues for Ollie is* based on a piano riff by William Smith, and features some splendid soloing on tenor sax by Ernie Watts. Domenic's solo has a distinctive modal jazz vibe reminiscent of one of his earlier guitar heroes, Lenny Breau. The third movement of the suite is an up-tempo blues by Domenic called *I'll Get My Own* and is followed by a funky instrumental, *The Greaser*.

Arranged by Gene Page and Domenic, TRICKY is an ambitious arrangement both compositionally and conceptually—the jazz elements are authentic, and the fluctuation between jazz-blues-funk are virtually seamless. Although there is not an abundance of singing on the album, Domenic's singing on TRICKY seems more confident than ever.

In L.A., Domenic continued to attract regular session work with different bands and artists including Canadian David Foster who would in years to come achieve great success as a record producer in Canada and the US. Foster and his wife, B.J. Cook, headed a band called Skylark, who had a million-selling single called *Wildflower*, the flipside of which was Domenic's *The Writings on the Wall*.

Donnie could cover it all with ease, grace, and pure talent! I had the honour and pleasure of witnessing this talent up close when, for a brief time, we played in the same band together, though mostly I was just a fan, marvelling at this huge Canadian talent. Thank you, Donnie Troiano, for gracing us with your monster talent!
- David Foster, composer, arranger, record producer, and music executive; email to Frank Troiano, November 2020

Drummer Eric "Mouse" Johnson, who worked with major artists such as Aretha Franklin, Chuck Berry, and Lou Reed had known Domenic since the Bluenote days in the sixties, and was now based in L.A. and had reconnected with Domenic.

Both Donnie and Smitty helped me a lot when I went down to L.A. In 1974, I started weekly jam sessions at the Josephina Club in Ventura. We had Jim Keltner on drums, David Foster on keyboards, Smitty on organ, Danny Kortchmar and Donnie on guitars. We were really cookin'! Donnie was a beautiful cat. He was straight-ahead, kind, very talented, and had a good soul. I would say that he was as good a person as he was an artist, a rare trait. When it came to session work, he knew what he wanted. He wanted the other players to feel him and then give it to him with their performances. He was fair and he provided space for development and so the sessions were fun and enjoyable. He was a positive guy to be around.
- Eric "Mouse" Johnson, drummer; interview with Frank Troiano, June 28, 2020

For whatever reason, many of the Toronto Sound musicians from the late sixties found themselves together in Los Angeles in the early seventies. Kenny Marco, guitarist with Motherlode and Dr. Music had shared the stage on numerous occasions with Domenic and the Mandala, and in 1973 ended up recording with Domenic in L.A.

The next venture was in Los Angeles, which was really eye-opening, because who did we run into there but Domenic, Whitey, and the rest of our fellow Canadians. We all seemed to follow similar routes and by strange coincidence Dom and I had been contacted by legendary producer Gabriel Mekler (Steppenwolf, Janis Joplin, and Three Dog Night) to record on the very famous, controversial label, Chess Records. The album featured Etta James and was recorded at The Sound Factory in Hollywood, California. Both Dom and I had the privilege of playing on her LP.

- Kenny Marco, guitarist—Motherlode, Dr. Music, Grant Smith and the Power; email to Frank Troiano, November 2020

Etta James' self-titled 1973 funk-blues-rock album features Marco on guitar along with William "Smitty" Smith on keys, and Kenny "Spider Webb" Rice on drums. 1973 also saw Domenic guesting on David Clayton-Thomas' self-titled effort released on RCA.

Singer-songwriter Brenda Russell, who had known Domenic back in Toronto during the Bluenote days moved to Los Angeles at about this time and credits Domenic for his loyalty and support.

In 1973, I moved to L.A. with my husband, Brian Russell, and I was made to feel at home by Shawne, Eric, Donnie, Smitty, Mouse, Steve, and many other Canadian musicians. They introduced me to David Foster, who gave my song writing career a big boost by his introductions to Earth, Wind & Fire and other bands. Periodically, we would all get together and jam at one of our homes. For the next two years Donnie remained a very good friend, and we got together frequently. I loved him like a brother. After he moved back to Canada, he would visit L.A. every year or so and he always made sure to look me up.

- Brenda Russell, singer-songwriter; interview with Frank Troiano, July 15, 2020

In the spring of 1973, Domenic initiated weekly jam sessions (featuring many of his fellow Canadians) at a Los Angeles Valley club called Cappy's, which attracted the attention of Michael Sherman of the Los Angeles *Free Press*:

We showed up there on a recent Monday night after being told by old friend Domenic Troiano that "a few of us are going to have a little fun, do a little jamming to keep our chops up." At the drums is Hoppy Hodges who is, says Dom, "an up-and-comer—a damn fine musician—he's been doing some session work with Feliciano recently." Organist William "Smitty" Smith first achieved a heavy rep in Canada as a result of his work with Dianne Brooks and the Soul Searchers, and more recently as a member of David Clayton-Thomas' Sanctuary Band. Warming up on piano and ARB is Skylark's David Foster and later, fellow Skylarker, vocalist Donnie Gerrard, will join the clambake. On bass is Willie Weeks (ex-Donny Hathaway, ex-Aretha) who might well be the finest around. Troiano and the group played for a solid hour before taking a break, but unlike many, it had some incredible moments which went far beyond the call of duty. It's a pity Cappy's wasn't packed to the pits. The music and the vibe were perfect, just floating there, with plenty to go around for any number of soul gourmets. Troiano isn't sure how regular the sessions will be insofar as he and his friends are concerned, but he does intend to do it as often as seems right.

- "Troiano Group Jams at Cappy's in Valley … Maybe,"
  Michael Sherman, Los Angeles *Free Press*, June 15, 1973

Most of 1973 and '74 were spent rehearsing, doing session work, and playing live locally. Domenic was now established and respected for his incredible technique and musicality. He was also making a concerted effort to clear his head of the dynamics of playing in a group. However "opportunity" was about to knock again, and within a matter of months, that would all change.

James Gang-Straight Shooter Ad—Dale Peters, Roy Kenner, Domenic Troiano, Jim Fox, 1972 (Troiano Family Archives)

CHAPTER 7

POWER IN
THE MUSIC

"Fret fever—it's the music that counts
Not who they think you are."
(*Fret Fever*, lyrics by Domenic Troiano)

The Guess Who—Gary Peterson, Domenic Troiano, Burton Cummings,
Bill Wallace, 1975 *(Troiano Family Archives)*

We did a couple of albums that I really feel pretty good about—very different from Guess Who albums. I know in retrospect (and die-hard Guess Who fans in that respect), I can understand why they wouldn't be that crazy about some of the stuff, because it was definitely not vintage Guess Who stuff—it was different. But I thought it was fun, and we had a good time doing it, and I think live, probably the band was at its best on the road during that period, from what the guys all told me and what they felt, and how hard they were working at it.

- Domenic Troiano; interview with Howard Mandshein, 92 CITI-FM, January 2005

Years later, Burton Cummings claimed that by 1974, he was thinking seriously of packing in The Guess Who. But the decision to leave the security of being the leader of one of Canada's established rock acts could not be easy. And while many fans blame the recruitment of Domenic Troiano for the demise of the Guess Who a year later in 1975, it's an all too convenient narrative.

Changes in direction are risky for an established group. When fan expectations are not met, the response is often negative. Domenic Troiano, the acclaimed "musician's musician," was intended to add a new-found credibility and musical sophistication to a group known for catchy, radio-friendly rock.

They got me into the band because they wanted to change things, probably a little too much for some of their fans, but for me it was interesting; it was a good experience.

- Domenic Troiano; interview with Martin Melhuish, June 19, 1997

The story of The Guess Who reads like a soap opera: personnel changes; bitter disputes; sex, drugs, rock and roll; disagreements over finances; and even politics and religion. All the while, the good old Guess Who, propelled and sustained by the distinctive voice of Burton Cummings, continued to make great records and churn out singles to a faithful fan base in Canada and parts of the midwestern US. Six different guitarists went through The Guess Who's revolving door from 1966 through 1975. The last was Domenic Troiano.

Starting in the early sixties as a Winnipeg-based, five-piece combo (originally Al and the Silvertones, becoming Chad Allan and the Reflections and then Chad Allan and the Expressions), The Guess Who under lead singer Chad Allan had a surprise hit single in 1965 with *Shakin' All Over*. Shortly after this success, Allan left the band. Burton Cummings, who had joined the group a few months earlier to replace pianist Bob Ashley, would take on the lead vocals. Cummings was a singer with a powerful, rare vocal range and a magnetic stage presence. It would take four years, but finally, in 1969, The Guess Who (comprised of guitarist and leader Randy Bachman, lead vocalist/pianist/flautist/rhythm guitarist Burton Cummings, Jim Kale on bass, and Garry Peterson on drums) struck gold with the international hit record *These Eyes*. This was followed by a succession of top ten singles including *Laughing, Undun, No Time*, and of course the number one single *American Woman*.

At the pinnacle of their success in May 1970, guitarist and lead writer Randy Bachman left the band in one of the most public and nasty break-ups in Canadian rock history, citing differences over musical direction and lifestyle. At the exact time of Bachman's departure, the single *American Woman*, and the album of the same name, were both at number one on the North American music charts.

Bachman was swiftly replaced with Winnipeg guitarists Kurt Winter and Greg Leskiw, and The Guess Who hit-making machine continued without skipping a beat through 1970 and 1971 with a string of follow-ups including *Hand Me Down World* and *Albert Flasher*. In 1972, Leskiw was replaced by another Winnipegger, Donnie McDougall, and that same year bassist Bill Wallace replaced Jim Kale. From late 1971 through early 1974 The Guess Who remained a popular draw through the American midwest, producing several great albums, but frustratingly, none of these releases realized the success previously achieved by their 1970 hit records.

By 1974, salt in the wound was added by Randy Bachman's stunning success with Bachman Turner Overdrive (BTO), who were cresting an incredible wave of popularity and record sales, scoring hits such as *Takin' Care of Business* and *You Ain't Seen Nothing Yet*. BTO specialized in basic meat-and-potatoes three-chord rock. Fans loved it, and everywhere they played, record sales went through the roof.

Meanwhile, The Guess Who's popularity had plateaued. Although they were in the midst of a multi-album deal with RCA, it did not help that the record company was either less interested or incapable of understanding how to promote their work. The band wasn't writing pop ballads like *These Eyes* anymore, or political tracts like *Hand Me Down World*. Songs such as *Those Showbiz Shoes, Glamour Boy, Lie Down*, and *One Way Road to Hell* were well crafted songs to be sure, but the depressive and introspective lyrical focus of these tunes doomed them from being hits. Burton Cummings was restless and by 1974, was openly candid about leaving the group, or possibly even exploring a career in film.

"I'd quit the band in two seconds," said lead singer-pianist-composer Burton Cummings recently, sitting up on the bed in his hotel room, "if I was offered the right movie role, that is."
- Burton Cummings, lead singer, pianist, composer; "Movie Bug Poses Threat to The Guess Who," Peter Goddard, *Toronto Star*, March 30, 1974

No sooner did word get out about Burton's interest, that a role was offered for a movie entitled *A Fool, a Fool, I Met a Fool* in which Burton would play a rock star and also write and record the soundtrack.

And Burton Cummings is having an oft-expressed wish come true. He'll play hero and The Guess Who will make the music for a movie titled *A Fool, A Fool, I Met a Fool*.
- "Guess Who," Richard Dumont, *Beetle*, December 1974

In the spring of '74, The Guess Who released ROAD FOOD, their eleventh album on RCA. The actual recording process had been frustrating due to guitarists Kurt Winter and Donnie McDougall, who seemed either not prepared or less than interested. Tales of arriving late to sessions, substance abuse, and festering resentments over creative control were all contributing factors. Along with Cummings' public musings about leaving

146

the band and making movies, tensions were high and relationships frayed. Something had to give, or The Guess Who was finished.

Domenic got the call in May 1974. Cummings, Wallace, Peterson, and producer Jack Richardson were convened at RCA Studios in Los Angeles, prepared to record the movie soundtrack, only to discover that neither McDougall nor Winter were ready. With the studio booked, Domenic Troiano was called in on short notice. Bill Wallace thinks that it might have been Jack Richardson's idea to bring in Troiano.

Burton was trying to do this film thing, and we'd done about three or four songs, and then I think Jack suggested that Troiano was around and he could try and puts some tracks on. I think we did *Your Back Yard* and *Sona Sona*... Anyways, he came in and everybody was pretty impressed with what he did! But I think it was Jack who just wanted to bring him down so we could see what he does.

- Bill Wallace, singer, bassist – the Guess Who; interview with Mark Doble, May 1, 2021

We went to Los Angeles to record some stuff for the soundtrack of a movie I was going to star in, which was subsequently cancelled. But anyway, I'd given the band some demo cassettes of the songs I'd written so they could learn their parts. What it boiled down to was Wallace and Peterson learned the stuff, but our guitar players didn't. When we got to L.A., they were so far out of the picture that the rest of us did those tunes as a trio and then phoned Troiano, just because he was right there in Los Angeles, and asked him if he'd like to play on the soundtrack. One thing led to another and he was in the band for good about a month later.

- Burton Cummings, lead singer, pianist, composer; "Guess Who," Jim Millican, *Sound*, May 1975

The ease with which Domenic stepped in and played his parts impressed the guys beyond belief. Suddenly, the solution to their frustrations was smiling and standing right in front of them in the studio, rapidly rolling out guitar patterns and lead licks without even breaking a sweat.

We all looked at each other like, "Wow, wouldn't that be something if we could get him in the group?" I had no opposition to that. I didn't want the group to be over quite yet.

- Burton Cummings, lead singer, pianist, composer; interview with Ralph Chapman, liner notes to FLAVOURS, The Guess Who, CD reissue, Iconoclassic Records, 2011

For Burton Cummings and The Guess Who, the timing was perfect. If they couldn't match BTO's sales success, at least they could raise the bar musically and go for a more sophisticated sound. Cummings, Wallace, and Peterson were more than capable. Adding a player of Domenic's talent and reputation would earn instant credibility.

Domenic was one of the finest talents, one of the greatest gentlemen—I mean, I knew who he was. I knew he was an immense talent and I knew the bands that he played for. To me, if I am replacing somebody in my band, I want the best guy and also a guy who is better than me, so that I can up my game.

- Garry Peterson, drummer; interview with Mark Doble, April 10, 2020

Initially, Domenic was reluctant. Having come out of a group situation with the James Gang, he wasn't so sure he wanted to be part of a band anytime soon. But The Guess Who was persistent. After numerous calls from Guess Who manager Don Hunter as well as Garry Peterson and Burton Cummings, Domenic acquiesced and agreed to join. Domenic and Burton would become the primary writers, and he would come on board with a full twenty-five per cent share in the band. Some have suggested that Domenic's decision to join was in part a cash grab. Frank Troiano does not disagree, noting that Domenic had not been earning serious money through any of his previous assignments (other than his short tenure with the James Gang) and joining a band with the status of The Guess Who would enhance his financial position, as would the guarantee of writing credits on subsequent albums. Money was a factor and Frank Troiano recalls several conversations with his brother, who agonized over his decision. Ultimately it was the commitment of Burton Cummings that sealed the deal for him to join The Guess Who.

I wasn't all that familiar with what the band was doing, but they'd always seemed to be trying different things and once I started talking with Burton we seemed to share a lot of similar views, mainly that he wanted to try to progress and grow and not just stay in the same musical rut.
- Domenic Troiano; "Guess Who," Jim Millican, *Sound*, May 1975

Years before, Domenic had played on Randy Bachman's instrumental solo album, AXE, recorded in Chicago in 1970, shortly before Randy departed from The Guess Who. Bachman had seen Domenic perform in Toronto in the late sixties and was impressed enough to invite him to record with him.

I heard about this cool guitar player who played a Tele and gigged in an R & B band called the Mandala. I got their album. Dom's guitar work was a cool mixture of funk/R & B and Lenny Breau stuff, all in one. We spent a few days in Chicago, jamming together. He was a great person with a beautiful spirit and was a true master of his own guitar style.
- Randy Bachman, lead guitarist/composer; "Domenic Troiano, Musician 1946–2005," Sandra Martin, *The Globe and Mail*, June 4, 2005

Garry Peterson also noticed similarities between Domenic and Breau.

He reminded me so much of someone that I played with early in my career when I was eighteen years old—a guitarist from Winnipeg by the name of Lenny Breau. And every time I saw him, his manner, his style, and his playing, I saw Lenny Breau. Lenny was dark haired, and their mannerisms when he talked—that was Lenny! For me it was kind of a déjà vu when he came into the band. I thought, "Man! This is just like playing with Lenny again! And that's a compliment to Domenic."
- Garry Peterson, drummer; interview with Mark Doble, April 10, 2020

For Bill Wallace, it must have been somewhat unsettling. Having joined The Guess Who in 1972 and establishing himself as the band's arranger as well as a principle song writer, Wallace was suddenly relegated to a secondary role.

He put me on my toes! He sort of took over the music of the band and I had been used to playing my own parts. But as soon as Donnie came

in, he'd go, "This is how the bass goes and it has to be like this, and it might have to fit with the guitar…" And I was busting my ass to keep up basically just to play his parts, and I got pushed to the side even as far as Donnie took over. He just started trying to organize the background vocals and stuff. He just came in and took over. But honestly, we were expecting him to, because we were looking for something like that. For me, it was a great learning experience.

- Bill Wallace, singer, bassist; interview with Mark Doble, May 1, 2021

But initially everyone, including Bill, embraced Domenic's arrival and eagerly championed how Domenic's musical leadership would take The Guess Who to the next level.

Troiano has really changed our attitude. We want to learn. A good musician never stops learning, but we had kind of packed that in and were willing to do the same show night after night, year after year. We've never had a guitar player who was capable of taking an extended solo the way Domenic can. He plays an infinite number of licks and never repeats the same thing. He's given us different flavours in the band because he's had more of an R & B influence during his life, whereas growing up on the prairies, we've had more of a Midwestern influence. So, The Guess Who sounds a little funkier and more centred around guitar lines and riffs, where I mainly wrote with piano chords before.

- Burton Cummings, lead vocalist, pianist, composer; "Guess Who," Jim Millican, *Sound*, May 1975

By the second week of June 1974, Kurt Winter and Donnie McDougall were no longer in The Guess Who, having been replaced by Domenic Troiano, who immediately flew to Winnipeg to spend a couple of weeks at Burton's, writing songs together.

Dom came up to my house in Winnipeg just after he'd joined the band. We started writing songs the same day he got there. And the first song we wrote, *Dancin' Fool,* turned out to be our new single. We just wrote every day for two weeks and came up with enough songs for FLAVOURS, and our next album as well.

- Burton Cummings, lead singer, pianist, composer; "The Guess Who Battle Obscurity With FLAVOURS," Dan Nooger, *Circus*, March 1975

Somewhat ironically, just as Domenic joined, The Guess Who had a hit single. *Clap for the Wolfman* (a novelty tune featuring a cameo performance by the notorious rock DJ Wolfman Jack) was their first top ten hit since 1971. But instead of touring to support ROAD FOOD, the band spent the latter half of 1974 performing North American venues, introducing the new guitarist to their loyal fan base. Domenic's presence was noticed by critics and audiences alike. Of their August 31 appearance at Toronto's Canadian National Exhibition, music critic Peter Goddard wrote the following:

By all the logistics of the rock business, the group should have been finished years ago, remembered only as a top forty hit record machine. But the band continues to evolve. They are erratic at times, but their new guitarist, Dom Troiano, is always interesting. And with Troiano last night stitching together the playing of bassist Bill Wallace and drummer Garry Peterson, and with pianist-singer Cummings keeping the momentum brisk, the results were as satisfying as any in the past.

- "Guess Who's Rock Banishes the Blues," Peter Goddard, *Toronto Star*, September 1, 1974

The CNE show was Domenic's first live performance in his hometown as a member of The Guess Who.

It was the 1974 CNE show. Donnie arranged a limousine to take us to the concert—Mom, Dad, Frankie, and me, along with Roy and my cousin Lucy. We drove through the Princes' Gates—we were right onstage for the show. Afterward, we joined the band at Sam the Chinese Food Man for a party. I sat beside Burton Cummings, who showed me how to operate chopsticks. He was so nice.

- Gina Troiano; interview with Mark Doble, June 30, 2020

The Guess Who—Raffaele Troiano, Gary Peterson, Pasqua Troiano,
Domenic Troiano, Burton Cummings, Bill Wallace, 1974 *(Troiano Family Archives)*

From reviews, the quality did not suffer under Domenic's influence. The following review appeared in the *Green Bay Gazette*:

Thanks to the addition of Troiano, standards like *Bus Rider, Albert Flasher, Undun, Sour Suite, Hand Me Down World*, and of course *American Woman* and *No Time* are more streamlined, while the timbre of Cummings' voice is as biting as ever. Even though he seemed to drown out Cummings' piano at times, the songs were rawer and more electric than before. Troiano's guitar imagery is the one ingredient necessary to cut the pressure in half and double Cummings' creative output. And

from the numbers played last night, The Guess Who's thirteenth album FLAVOURS should be just the beginning.

- "Guess Who Gives its Best," Mark Moran, *Green Bay Gazette*, November 30, 1974

FLAVOURS was recorded during several stops to Nimbus 9 Studios in Toronto in July 1974. Interestingly for Domenic, FLAVOURS was his first full-length album recorded entirely in his hometown. Domenic was eager to share his exciting new experiences with close friends and family. Gina Troiano recalls bicycling from Sammon Avenue to Hazelton Avenue, carrying a homemade pizza to the studio to be shared while the band ran through countless renditions of *Dancin' Fool*. Younger cousin, Anthony Ferrara, was also there that day.

One of my fondest memories as a young teenager in the summer of '74 is Donnie taking me to the Nimbus 9 Studio in Yorkville to watch The Guess Who record FLAVOURS. I didn't recognize that I was in the presence of greatness: true Canadian music icons. Not just the band, but legendary producer Jack Richardson. That day, the mood was good and I remember Cummings joked around a lot and he would break into songs, swearing a lot, but it was funny! (I was fourteen.) That day, they were doing take after take of *Dancin' Fool*. Donnie was playing amazingly. I'm forever grateful to my cousin Donnie for including me in this special part of his musical journey.

- Anthony Ferrara, cousin; email to Frank Troiano, May, 2020

Jack Richardson had to have been thrilled. The band came into the studio fully prepared and well-rehearsed. Troiano could deliver solo after solo, each one different and perfect. The newfound musicality, discipline, and positivity were a distinct contrast from recent Guess Who sessions. Lastly, the material was refreshing, funkier, and upbeat. Nobody was sulking. Bill Wallace once stated, *"The studio is where we became friends."*

FLAVOURS—the name of the album was deliberately intended to convey the band's stylistic versatility. All nine songs were written by Cummings and Troiano. And even though musical variety was a feature of most Guess Who albums, it would be hard to find a collection of songs more diverse in style from one another: hard rock, country, blues, gospel, jazz, pop ballad, and even some fusion. Domenic was putting his own stamp on things and the rest of the band was on board. Cummings raved that this was their best album since 1970's SHARE THE LAND.

Dancin' Fool was probably the most "Guess Who-ish" song on the record, with a pulsing guitar riff and a riveting vocal. Sequenced as the album's lead-off track, it was sublimely catchy, and an immediate notice that the new partnership could play the singles game, gifting the band with a more than worthy follow-up to *Clap for the Wolfman*. (*Dancin' Fool* would be the band's last single to break the Billboard Top Forty.)

Hoedown Time is the kind of single that never was, from the absolutely exquisite bridge and Domenic's layered acoustic guitars to the epic solo lasting ninety seconds. *Hoedown* was "Exhibit A" that the band had found an extraordinary, visceral, dynamic player!

Seems like I Can't Live with You (But I Can't Live Without You) is an unapologetic foray into country and western music. Dedicated to the departed country rocker Gram Parsons, Burton's utterly countrified vocal is terrific. The tune is also notable for the only occasion Domenic performed or recorded a mandolin solo.

I tried to sing it like a western singer, but to make it sound authentic, not phony. That's why we just did it very simply, with my piano and Domenic on mandolin, instead of with the fifty steel guitars you'd expect. I really enjoyed singing the song, but the other guys won't let me do it live.
- Burton Cummings, lead singer, pianist, composer; "The Guess Who Battle Obscurity with FLAVOURS," Dan Nooger, *Circus*, March 1974

Dirty is one of Cummings' favourite tracks from FLAVOURS and was one of the tunes performed during the 1974 summer tour.

Dirty—Good rocker, all built around Troiano's guitar riff, still has some grit, this one. But at times, it sounds like the singer's trying a bit too hard … nonetheless, this one I like.

- Burton Cummings, lead singer, pianist, composer;
  Facebook post, December 22, 2019

Featuring some of Cummings' most vitriolic lyrics ever, *Long Gone* builds on rhythm and tempo shifts. Domenic delivers with several blues-inflected extended solos while Peterson's percussion work is absolutely amazing. Wallace's fluid bass lines synchronize beautifully with Peterson, and Cummings' manic keyboard near the end adds to the intensity. It's a tour de force, a fine composition, expertly performed, and was one of the first new things The Guess Who used to showcase Troiano to their fan base during the 1974 summer tour.

But *Long Gone* was perceived as a serious departure. The song became a lightning rod, doing nothing in terms of winning back those long-suffering Guess Who fans who desperately wanted the band to return to a more basic rock and roll approach. *Long Gone* proved, if anything, the band was moving the bar again in terms of what it was willing to try.

FLAVOURS was released in November 1974. The single *Dancin' Fool* made it to number twenty-eight on the Billboard charts. *New York Times* columnist David Fandray raved about the album and the new Guess Who sound.

In the past, changes in membership have not affected The Guess Who sound. Troiano, however, seems to be Cummings' match. The two have co-written all of the songs on FLAVOURS, and the result is a surprisingly heavy Guess Who. This is a bit jolting at first, but the band wears this new sound well. There is a punch here that has been missing since the days of *American Woman* and *No Time*. Cummings' voice and keyboard skills are both up to the task of giving the band's sound this new depth. What is really amazing, however, is the depth added by Troiano's guitar skills. He is clearly the best guitarist in The Guess Who lineup, and would have to be considered a formidable guitarist in any situation.

- David Fandray, "Exit Column," *The New York Times*, 1974

Even RCA was suddenly interested! Canadian industry magazine *RPM* reported in January 1975 that the label was conducting one of their most intensive promotional campaigns in support of FLAVOURS. The Guess Who flew to Holland to film a lip sync promo for *Dancin' Fool*; and in January, to New York City for appearances on the *Midnight Special* television show, along with live radio broadcasts at the Bottom Line and Electric Ladyland Studios, all with the intention of growing the new Guess Who brand.

One thing musically, since Domenic has joined the band, I think he's brought the calibre of the music up considerably, because there's far more emphasis now on practising and experimenting, and working with sounds and progressions and musical patterns, etc. It's becoming more of a "band," rather than just a record-making machine, which we were for awhile, and then we tried to do our own experimenting—but we were floundering for a long time. Now we've got a good, solid group. I think everyone is doing their job to the best of their ability, and I see a lot of good things in the future for us.

- Burton Cummings, lead singer, pianist, composer;
  interview with Johan "Mosse" Vikstedt, CEO of Discophon, the
  Finnish branch of RCA Records, January 1975

In early January of 1975, The Guess Who was scheduled to perform a live broadcast in quad sound on WQIV FM at Electric Ladyland Studios in front of a small audience. At the sound check in the early afternoon, Donnie's Marshall amps were too powerful for the studio setting. He needed an old Fender amp in order to get a warmer sound. He considered his options and decided to call his old guitar buddy, Rick Derringer, who lived in New York City and was an avid guitar and amp collector. Rick was in town and said that he would send over a couple of old Fender amplifiers to the studio. Within an hour, a cube van showed up containing about a dozen old Fender amps (blond, tweed) packed in flight cases. Donnie was totally floored. After trying two or three of them, he found one that was just right. The Guess Who went

on to perform one of their finest live shows later that day. Derringer to the rescue!

- Blaine Pritchett, sound technician; interview with Frank Troiano, December 15, 2020

The Electric Ladyland recording is amazingly clear sounding, reportedly the first ever "quadraphonic" simulcast and certainly worthy of a commercial release.

Unfortunately, in the midst of what seemed at last to be an upward trajectory, *Rolling Stone Magazine* reviewer Jim Miller wrote a review of FLAVOURS that could only have made the band members cringe.

Sadly, someone missed a turn somewhere down the line. The sweetness of Cummings' vocal fails to mesh with the misplaced complexity of Troiano's playing, and the new lineup seems eager to forego the pleasures of pithy pop—which, after all, is what The Guess Who have always excelled at. Instead, we get sheer embarrassments like Cummings trying to sing C & W (*Seems like I Can't Live with You, But I Can't Live Without You,* dedicated to the memory of Gram Parsons) and Troiano trying to "stretch out" (on *Long Gone,* which also features such pungent lines as "I guess you've always been a power hungry specimen"). RCA's advance flak on *Long Gone* waxed eloquent: "Troiano really gets loose with an eat-your-heart-out Mahavishnu John McLaughlin guitar lick." Eat your heart out? Make mine BTO, please.

- "Flavours," Jim Miller, *Rolling Stone Magazine*, March 27, 1975

Miller's fixation on The Guess Who as a "pithy pop" group is hardly fair and fails to acknowledge the band's evolution into a more "album oriented" unit that started as far back as 1970, after Randy Bachman's departure.

But if the reviews were mixed, the stated issue was the "difference" in style rather than the quality of the music. This criticism is misplaced. From WHEATFIELD SOUL and every album after, stylistic variety was a Guess Who cornerstone, and in that respect FLAVOURS was nothing new. And while *Long Gone* may have been something of a departure, it is hard to imagine any of the other eight songs on FLAVOURS out of place on any of their previous albums. Sales of FLAVOURS were respectable and the Guess Who returned to Nimbus 9 in early March 1975 with a sense of optimism to record their follow-up to FLAVOURS.

Rock writer John Einarson was in attendance at the sessions and recalled an overall positive vibe during the recording process. Band members were upbeat, engineer Brian Christian kept the mood light with his humour, and the guys were generally positive. (Iconoclassic's 2014 CD reissue of POWER IN THE MUSIC includes a bonus recording from the sessions in which all of the band members are obviously enjoying themselves, jamming on old rock and roll and light-heartedly "kibitzing.")

POWER IN THE MUSIC was more a focused rock album. Leading off as usual with a buoyant rocker, *Down and Out Woman* set the tone. The band would open their shows with this number during the 1975 summer tour.

Women took things down a notch tempo-wise, with some nifty harmonies over a gorgeous and reflective acoustic guitar accompaniment.

I'm more conscious of lyrics. My strength lies in words. You should be able to do with lyrics what a player improvises with notes. You should be able to play a progression and just sing to make it rhythmically correct. I've done that with a million songs. An example on this album is *Women*. We sat in the living room and Dom would say, "Sing whatever comes into your head." And I said, "Alright, I'll sing this. How does this grab you?" It was the first thing I did and we left it like that. It seemed very logical. It turned out different than I thought it would. It just jelled in the studio.
- Burton Cummings, lead singer, pianist, composer;
  Guess Who—Power In the Music Promo, Larry Leblanc, 1975

The hook-laden *When the Band Was Singin' Shakin' All Over* is defined by a pounding bass riff, a raunchy guitar lick, and a full-on screaming lead vocal joyously recalling the good old days. The song goes full-tilt from start to finish and is over far too soon.

In writing the song, I flashed on going to see The Guess Who when I was still in high school in 1959, before I was in it. It was a magical time in

my life. That was a more innocent time for everyone. Anyway, this riff kept floating in my mind and we just kept messing around with it. We took it to practice, started playing with it, and for some reason I started playing the high, high right hand on the piano. It reminded me of their song *Shakin' All Over*.

- Burton Cummings, lead singer, pianist, composer;
  Guess Who—Power In the Music Promo, 1975

To this day, Cummings is full of praise for the chord progression Domenic devised for *Dreams*. Featuring poetic lyrics inspired by various dreams Burton had, it is arguably one of the most magnificent and well-crafted ballads in The Guess Who repertoire.

Dreams—it probably wouldn't have happened if it hadn't been for Troiano's guitar licks that start it all off. I listened intently to those guitar riffs and really absorbed the rhythm of them on Handsart Blvd. in Winnipeg … wrote all those lyrics quite quickly actually. Of all the GW records, this is one of my absolute favourites, although ironically, Domenic didn't really care for it that much. I guess it wasn't out there enough for his tastes.

- Burton Cummings, lead singer, pianist, composer;
  Facebook post, December 22, 2019

Rich World Poor World is another hard-driving number with complex rhythmic shifts and unusual chord changes. The opening guitar lick for *Rich World Poor World* was reworked from an unreleased Bush tune, *Wicked Woman*. The soloing is spectacular and Cummings delivers yet another lyrical diatribe about the state of the world, singing sarcastically about the plight of the privileged in contrast to children living in abject poverty with neither food nor medicine. When performing live, the band would exchange riffs from *Long Gone* and allow Peterson an extended drum solo. Another interesting feature of the live performances was a slide show displaying images of Richard Nixon and Jackie Onassis contrasted with pictures of hungry children. *Rich World Poor World* continued to showcase the musicianship of The Guess Who and convey to listeners that *Long Gone* was hardly a one-off.

Roseanne is a rollicking piano rocker featuring some frenetic playing by Burton and some tasty vocal harmonies; a legitimate choice for a single that sadly failed to chart.

Coors for Sunday features Troiano at his bluesy best. Cummings almost whispers as he croons the lyrics in a slow burn against Domenic's masterful guitar lines. The playing is restrained and there isn't a note out of place.

Coors For Sunday—here again, this song would never have happened were it not for Troiano playing me that guitar riff and saying "Got anything for this?" And he sure did a spectacular guitar solo in this one ... yes he did ...
- Burton Cummings, lead singer, pianist, composer;
  Facebook post, December 22, 2019

Windsor Star columnist John Laycock was glowing in his review.

What has grown is the fullness of the music. The Cummings-Troiano hybrid has remarkable clarity and finesse. *Roseanne* and *Down and Out Woman* are stirring rockers; *Dreams* enhances the melodic beauty of Cummings' remarkable voice; there's a tribute to Coors beer, justly deserved; no rocker will argue with *Power in the Music*; a sense of the past in *When the Band was Singin' Shakin' All Over*; and a glimpse of the future *Women*. Their new album continues the impression of their last one, FLAVOURS—that the band is now at its peak.
- "POWER IN THE MUSIC—Review," John Laycock,
  The Windsor Star, 1975

To kick off the 1975 tour, on April 15, The Guess Who played to a capacity audience at the Winnipeg Playhouse Theatre in a show that was simultaneously broadcast on CFRW-FM. In 2018, European label Orbit Records released the concert as a two-disc set entitled THE GUESS WHO LIVE IN '75. The set list is decidedly Cummings-Troiano heavy, featuring an equal measure of tunes from both POWER IN THE MUSIC and FLAVOURS.

However, as the tour progressed, audiences were less enthused. That Troiano was still an amazing talent was undeniable. But fans clearly preferred the old hits. An *Edmonton Journal* review was particularly scathing.

What he got mostly, was lead singer Burton Cummings singing about Asian babies with bloated bellies in heavy metal rock songs like *Rich World, Poor World,* a Guess Who newie that typifies the group's new musical direction. They tuned out during the heavy stuff. Waiting patiently for the more familiar tunes ... when he gets to preaching like he has in the past, the results are disastrous. Of the new stuff, none of it stands out as particularly pleasing or enjoyable.

- Night of Musical Preaching, Joe Sornberger,
  Edmonton Journal, July 24, 1975)

Live recordings of The Guess Who from the 1975 summer tour reveal a band that was probably more polished and refined than any time in its history. The rhythm section is in sync, Burton's keyboard skills were more than solid, and if his singing seemed a little subdued on record, in live performance he would let loose, exploiting his amazing vocal range at full volume and value. Domenic's guitar wizardry and dexterity was also on display every night.

Still, The Guess Who soldiered on through the summer, delivering their full two-hour set chock full of new material interspersed with classic hits. Notable dates included a rain-drenched concert at Toronto's CNE Stadium on August 31, at which the four members marched onto the outdoor stage wearing rubber-soled footwear amid the pelting wind and rain and proceeded to deliver their entire set without dropping a song. Two weeks later, The Guess Who would play their final concert at the Montreal Forum.

In Montreal on September 14, 1975, at the Montreal Forum was when I first met Domenic while he was with The Guess Who. My friend back in the day, Burton Cummings, introduced me to him. It would turn out to be the last Guess Who concert with Burton Cummings featuring Domenic. I still remember how gentlemanly he was, given he was busy and it was close to showtime. I watched most of the concert from the side stage near the amps.

- Susan Finkler, fan; email to Frank Troiano May, 2020

POWER IN THE MUSIC did not yield a hit single. Audience numbers declined, and for the first time, some concerts were cancelled mid-tour.

And while FLAVOURS had outsold ARTIFICIAL PARADISE, #10, and ROAD FOOD, the numbers for POWER IN THE MUSIC were disappointing. By the end of the summer, the band was exhausted. Burton Cummings explained to Jim Millican: *"This last tour was just too long. About five weeks is my limit, but this one was about nine and everyone started getting a little crazy toward the end."* At its conclusion, Bill Wallace gave his notice to leave The Guess Who.

Now that Bill has two children that are growing up, kids he's basically been away from since they were born, I think it's bothering him and it's reflected a lot in the way he was on tour, he was kind of edgy and really just not wanting to be on the road anymore. There are no hard feelings between Wallace and ourselves. Basically, it was his decision.

- Burton Cummings, lead singer, pianist, composer; "The Guess Who Controversy," Jim Millican, *Record Week*, October 20, 1975

Fifteen months earlier, at the time of Domenic's joining, The Guess Who was enjoying the top ten success of *Clap for the Wolfman*, a tune penned primarily by Wallace. In his three years, Bill had become a lead writer as well as an arranger for the band. Suddenly, Domenic became The Guess Who's de facto music director, requiring a greater rehearsal discipline, co-writing all of the new material, and having input into how the other players would approach their parts. As Bill explained to Winnipeg author John Einarson:

I was sort of intimidated by Troiano. He came in and the music was all set and we had to learn what he wanted. Troiano took control and called the shots. He wanted to Torontosize the band.

- Bill Wallace, bass guitarist; John Einarson, *AMERICAN WOMAN— The Story of The Guess Who*, Quarry Press Inc., Kingston, Ontario, 1995

Despite initially and publicly embracing the changes, one can only surmise that it could not have been easy, suddenly being relegated to a less prominent leadership role within the ensemble; and this (along with the less than satisfying and exhausting POWER IN THE MUSIC tour that summer) could very well have contributed to Bill's decision to leave.

Interestingly and somewhat ironically, in 1982, Domenic and Bill reunited when Domenic produced two excellent albums by Bill's Winnipeg band, Kilowatt (which also included fellow Guess Who alumnus Greg Leskiw). As Burton stated, there were no hard feelings with Bill. Bill would rejoin The Guess Who twenty-five years later with Cummings, Randy Bachman, Garry Peterson, and second guitarist Donnie McDougall in a three-year extended reunion tour of North America, which yielded the live album (and concert video), RUNNIN' BACK THRU CANADA.

In the liner notes to the 1988 CD release TRACK RECORD—THE GUESS WHO COLLECTION, long-time Guess Who producer Jack Richardson shared his thoughts on Bill's departure.

Bill Wallace indicated he would be leaving the band, and I believe that this was the catalyst that solidified Burton's decision to continue his career as a solo artist.
- Jack Richardson, producer for The Guess Who; "TRACK RECORD— THE GUESS WHO COLLECTION," Liner Notes, 1988 BMG Music

Following the '75 tour, Burton continued to be positive, even publicly speculating as to how they would replace Bill on future Guess Who recordings, defending their musical direction, and looking to the future.

I've been experimenting with a lot of vocal effects, looking for different sounds. We want to try and mix it up a little more. I think there's been too much sameness on all of the cuts as of the last three albums, and I'm looking for a little more diversification. Troiano has been moving into more sounds on guitars and synthesizers and I'll be into more keyboard things.
- Burton Cummings, lead singer, pianist, composer; "The Guess Who Controversy," Jim Millican, *Record Week*, October 20, 1975

But a month later, In November, Burton officially disbanded The Guess Who. Burton would go on to a successful career as a solo artist, and even eventually star in a movie (*Melanie*, 1982).

After an initial break from the music business, Bill Wallace resumed playing and recording in Winnipeg bands, including Crowcuss and

Kilowatt, and Garry Peterson joined an R & B group called Delphia, with Troiano alumnus Roy Kenner on lead vocals. Domenic would move back to Toronto and resume his career as a solo artist.

Garry Peterson once shared his frustration that they did not give the Troiano experiment more of a chance, as he felt that the group was just getting comfortable with the new sound and better things in the future were inevitable.

If you listen to some of the things that we produced on those albums, and listened to the music, and listened to the chord progressions, you have to get excited about it. We created some great music. Unfortunately, we didn't have enough time to fully develop the writing. Domenic knew a lot about promotion. Because of Dom, we were dressing and looking better. We were cleaning up our act, rehearsing more, and we were a tighter unit. Suddenly we were disciplined again! Who knows what we would have done if we had been together for a longer period of time?
- Garry Peterson, drummer; interview with Mark Doble, 1999

Although Roy Kenner was not involved with Domenic's tenure in The Guess Who, no one worked more closely and was more familiar with the dynamics of Domenic's musical leadership in a band setting. Forty-five years after the fact, Kenner provided a pertinent observation from his own experience that is likely more than fair and may accurately characterize Domenic's impact within The Guess Who at the time.

If Domenic's greatest strength was his obsession and dedication to his musical craft, it was also his greatest weakness. He would go right over top of you because he already had five different ideas or approaches while you were still working on one. You had to be on your game to keep up. Donnie could make you feel intimidated, but it was never on purpose. Once you stick him into an environment where he is part of the unit, things get dicey with those who are used to being in control. You praise the guy for making you better, because when you play with him, he makes you play better, but after a while, you can start to resent his dominating nature.
- Roy Kenner, lead vocalist; interview with Mark Doble, July 4, 2020

164

With The Guess Who's impressive string of singles and albums, all defined by the incredible and distinctive vocals of Burton Lorne Cummings, and even with the support of long-time drummer Garry Peterson, it is hard to conceive of The Guess Who carrying on in a musical direction that Burton didn't fully endorse. In 1975, The Guess Who was *his* band. And it was *his* decision to end it.

Musical partnerships are difficult to maintain at the best of times. The complementing differences that bring two parties together over time become less complimentary and increasingly divisive. It is difficult to imagine two musicians who were more opposite in their approach, but in their brief year and a half together, Domenic Troiano and Burton Cummings created two impressive albums of music and a stage show that was polished and always satisfying.

Jack Richardson once said, "Domenic Troiano is probably the greatest guitarist in Canada, but he doesn't have a commercial bone in his body." At the time, I thought he was slamming Donnie. But later on, I realized that Jack was right and he was just stating facts. Donnie didn't want to rehash what someone else has already done. Donnie was his own man and he was determined that he was going to play what he wanted to play.
-   Blaine Pritchett, sound technician; interview with Mark Doble, July 21, 2020

In discussing his time in The Guess Who, Domenic Troiano was gracious:

"I have to say that I thoroughly enjoyed my time in The Guess Who; playing with the guys and writing some neat tunes."
-   Domenic Troiano; Conversation with Mark Doble, 1999

We played a lot and it was always fun! We had a good time. And they were good guys to hang with. Those couple of years were probably the best years they had in terms of playing live. When I was in the band, they were really working hard, it was very professional, the whole stage show kind of changed, and it was good; probably a couple of their best years of playing and touring. I enjoyed The Guess Who.
-   Domenic Troiano; interview with Martin Melhuish, February 9, 1996

The narrative that blames Domenic Troiano for The Guess Who's demise is simply unfair. Cummings has since stated he had been contemplating a solo career for well over a year prior to actually disbanding The Guess Who. Burton, Bill, and Garry were well aware of Domenic's talent and reputation and were consciously all in with the decision to recruit him. With Troiano, The Guess Who was a tighter and better performing unit both onstage and in the studio. The writing team of Cummings and Troiano produced two very satisfying albums. While some may disagree with this assessment, it can be reasonably argued that FLAVOURS and POWER IN THE MUSIC were as artistically strong and commercially accessible as anything the band had put out in the previous three years. And although Troiano may have had a funkier edge in his writing, most, if not all of their songs would have complemented any of the pre-Troiano Guess Who albums.

Some fans in retrospect blame Troiano for being too "jazzy" for The Guess Who, a band whose catalogue included such obvious jazz-inflected tunes as *Undun, 969, Moan for Joe, Grey Day,* and *Straighten Out.* Variety was a cornerstone of Guess Who albums. All bands ultimately break up. After ten years and thirteen albums, The Guess Who was exhausted and Burton Cummings was rightfully eager to embark on a solo career. While Domenic may have been the *excuse,* he was not the *reason* for The Guess Who disbanding.

In 1983, Domenic appeared and performed with Burton in a local Hamilton, Ontario, television (CHCH) production called "In Session," featuring Cummings and Don Everly.

In 1996, Domenic was inducted into the Canadian Music Hall of Fame. The master of ceremonies for the induction was none other than Burton Cummings, who acknowledged and thanked Domenic for the music they wrote together in The Guess Who.

I happen to know our next inductee into the Hall of Fame very, very well. During the last two years I was in The Guess Who, Domenic joined our band, and we ended up writing all the songs on the albums FLAVOURS and POWER IN THE MUSIC. I was living in a rather large house in Winnipeg and Domenic came out and stayed with me for a

couple of weeks at a time. We'd get up in the morning, make very, very strong coffee, and just sit and play, and sing, and trade riffs, and trade lyrical ideas all day long. He opened my head up to a new method of song writing. I'm very proud of the two albums we co-wrote, and I have great memories of Domenic!

-   Burton Cummings, lead singer, pianist, composer; Canadian Music Hall of Fame Induction Ceremonies, 1996

We were travelling around the world, we were having a good time, I just kind of enjoyed the rock and roll life for a couple of years. Burton decided to leave and obviously, for all intents and purposes, that was the end of the band, but Burton had to do what he had to do. For me it was about right, because my two-year run was coming to an end and I was getting a little antsy. It was perfect timing. And I wanted to get back into more of the funkier side of things and that. I was also really feeling that I wanted to move back to Canada at that point. I really missed my family, so it also kind of closed a couple of chapters for me. The end of The Guess Who sort of signalled the end of L.A. I went back to L.A., I was there for a couple of months, and moved back to Canada at the end of 1975.

-   Domenic Troiano; interview with Martin Melhuish, February 9, 1996

The Guess Who, 1975 (Troiano Family Archives)

CHAPTER 8

INDEPENDENCE

"A tumbleweed keeps rollin'—an eagle flies anywhere
Don't tie me up—don't hold me down—I'd rather play it solitaire
I need my independence, baby."
(*Independence,* lyrics by Domenic Troiano)

Domenic Troiano band—David Tyson, Keith Jones, Jacek Sobotta,
Domenic Troiano, Paul DeLong, 1977 (Troiano Family Archives)

I was going to the University of Western Ontario. There was a great music club in downtown London called Fryfogle's, and the Domenic Troiano Band was coming to play. I was a student at the time, but I couldn't miss this. The place was packed and humming with anticipation. The band got in place first, and then Domenic came out in a black karate top and trademark beret. They kicked off the set with *Burnin' at the Stake*. It still gives me shivers. The whole set was electric and Dom's playing had risen to a truly artistic level. He was a virtuoso on the instrument. He got sounds out of that BC Rich that I had never heard from a guitar before.

- Lance Anderson, keyboards and producer; email to Frank Troiano, April, 2020

The very first time I got to see Domenic play live at the Colonial Tavern in Toronto with his band was absolutely spectacular. That beautiful full sound, the incredible musicianship from every band member; I was completely mesmerized. I couldn't believe that those songs from the album could sound even better live. And of course, Domenic was completely in control, with the entire crowd in the palm of his hands.

- Johnny Rutledge, singer, songwriter; email to Frank Troiano, August 2020

This time around, Domenic wanted something more long-lasting. From 1965 through 1975, Domenic seemingly changed things up and reinvented himself professionally every fifteen to eighteen months. Indeed, if you split the Mandala years into two (the George Olliver period, and the Roy Kenner years), consider the lengths of time in Bush, the James Gang, and finally, The Guess Who, there is a striking similarity in the respective shelf lives of each project. This time around, Domenic wanted something more long-lasting.

I like all kinds of music, and I've never been one to try to get locked in a corner. I hope I never do. I think there's good in all kinds of music, and I think the music is transcended by the players and their energy. They're into what they're doing. If it gets to you on some level emotional, physical, or mental, that's what you go for. Energy's a very subtle thing. When Segovia plays, there's an "energy"; a different kind of energy than Ted Nugent, but an energy nevertheless. And I think what people pick up most in music is that energy, regardless of the kind of music being played.

- Domenic Troiano; "Fret Fever Becomes an Epidemic,"
  J.J. Linden, *RPM Weekly*, August 1979

Domenic craved the independence of a solo career, being true to himself even if it meant less money; and, even as the invitations continued to pour in to join world famous, established groups. He also made the decision after The Guess Who to relocate his home base back to Toronto from L.A.

Sometime in 1975, I was sitting with Donnie in the kitchen of the house on Sammon Avenue. While we were talking, he excused himself to get a call from the telephone down the hall. After awhile, he returned to the kitchen and mentioned that he was speaking with Alice Cooper. Apparently, he asked Donnie to join him on his upcoming WELCOME TO MY NIGHTMARE tour and, to my surprise, Donnie declined the offer. I believe after The Guess Who disbanded, he was planning to do some solo projects. What impressed me by this decision was Donnie always stayed true to himself. He didn't seem to care too much about attaining fortune and fame and that's why, in my eyes, he was a respected musician amongst his peers and fans.

- Joe Ferrara, cousin; email to Frank Troiano, April 2020

Blaine Pritchett had by now worked closely on and off with Domenic for nearly ten years as his sound and equipment man. When Domenic joined The Guess Who, he stipulated that Blaine would be part of the crew. He trusted and valued Blaine enough that after The Guess Who when it came time to put together his new band, Blaine was centrally involved.

A lot of people were intimidated by Donnie. Donnie didn't want to be the Canadian version of Eric Clapton. He was his own man and he had his own style. It was his band and Donnie knew what he wanted, but

he was never belligerent or anything like that. I never saw him have a harsh word for anybody.
- Blaine Pritchett, sound technician; interview with Mark Doble, July 21, 2020

Domenic's new band would be *very* good—with every player able to meet exceptional musical expectations, both live and in the studio. Auditions were rigorous. Domenic quickly put together a basic band of Fred Mandel and Dave Tyson (both keyboard players!), bassist Keith Jones, singer, Wayne St. John and drummer Jimmy Norman.

I don't want five robots in the band. I want guys who can play. We get ideas, get a tune together, and I like leaving guys room to stretch out. If you have good players, you want them to stretch out. You don't want to stifle what they're doing.
- "Domenic Troiano," Frank Emmerson, *Tempo*, July 1977

His standards were high, but he conducted his auditions with a caring integrity that took notice, and at his first audition, keyboardist Dave Tyson was immediately struck by this.

The first thing I observed about Domenic was his character as a human being. He was a meticulous and attentive person. I have learned through the years as a musician that the way a musician plays their instrument is a reflection of how they are as a human being. Domenic clearly was a great listener and paid close scrutiny to detail. But he never let that override the beauty of random spontaneity. He was quick to be quiet and listen and quick to respond in kind. So my first audition felt really comfortable to me. There was a full complement of players that day, and Domenic wasn't at all a selfish player. He went out of his way to support everyone and bolster them as best he could. He brought incredible energy to every note he played, never faltering. What a constant joy it was to play music with him.
- Dave Tyson, keyboards; email to Frank Troiano, April 2020

Dave Tyson would be a mainstay on all three of Domenic's Capitol Records albums and as part of the performing band from 1976 through 1979. In the 1980s, he would join the Doobie Brothers, Alannah Myles, and Eddie Schwartz. The other keyboard player, Fred Mandel, reflected on the experience of playing in the band.

Almost every night was an incredible musical tour de force with Donnie and the band. I was in the original lineup consisting of Donnie on guitar and vocals of course, Dave Tyson (keyboards), Keith Jones (bass), Jimmy Norman (drums), and myself on keys. Wayne St. John joined on vocals later on. Dave Tyson and I shared keyboard duties and played four-part horn arrangements with our two Korg synthesizers. It was a rocking little ensemble and we played to mostly packed houses around Ontario. I remember we opened for Santana in Ottawa, which was one of our bigger gigs. We also played a live FM broadcast from the El Mocambo, and the crowd was lined up around the block on a cold winter night.

- Fred Mandel, keyboards; email to Frank Troiano, April 2020

Winston Meyer, drummer and fan, recalled a memorable show at Grant Hall at Queen's University, where Domenic's remarkable improvisatory ability and on-the-spot performance agility came to bear.

It was a rather informal entrance. Domenic sauntered onstage and plugged in his guitar. Immediately, his amp experienced a grounding problem. Almost comically, the sounds of a local radio station were uncontrollably pouring from the speakers. For a few moments some roadies jostled with the equipment, to little avail. Then, as if resigned to the circumstance, Domenic threw his guitar strap over his shoulder and started playing with the music on the radio. Within seconds, the whole band was laughing and playing along. Hardly a great entrance! Then again, maybe it was the ultimate professional entrance. I will always remember the beginning of that performance. Of course, roadies are able to fix any problem with wire cutters and/or electrical tape. Before the radio accompaniment had completed its first song, the grounding problem was fixed. The evening highlighted the tracks from the newly released album BURNIN' AT THE STAKE. I was awestruck. To this day, I rank that performance as one of the most exciting concerts I have ever

experienced. The energy, the creativity, the adrenalin! The hall was on its feet for the entire show.

- Winston Meyer, drummer; email to Frank Troiano, June 2020

The records were great, but the fluid, ever-evolving live act was something else entirely, reflecting Domenic's desire for a less-structured, agile, and more creative performing unit.

The last couple of bands I was in, it was a very set-formatted thing. It's fun, but it gets boring after a while. With this new band, in a lot of our tunes we have the intro, we have the ending, and the general idea of where we're going, but within that framework it goes a lot of different ways. I guess that's the jazz orientation.

- Domenic Troiano; "Rock Guitarist Pulls Together New Image," Matt Radz, *Montreal Star*, September 27, 1977

The music for Domenic's first solo album following his exit from The Guess Who would be decidedly different.

BURNIN' AT THE STAKE was recorded at Automated Sound Studio in New York. Domenic was able to attract such high-powered talent as the Brecker Brothers. Randy (trumpet) and Michael (saxophone) Brecker were quickly gaining status with their brand of jazz-fusion-funk, playing with such diverse acts as Frank Zappa, Frank Sinatra, and Blood, Sweat & Tears; and star saxophonist David Sanborn, whose resume included Steely Dan, Stevie Wonder, and The Rolling Stones, to name just a few. The band also included drummer Steve Ferrone (Average White Band and Tom Petty) and New York City bassist Neil Jason.

What I do remember is how much fun me and Steve Ferrone and Dom had at the sessions. BURNIN' AT THE STAKE was a very early highlight in my career, and I loved those sessions. Super musical, very hip, and he was just a sweetheart to all the cats there every day!

- Neil Jason, bass guitarist; email to Frank Troiano, May 2020

BURNIN' AT THE STAKE was released in August 1977 on Capitol Records. The front of the album jacket is a full headshot of Domenic wearing his beret. On the back cover, beside the black and white photo of Domenic standing in front of a poster for a bull fight is the track listing, below which is inscribed: *"This album is dedicated to Ralph and Pasqua Troiano."*

The songs are expansive and thoughtfully conceived, with only two up-tempo tunes (*Burnin' At the Stake,* and *Rock and Roll Madness*). The keyboard-dominated tapestry is rich with musical colours, and Domenic paints solo guitar lines like an artist. The reviews were positive.

Domenic Troiano's third solo album places him in the jazz-fusion genre for the first time. Co-producer Randy Brecker's touch is so sure that the record sounds more like a Brecker Brothers' album than anything else Troiano has recorded. But Troiano handles his end of it, and it's as good a fusion album as you're likely to hear. He's never played better than he does here, so he may now receive the widespread recognition that has always eluded him.

- "Review: Burnin' at the Stake," John Swenson, *Rolling Stone Magazine,* October 1977

BURNIN' AT THE STAKE is vintage Bluenote stuff, but with all the extra gloss producers Richard Landis and Randy Brecker (of the Brecker Brothers) could give it. Sometimes too much gloss is evident, as in an instrumental called *Lonely Girl,* a pretty enough tune that sounds all too much like synthetic disco. Troiano likes this gloss, though. He likes to think of his music as "futuristic space blues," whatever that means, and one can imagine he views the perfect sheen of *BURNIN' AT THE STAKE* as the ideal product of the clockwork precision of his band.

- "It's Almost too Glossy but Troiano's Album Catches Fire Anyway," Peter Goddard, *Toronto Star,* September 1977

The songs are well-crafted, from the plaintive *Peace of Mind,* the unabashed disco of *Savour the Flavour,* the upbeat *Master of Concealment,* and the full-on R & B of *I'd Rather be Your Lover.* If *Willpower* is too slick for reggae, the George Benson-ish jazz instrumental *Lonely Girl* is authentic and satisfying.

Rock and Roll Madness hearkens back to Domenic's days in Bush, reflecting on leaving Toronto for "the land of the sun." It is certainly the rockiest tune on the album, driven by a raunchy guitar riff.

But Domenic saves his best for last in the closing number, the magnificent *The Outer Limits of My Soul*. A hauntingly "spacey" synthesizer lick colours the corners, Domenic sings expressively, his guitar solo is restrained but powerful. Shawne Jackson delivers a classy, midrange lead vocal on the second verse and chorus that almost steals the show until Domenic joins in with her on the bridge. The tune finishes with the evocative synthesizer lick exploring into a fade-out. *Outer Limits* is one of the finest songs Domenic has ever written and composed.

For Randy Brecker, recording and producing BURNIN' AT THE STAKE with Domenic Troiano was memorable and satisfying.

We really hit it off on a personal and musical level right away after I heard him and his band. It was just one of those nights where you weren't prepared to hear someone play that great, music that was "right up your alley" so to speak. We stayed in touch, and when it came time to record his first record for Capitol, he thought of me to produce it. I had "produced" the first Brecker Brothers record and done a couple of other productions for Columbia Records. Richard Landis was also brought on board. Donnie had some great tunes, so we put a fine band together, and the result was the album BURNIN' AT THE STAKE released in 1977 with a burning band and great original tunes and dynamic playing and singing by Dom and the band. The best way to produce someone like Dom was to stay out of the way as much as possible, and that's essentially what we both did. He was just totally prepared and really didn't need us!
- Randy Brecker, trumpet, producer; email to Frank Troiano, May 2020

BURNIN' AT THE STAKE was promoted heavily in Toronto. On April 24, 1976, the Domenic Troiano Band made their official Toronto debut performing at the legendary El Mocambo with the last set of the evening broadcast live on CHUM-FM radio.

I felt comfortable with these bands. James Gang was more of a hard rock band and The Guess Who was more pop, and I had fun playing with them. But after awhile it just stopped being fun. That's not to knock the guys. They were into what they were doing and that's fine. But what I have now is a musical jamming situation. We're not doing the same things at all, we're constantly changing. There's certain tunes off the album that change drastically when we play them live. It's that kind of band.

- "Troiano is 'Burnin' at the Stake,'" *Music Express*, October 1977

One person who attended the Elmo gig and was seriously influenced was Randy Muise, guitarist/songwriter/vocalist who fondly recalled that special night and meeting Domenic.

We went early and I sat a few feet away from the left side of the stage where Domenic was playing his beautiful, custom, ocean-blue BC Rich. Domenic's playing technique was impressive, from his blistering solos to his gentle octave approach, he was on top of his game that evening and the audience was so appreciative. I couldn't take my eyes off this incredible guitar he was playing and how he masterfully used every knob and switch and made it sound like twenty different guitars throughout the evening.

After the concert, he took a couple of minutes to explain to me how all the inner electronics worked. That small interaction of his valuable time showed me how wonderful a person Domenic was. It affected me in such a positive way that the next day I went down to Long and McQuade and purchased a custom BC Rich Seagull, which I'm proud to say, I still enjoy playing forty years later.

- Randy Muise, musician and fan; email to Frank Troiano, July 2020

That fall, Q-107 (CILQ-FM), the other major rock FM station in Toronto also broadcast LIVE AT THUNDER SOUND; an in-studio concert for radio. A limited promotional vinyl pressing of the broadcast was issued to Canadian radio stations.

Shortly after the release of BURNIN' AT THE STAKE, Domenic decided to change up some of the personnel in the touring unit, including recruiting bass guitarist Bob Wilson.

The manager of Fryfogle's called and said that Domenic was making changes to his band and was looking for a drummer and bass player. He asked if I was interested in auditioning. I passed on my number and never expected anything to come of it, and then a week later Domenic called me at my mom's house in Chatham and invited me to come to Toronto to audition. I was absolutely shocked that he had called me, as well a bit intimidated.

I went down to Toronto two or three days later and we rehearsed at Stop 8 Music on Danforth and after a few days Domenic offered me the job—I was absolutely floored. At the age of twenty-four, I was joining the likes of Dave Tyson on keyboards, Jacek Sobotta on keyboards, Paul DeLong on drums, and the amazing Domenic Troiano.

Domenic was a great guy—he was sweet, no nonsense, calm; just a grounded, blue-collar individual. He was always in charge and knew exactly what he wanted. He believed in practice makes perfect so he stressed long rehearsals. He was a real pro and he expected all the players to up their game and get their shit together. At the same time, he was patient, never critical, and led by example. He was a great mentor too and we learned a lot. He told me that if I continued to work hard that I wouldn't recognize my current level of playing the following year.

- Bob Wilson, bass guitarist; interview with Frank Troiano, June 24, 2020

LIVE AT THUNDER SOUND was also the first show for roadie and sound technician Dave Gardon, who worked with Domenic from 1977 through 1979.

Donnie's band was a smoking hot band without equal in Toronto. I signed on at two-hundred dollars a week (seven day weeks!), and mainly did the lights. Every night was a little bit special because it was never the same. He seemed to cover new territory every time he stepped onstage.

Donnie chose great players, always. He worked them hard in rehearsal and always spurred them to be creative with their solos each night.

- Dave Gardon, technician; email to Frank Troiano, April 2020

The LIVE AT THUNDER SOUND broadcast/recording also introduced listeners to Toronto drummer Paul DeLong, who would continue to be associated with Domenic for years to come.

I first met Donnie sometime in 1975 or '76. He came back to Toronto after playing with The Guess Who, with the intent of starting his own band. So, he was checking out a lot of players! I was doing a house gig backing up strippers at Stage 212 down at Jarvis and Dundas, and Donnie came down and sat in with the band. I guess someone had told him to check me out. Anyway, I think he liked my playing, but I wasn't quite ready for that band yet. I auditioned for him a couple of times, but I was so nervous that I blew it! So, he formed his band, which was great, and I thought to myself, "maybe one day ..."

The original rhythm section in that band came and went, and then Donnie was looking for a new drummer. I think I auditioned again, but I still blew it! So, Donnie hired another drummer, but he didn't quite work out, and one day there was a knock on my door and Donnie said, "You have the gig, whether you want it or not!" Quite a shock! So, that was it.

Our first gig was at the El Mocambo and I was shaking, I was so nervous. But I did okay, and Donnie turned around to me every few tunes, tapped on my tom-tom and said, "Alright, DeShort!" He liked to call me DeShort! After the gig, he said he was really proud of me. He was such a sweet guy that way. This was the fall of 1977 and I was just twenty-four years old. There was a lot I had to get used to. We did a live radio show at Thunder Sound in Toronto; that went well, too. I have the memory of listening to the playback in the control room of Thunder, and Donnie turning to me and saying, "Somewhere out there in radio land, there's a young drummer listening to your great playing."

We were on the road a lot, in Canada and the US, the band in Donnie's van and the crew in the equipment truck with the stage gear. We had such a blast, and Donnie loved the hang too. When it came to business, Donnie wouldn't take any shit from anyone. I've seen club owners try to short-change him, and Donnie wouldn't back down until he had the money that was owed to him.

He could be hard-nosed with me, too. I was young and foolish and very immature, and quite a few times he would say, "Oh Paul, grow up!"
- Paul DeLong, drummer; email to Frank Troiano, April 2020

Today, Paul DeLong is Canada's most prominent touring and session drummer. He has played with Kim Mitchell, Lighthouse, David Clayton-Thomas, Roger Hodgson (Supertramp), and Rik Emmett (Triumph). He is actively involved in musical theatre, teaching musical technique at Humber College (Toronto), as well as performing with his own jazz-fusion group and the highly acclaimed tribute bands Brass Transit (Music of Chicago) and Pretzel Logic (Steely Dan tribute).

Domenic's second Capitol Records album, THE JOKE'S ON ME, was recorded in early 1978 at Toronto's Sounds Interchange, and was different from the previous record in almost all respects. Recorded in Toronto, produced by the acclaimed Canadian rock producer Terry Brown (Rush, Max Webster, Klaatu), and while BURNIN' AT THE STAKE featured fifteen different singers/players in supporting roles, THE JOKE'S ON ME had no guests. The five-piece band included Domenic on lead vocals and guitars, Dave Tyson on keyboards and vocals, Jacek Sobotta on keyboards, Keith Jones on bass and vocals, and Paul DeLong on drums. If the sound was still slick and clean, it was also punchier, with songs constructed on a solid rock foundation.

The title track, *The Joke's on Me*, is founded on a slow but menacing bass/drum riff. Domenic's vocal reflects a disorientation of sorts both tonally and in his phrasing that suits the lyrics perfectly. There are two instrumentals: *Spud*, a bouncy question and answer session between guitar and keyboards that came out of an instrumental jam from Domenic's Guess Who days, and the melodic and emotional *Eleanora Fagan* (the original name of the American jazz singer Billie Holliday).

Maybe the Next Time is optimistic and bouncy, and *Here Before my Time*, about the trials and tribulations of a guitarist/gunslinger slightly ahead of his time, may be the most biographical number on the album.

Road to Hell/War Zone is a prog-rock manifesto driven by a schizoid drum beat shifting from duple to triple time and back throughout the *Road to Hell* portion. *War Zone* is sustained with a more basic midtempo rock beat and features extended soloing. *Road to Hell/War Zone* was a set list staple going back to the release of BURNIN' AT THE STAKE, and so, by the time of the recording, was both well-rehearsed and well-explored.

The final song on the album, *Look Up,* is perhaps Domenic's most spiritually-themed lyric, about how faith in a higher power can sustain you during periods of uncertainty. *Look Up* is an optimistic, sublime song of triumph dressed with chorale-quality harmonies.

Twenty-eight years after the recording was made, Terry Brown recalled the sessions.

I remember having a great time making the record with Domenic and the band, because it was such a hot group of players. It was pretty straightforward, because we did so much live, off-the-floor. Domenic wasn't really into doing tons of overdubs. I think there was a certain amount of hesitancy on his part to cut vocals, but I think he did a great job. Who better to sing these songs but him, quite frankly. I think he was more comfortable when he was behind the guitar, to be honest. That was really where he was at his best, and he definitely had the ability to do it.
- Terry Brown, producer; interview with Jeremy Frey, Troianomusic.com, July 2005

An Edmonton reviewer observed the following shortly prior to the commercial release of THE JOKE'S ON ME:

Troiano may be Canada's premier electric guitar player ... Troiano showed more of himself than was evident on his BURNIN' AT THE STAKE album. That record was dominated by elaborate horn section arrangements, and Troiano's live versions of that material showed how

unnecessary and cumbersome those arrangements were. Much of the excitement stemmed from Troiano's new songs taken from an album called THE JOKE'S ON ME, which is scheduled for release April 1. At least, that's what Domenic said. The songs were a distinct cut above the BURNIN' AT THE STAKE material, and gave Troiano the room he needed to stretch out and show just what he could do.

- "Troiano: An electric performer," Paul Hepher, *The Albertan*, March 1, 1978

Headliners for whom he was opening would frequently invite Domenic to join them onstage. In addition to appearing with the great Carlos Santana following his opening act at Maple Leaf Gardens, Steve Miller invited Domenic to join him onstage at the Ottawa Exhibition in August 1978. Donnie was always up for the challenge.

Miller made no secret of his blues roots. The two straight twelve-bar instrumentals that he performed were definite highlights. The second number, with Domenic Troiano, showed the marked contrast between the two; Miller played in a classic B. B., Albert King style while Troiano ripped the style apart, shredding the tune like confetti and prompting Miller into a little behind-the-back playing as a form of supplication. It was the kind of humour that wins you right over.

- James Hutton, "Steve Miller and Domenic Troiano at the Ex," *Ottawa Revue*, August 31–September 6, 1978

Although Domenic's first two Capitol albums received positive reviews, record sales were disappointing. Still, Domenic was uncompromising.

To begin with, you've got to be happy with what you're doing, and I am. I mean, obviously, everyone wants to sell a million records, but in my case I only want to do it within the framework of the music I want to play. I get the thing of "your stuff isn't commercial," but I think people in the record business and the radio business underestimate the general public. The radio guys say, "Well man, it's not that we don't dig what you're doing. We think it's great, and if we could play what we like, your music would be on the radio right now." I mean, how can anyone assume that they know what so many people want to hear? Maybe they

do, but I doubt it, when I hear the same fifteen records getting played over and over on the radio day in and day out.
- Domenic Troiano; "Guitarist has had a Busy Career", CP, *Ottawa Citizen*, October 1978

Recorded at Toronto's Sounds Interchange between November 1978 and January 1979, FRET FEVER was a response to the lack of success of the previous two records. Rebranding his band simply as "Troiano," denoted more of a "group" as opposed to a leader with a supporting cast, Roy Kenner was also back on lead vocals. With shorter songs and less soloing, the focus was on crafting a more commercially viable "band" sound. It was also the first time Domenic had chosen to produce his own record.

People used to think of it as being me, so we figured maybe if we short-ened the name, people would assume it's a group. … It is me. I'm not trying to get away from that. I'm just trying to get that band feeling across. I don't think there's any better situation than to have an actual band that works together, especially when they're good players.
- "Domenic Troiano—Fret Fever Becomes an Epidemic," J. J. Linden, *RPM Weekly*, August 1979

FRET FEVER opens with the killer track, *South American Run*, a full-blast guitar rocker, power chords, and a lead solo that is so hot you can feel the steam rising off the fret board. The song also serves to announce Roy Kenner back in charge of the lead singing duties, and his performance on *South American Run* is bold and fun. The next tune, *Ambush*, is a hard rock, flashy instrumental reminiscent of the work Domenic did on TRICKY.

He had the instrumental *Zingaro*—Donnie wanted the prelude to be a vocal story referring to the drug trade. He told me he was thinking of a title, *South American Run*. So, I started thinking up all the ways to combine names of places and double-entendres to make that point for him. I thought it was a neat tune.
- Roy Kenner, lead vocalist; interview with Mark Doble, July 4, 2020

The upbeat, disco-tinged *We All Need Love* became the hit single, set in motion by the joyous, anthem-like singing of Kenner. In fact, Kenner's performance "makes" the song. The number received considerable radio airplay across Canada and also attracted attention in various European markets (including Italy), and became almost a signature tune for Domenic in the future. Domenic has been referred to as "a musician's musician," a title often attributed to an artist who is recognized by his peers for his skill and advanced musicality, but unfairly neglected by the record-buying public, who enjoys great artistic success without the advantage of a hit record. But, the success of *We All Need Love* signalled the exception to that rule for Domenic!

DT finally writes one that clicks, and it's his most successful and most-covered single. I actually like my vocal on this one, and feel blessed that I got to do this one with Donnie.
- Roy Kenner, lead vocalist; interview with Mark Doble, July 4, 2020

We All Need Love was subsequently covered by several other artists including Ebony (1983), Karen J. Ann (1988), and in 1998 an Italian-language cover *(Angeli Noi)* was recorded by Mietta for her album LA MIA ANIMA. By far the most commercially successful recording of *We All Need Love* was by Italian Eurodance group Double You, who released the song (off of their debut album WE ALL NEED LOVE) in 1992, peaking at number one in Belgium and becoming a top ten hit throughout Europe.

The autobiographical *Fret Fever* sung by Domenic references Domenic's childhood listening to R & B on the radio, developing a love for the guitar (fret fever) and becoming a rock star. *Brains on The floor* is a humorous blues-reggae in which the hungover hero bemoans his state and includes a neat synthesizer solo at the end.

The album concludes with three short instrumentals: Dave Tyson's *Victim of Circumstance,* the only non-Troiano composed piece on the album, a fast-paced number featuring some great keyboard and melodic guitar. The slower paced *Achilles* soon became a favourite instrumental for live performance. It's almost as if, after creating an album with virtually no soloing, at last the guitarist is allowed to indulge. *The End* is more a coda than an actual song lasting for mere forty-three seconds and consisting entirely of a repeated rising and falling arpeggio pattern.

The purpose-built, radio friendly FRET FEVER is Domenic's most commercially accessible record, with good writing, creative arrangements and a surprising but deliberate avoidance of extended guitar pyrotechnics. It's also Roy Kenner's best collaboration with Domenic.

It's no wonder Domenic has FRET FEVER. After listening to just the first cut, *South American Run,* you shouldn't attempt to take the LP from the turntable "sans oven mitts"... FRET FEVER is subject here to almost any cliché depicting an outrageously talented guitarist who has the ability to "burn down the mission" on *South American Run*, blow 'em away with sixteenth notes on *Achilles*, and the smarts to lay back in a reflective song such as *It's Raining, It's Pouring.*
-    "Troiano—Fret Fever," *Canadian Musician*, October 1979

Rob Gusevs was recruited to play Keyboards for the FRET FEVER tour. Rob had been a fan of the Mandala since listening to them on his transistor radio as a child. In 1976, he joined Shawne Jackson's backing band and met Domenic through that association.

Through the times we played together, Donnie was always encouraging and supportive. Food sometimes acts to bring people together, and it wasn't long before Donnie noticed that I enjoyed eating out. Whether it was going to Sai Woo's at 2:00 or 3:00 a.m. after a gig or a jam, or having some of his mom's *taralli,* I knew that food and family (his folks, Shawne, Gina, and Frank) meant a lot to him! Donnie was a gifted musician—focused and driven, and a gentleman throughout.
-    Rob Gusevs, keyboard; email to Frank Troiano, June 2020

In 1979, Troiano played at the El Mocambo again in a concert simulcast over City TV and CHUM-FM. Watching Kenner and Troiano perform together along with the rest of the band is a treat. Some of the video from this performance can now be found online. Roadie Dave Roberts was hired as part of the crew.

I was hired in 1979 by Donnie, and the band rehearsed at the Twelfth Fret Guitarist Pro Shop in the upper beaches in the midsummer. Roy Kenner had joined the lineup and Rob Gusevs had replaced David Tyson. Bob Wilson and Paul DeLong remained in the band. Our first performances were at the band shell at the CNE, at the Ontario Place Forum, and at clubs around TO. We then went on the road to Quebec City, Montreal, Kingston, London, Hamilton, Ottawa ... In Kingston, we performed at Dollar Bill's and on September 18 we did a live broadcast on the local FM station. On October 6, we did a live simulcast on CHUM- FM and City TV. The Elmo was absolutely packed and there was a real buzz of excitement in the air. David Clayton-Thomas and many other high-profile musicians were there to take in the show. Donnie was the nicest, friendliest, and most professional musician that I have ever worked "with" (not for). He took time to talk to all of us, didn't put us down, and treated us respectfully, but it was always clear that he was the leader.

- Dave "DR" Roberts, roadie; interview with Frank Troiano, May 2020

The recording from the Kingston FM broadcast is exquisite. The playing is flawless, and the band's improvisational chops are fully put to the test. And if the FRET FEVER album seems to lack extended soloing, here Domenic is unrestrained and seems to be at the top of his game. However, the style of the show had become less interesting to the lead singer.

Toward the end of the FRET FEVER tour, where we did a live simulcast—video and radio broadcast from the El Mocambo—at that point, Domenic was frustrated, I was frustrated, the band was frustrated, and I said to him, "I love you to death, you're like a brother to me, but I can't do this anymore." I'd finally realized what I am is a lead singer, and I can't be a guy that sits around on a stage for fifteen or twenty minutes while the band goes off into basically what's fusion/jazz music. I love to listen to it, but I don't want to be a part of it. I said, "I don't know what you want to do. You got me in the band to be the singer because you wanted to go back to doing shorter tunes, but here we are doing long stretch-outs again." And he said, "Well, I'm not sure what I want to do anymore either." Domenic and I certainly parted on good terms.

We knew that we would work together in the future, and of course, ultimately, we did.

- Roy Kenner, lead vocalist; interview with Mark Doble, November 27, 2020

By 1979, almost as a reaction against perceived excesses of disco, popular music was simplifying, purging, and embracing a more basic in-your-face punk rock/new wave sensibility. Disco and R & B were not the only casualties. Many mainstream rock acts needed to adjust or fade away, consequently, the timing of *We All Need Love* was unfortunate. In the fall of 1979, Domenic disbanded "Troiano." It would be a year and a half before he fronted a band again.

A 1996 CD compilation of the three Capitol Records was released called TROIANO TRIPLE PLAY, and included a beautifully extended mix of *We All Need Love*, as well as two previously unreleased numbers, the instrumental jam *Gypsy*, and the eleven-minute blues-vamp *Draw Your own Conclusions*.

The Capitol years provided some great music. Domenic's playing and performance ethic had a profound influence on many young musicians, such as guitarist Frank Cosentino.

When I first witnessed Dom live in action, he was doing things on guitar I had only heard from records coming out of the States and England. Here he was doing it all in real time and right in front of me! For this young upstart, it was powerful medicine! I began to follow his every move. This was a time where musicians would congregate at local music stores to get the latest news on the players making big noise at the time. Dom's name was always spoken in hushed reverence.

- Frank Cosentino, guitarist; email to Frank Troiano, April 2020

The title of this chapter, "Independence," is taken from a song subsequently recorded and released by Domenic's power-trio, Black Market. The Capitol Records years were all about Domenic exercising his creative and musical independence.

By February of 1976, the first incarnation of the Domenic Troiano Band was in place. The next four years were some of the most creative and exciting times of my life. I was surrounded by great musicians who gave the band their heart and soul. Even though members changed from time to time, the level of musicianship and friendship stayed high. It was wonderful to have a group of players that were always ready and able to experiment and develop new ideas. I will always look back at this time as a special period of my life. Thanks for listening.

- Domenic Troiano; liner notes to "Troiano Triple Play," EMI Music Canada, February 1996

Changing stylistically from one album to the next is a risky play that often challenges a fan base. Domenic was not interested in standing still or finding something that works and playing it to death. His modus operandi was all about musical evolution and continuous change for the better. A new decade was dawning, and Domenic was determined to be vitally involved in what was to come.

Troiano—Rob Gusevs, Bob Wilson, Roy Kenner, Paul DeLong, Domenic Troiano, 1979 (Troiano Family Archives)

188

CHAPTER 9

CHANGING OF THE GUARD

"What did you gain? What did it mean?
You were slowly destroying everything that you see
And I think it's time for the changing of the guard
Yes, I think it's time for the changing of the guard."
(*Changing of the Guard*, lyrics by Domenic Troiano)

Black Market—Howard Ayee, Ed White, Domenic Troiano, 1981
(Troiano Family Archives)

Being onstage for me has never been the most comfortable thing. The music was the thing for me. I had as much fun, if not more, rehearsing than I did at the jobs. There were a lot of nights where if I could have played behind the amps or from the dressing room, I would have been real happy. There are guys who love to perform. That's what they do. I never felt comfortable with that.

- "Domenic Troiano—From Soul Crusade to Night Heat," Martin Melhuish, *The Record*, March 11, 1996

The emergence of punk rock in the late '70s represented a defiant "cleansing of the palate," eschewing the excesses of progressive rockers like Pink Floyd and Genesis with their respective "concept" albums containing fifteen to thirty minute quasi-symphonic opuses. Similarly, it was also away with the glitter balls and Saturday Night Fever—disco was dead.

There was directness in the new music—nonpretentious, three-minute songs, delivered straight up with little or no extended soloing. And while one could never describe Domenic's Black Market as a "punk" band, CHANGING OF THE GUARD represented an attempt to revitalize and adapt to the new wave sweeping through popular music.

I wanted to approach this as a band project. I like playing with bands rather than the solo career thing. In the past, record companies have always told me that my music was too jazzy to be rock, too black to be white, but this album just turned out more direct. The record is quite song-oriented compared to some other things I have done.

- Domenic Troiano; "Selling his Wares on The Black Market," Chris Churchill, *Music Express*, 1981

Domenic readily acknowledged that a stripped-down, back-to-basics trio format would also require more of himself and less reliance on supporting elements—the guitar playing would be front and centre.

Change—as defined by Troiano's career—meant going through a half-dozen rock bands in a twelve-year period, starting his own band in 1976, dismantling it, and going back to a trio format. "Last time I played with a trio was the James Gang. The challenge is you have to play

more. With so few guys, you can change things, it's much more open, there are fewer arrangements to worry about."

- Domenic Troiano; "Challenge a Hallmark of Troiano's Career," Teresa Mazzitelli, *London Free Press*, September 24, 1981

Robert Charles-Dunne, founder of El Mocambo Records, was distinctly honoured to have Domenic Troiano record on his new fledgling company.

I had known Dom for a decade before we conspired to release his newest project, an album he wanted to release under the band name Black Market. Sadly, using that name was like trying to break an album by an unknown artist, undervaluing Dom's remarkable talent by failing to disclose the name of the super-talented guitarist responsible for the album. Upon realizing this, we had the front of each album stickered with "Featuring Domenic Troiano," but it was too late. The album was called CHANGING OF THE GUARD and we decided we would rent some camouflage military uniforms and shoot the cover in a Toronto military armoury, who loaned us unloaded weapons for the shoot. Because El Mocambo Records was a young label with a limited budget, Dom insisted that we commit to spending $10,000 on promoting it. It was a large sum for a small label, but he was a world-class artist, so I eagerly agreed.

- Robert Charles-Dunne, El Mocambo Records; email to Frank Troiano, April 2020

Recorded at Phase One Studios in Toronto for Domenic's "Black Market Records" label, the album was produced by Domenic and released on El Mocambo Records. The band consisted of Domenic on guitars and lead vocals, drummer Paul DeLong, and Bob Wilson on bass. Guest artists included Shawne Jackson, Prakash John, and Roy Kenner on background vocals. Despite these familiar faces, Domenic was shifting directions.

People have a tendency to remember you from your last album, and my stuff during the Capitol period had a lot of variety in its influences. There was rock and jazz and some lighter blues, plus a lot of rhythms. Black Market, hopefully, will remind people that I've been playing hard-edged, aggressive music for twenty years. I've been rockin' since

high school and I don't intend to stop now. As a three-piece band, Black Market can't get too fancy, but it can sure be intense.

- Domenic Troiano; "Black Market," El Mocambo Records Inc., Press Release, 1981

The title track charges right out of the gate with a ferocious bass guitar hook. *Turn Back*, is statelier, with an enticing backbeat and lyrics reminiscing musical days gone by.

Oh Carol has a jaunty fifties feel complete with shooby-doo-wap harmonies recalling Chuck Berry, and references listening to music back in the old days. *Doctor Love* follows with a catchy boogie woogie hook, great harmonies, and a vicious lead guitar solo.

Dr. Dee Jay's Band, a bouncy pop song, was selected to be the first single, and was promoted by a video in which Domenic and the band were dressed in combat fatigues.

Other notable numbers include the midtempo *Independence,* which moves along to a catchy rhythmic "chucka chucka" pattern, along with the closing number, *The Shooter*, a rapid-fire, lickety-split power trio attack that is over way too soon.

Domenic would take Black Market on one cross-Canada tour, for which he enlisted the services of bassist Howard Ayee.

The Black Market LP had already been recorded, but he wanted to do some videos and prepare for the tour, so Ed White on drums joined Donnie and me for a lot of practising at his home in Agincourt. We completed the videos and went out on the road from coast to coast. We were well received and had a lot of fun, but the LP had very little airplay and mediocre sales. When we got back, we rehearsed for a short time, but Donnie soon realized that it was time to take a break from live music and having a band.

- Howard Ayee, bass guitarist; interview with Frank Troiano, April 2020

Paul Gruenwald was a promo rep for El Mocambo Records and was assigned to accompany Black Market on their western Canadian tour from Vancouver Island to Winnipeg.

After a radio show in West Vancouver, I got the coolest compliment of my life. Donnie said to me, "Paulie, I've been signed to seventeen different record companies and everyone had at least one promo guy that I had to deal with. I've never had one that I liked more than you, man. You did such a great job and I had so much fun, that if I ever go on another tour, I want you." That was so cool, I thought. Little did I know that he really meant, "Buddy, you are the guy from Winnipeg west, so you are going with me for the rest of the tour!" I did, and a couple of weeks later I flew home from Winnipeg."
- Paul Gruenwald, promo rep; email to Frank Troiano, April 2020

Paul and Domenic would remain friends for life. Robert Charles-Dunne attended Black Market's first live performance in Vancouver in 1981.

I will never forget that show, the awesome sight of Dom playing lead and rhythm simultaneously, all while looking round the room—I was struck by his uncanny ability to move a song along, playing two guitar parts at once!
- Robert Charles-Dunne, El Mocambo Records; email to Frank Troiano, April 2020

Domenic's capacity for playing multiple and intricate lines with precision, sounding like two (or even three) guitarists at once served him well. It is a fact that over his entire performing career, Domenic never belonged to a band with a second guitarist.

As Black Market toured eastern Canada, Scotty Brown joined the stage crew for the remainder of the tour.

I had heard of Domenic, but had never seen him perform. He put on an impressive guitar clinic for the veteran Nova Scotian musicians who were fawning over his guitar playing. I got talking with Domenic after the show and he said that the band needed an extra crew member for about three weeks. I agreed to join them, and after finishing off

in Halifax, we performed in Sydney and then on to Moncton and Fredericton, at which point they went west to Quebec and back home to Ontario.

- Scotty Brown, roadie; interview with Frank Troiano, May 16, 2020

Scotty would continue to work with Domenic in future engagements, including the 1996 Juno awards, as well as Domenic's final appearance at The Orbit Room in 2004.

Despite Domenic's willingness to change up the sound, fans and the press were quick to dismiss Black Market. El Mocambo Records invested heavily in the promotion, but the experiment would be discontinued after CHANGING OF THE GUARD, their first and last commercial release. It would also represent the final album of original music by Domenic Troiano. Which is a shame; as much as the record was a competent collection of good songs, it did not represent his best work.

Dom continued to play, record, produce, and create music for the rest of his life. There were avenues to explore other than that of a touring recording artist.

From the mid-1960s, Domenic was experienced and at ease in a studio setting. There are dozens of unreleased demo recordings of the Mandala as evidence of a considerable amount of time spent in a studio.

Adding to his resume, Domenic regularly recorded with other artists, such as David Clayton-Thomas (1973), the James Cotton Blues Band (1970), Bonaroo (ex-Doobie Brothers) (1975), Canadian R & B/disco group Sweet Blindness (1977), and Dick Wagner (guitarist/sideman with Alice Cooper in the '70s) (1977). One of Domenic's keyboard players at the time, Fred Mandel, recalled working with Domenic on Dick Wagner's solo album.

Dick was musical director of Alice Cooper's band as well as co-writer on some of his biggest hits, including *Only Women Bleed* and quite a few others. Dick respected Donnie's playing and the two of them worked really well together on the album. One day Dick approached me privately in the studio and asked if I would like to join the Alice Cooper band and go out on the road with them on tour. I was somewhat torn,

as I loved playing in Donnie's band with my friends so I decided to ask Donnie for his advice. Being the generous and thoughtful person he was, he advised me to take the gig.

- Fred Mandel, keyboard; email to Frank Troiano, April, 2020

Fred Mandel ended up working with some of the most popular musicians in the world, including Elton John, Supertramp, and Queen. It is interesting to note how many of Domenic's fellow and former bandmates typically moved on to bigger and better things after their tenure with him.

In 1972, I went on to perform with the Rascals, Lou Reed, and finally Alice Cooper. Several of the musicians in these bands were Domenic's ex-bandmates: Joey Chirowski, Fred Mandel, Whitey Glan, and Prakash John. I could see a common thread with all of them, they had been through Domenic's musician's boot camp, which meant lots and lots of practice and rehearsals. They were all ready and eager for musical combat.

- Danny Weis, guitarist; interview with Frank Troiano, May 2020

In addition to appearing on various records, Domenic also started producing other acts. One of the first artists Domenic produced was Shawne Jackson in 1974–75. Domenic's connection to the talented singer Shawne Jackson went back to the days at the Club Bluenote.

I was in a girls group called the Tiaras. Donnie and I were soulmates from day one. We instantly became friends. We would go out to dinner together, and never ran out of things to talk about. Even though we were both very young, and I just wanted to be good friends, I always knew he loved me. My mother came to hear us at the Bluenote and said to me, "That guitar player loves you, Shawne." My mother always loved Donnie and thought he was the perfect guy for me.

- Shawne Jackson, vocalist; interview with Mark Doble, June 19, 2020

For Domenic, it was love at first sight, and he became committed to the idea of one day recording and producing her as a singer. Shawne has an extraordinary singing voice. However, even with this talent, it was

Domenic who had to encourage her career, without which, Shawne now acknowledges, she probably would not have pursued a career in music.

I never wanted to be a singer. It was just something I did. Donnie would push me to sing. Every time I came back to music, it was because of Donnie. But I could take it or leave it.
- Shawne Jackson, vocalist; interview with Mark Doble, June 19, 2020

Shawne's powerful and expressive voice found its way onto many of Domenic's solo albums, sometimes taking a lead vocal. In 1974, while they were in L.A., Domenic recorded and produced (with Keith Olsen) the single *Just as Bad As You/He May Be Your Man*.

I left Toronto for New York in the late 1960s to work in the fashion industry. And then, Roy Kenner's girlfriend convinced me to move to Arizona and I worked for her as a dressmaker for about three years. Out of the blue, Donnie called me to come to L.A. He had studio time booked. "I want you to sing the song I've written for you. It's called *Just as Bad as You*. I told him I wasn't singing anymore. He said, "I don't care—I think it's a great song and I think you should try it." I went in and recorded the song and then returned to Arizona because all my stuff was there. Then Domenic called me again: "*Just as Bad as You* is a hit, and now you have to come out and promote it!"
- Shawne Jackson, vocalist; interview with Mark Doble, June 19, 2020

Domenic wrote the A side and co-wrote the B side with Shawne. The pop/R & B crossover single was a hit on both sides of the border, reaching number ten on the Canadian charts.

Shawne Jackson, Domenic Troiano, Sam "the Record Man" Sniderman, 1975
(Troiano Family Archives)

In 1975, Domenic produced Shawne's self-titled solo album. Shawne's vocal parts were recorded at Toronto Sound and Phase One Studios in Toronto, while the instrumental bed tracks were recorded at Sound City Studio in California.

I was in Toronto, Donnie was in L.A., we would write songs together. We would set the keys by singing over the phone. Donnie recorded all the bed tracks in L.A., I was not there for any of it. That was a little weird for me. As a producer, he had definite ideas in mind and expressed himself really well. With me, he was very gentle.
- Shawne Jackson, vocalist; interview with Mark Doble, June 19, 2020

Domenic has composition credits on seven of the nine songs. And apart from the fact that Shawne sings all of the vocals and it is her album, Domenic's musical stamp is all over it. From the production, co-writing, playing guitar, it is very much a Troiano album—pop-funk, R & B, and a touch of soul. Dom also arranged to have Shawne open for The Guess Who during their final tour in the summer of 1975. Grant Slater, keyboardist in Shawne's band recalls:

John David Redmond was putting a band together in Toronto to back up Shawne Jackson—a very talented singer, particularly popular in the R & B scene. Her album had just been released, and the single, *Just as Bad as You* was getting lots of airplay. Shawne's album was produced by—you guessed it—Domenic Troiano. Lo and behold, a few days later I found myself in Toronto, rehearsing with Shawne as a member of her backup band.

Shawne and the band became increasingly popular in the Toronto music scene, and we were thrilled to have the chance to open for Ray Charles at Hamilton Place. But the magic didn't end there. We were offered another opening position. This time it was with The Guess Who. During that period, we also did a handful of Ontario gigs with Burton and the boys, the highlight being the CNE Grandstand in Toronto in the summer of '75.

- Grant Slater, keyboards; email to Frank Troiano, April, 2020

Grant Slater would enjoy a remarkable musical career playing with such notables as Etta James, David Clayton-Thomas, Colm Wilkinson and others.

The catchy single *Get Out of the Kitchen/Don't Wait for Tomorrow* (both co-written by Jackson and Troiano) was released in December, but didn't enjoy the same success as *Just as Bad as You* had a year earlier.

Shawne recorded another single in 1982. *Come Back Boy/Can't Stop Thinking About You*, both Jackson-Troiano originals, were very much "Eighties synth-infused pop with a hint of R & B."

In 1976, Shawne and Domenic became a couple when he moved from Los Angeles back to Toronto, and they were finally married on February 3, 1985, honeymooning in Ocho Rios, Jamaica. Shawne and Domenic separated in 1995 and divorced in 1998. However, they continued to be close for the remainder of Dom's life.

With no more touring, Domenic suddenly had more time and Gary Katz (Steely Dan) jumped at the opportunity to involve him in several projects with some big-name artists.

Domenic finally had some free time to do some session work in the early '80s. I produced both Diana Ross and Eye to Eye in '82 and Joe Cocker in '83. He came down to NYC to record on several of the cuts for all three LPs. A couple of times we hung out at my house, and I will always remember his trademark beret. In addition to being an exceptional and tasteful guitarist, he fit in perfectly with the other session players. He was easy to work with and the recording sessions ended up being lots of fun and they felt as if we were a bunch of friends just chilling.
- Gary Katz, producer; interview with Frank Troiano, May 2020

Katz had long sought to work with Domenic (since the formation of Steely Dan in 1972), and although Domenic had previously not been at liberty to join up, his regard for Katz as a musician and producer was high, and he was pleased to finally work with him.

Troiano friend and fan Craig Webb recently related a conversation he and Domenic had regarding a session Domenic had attended in New York for Donald Fagen's first solo album, THE NIGHTFLY.

I remembered my discussion with Domenic Troiano at the Club Bluenote back in the '80s when he told me he'd just got back from NYC trying out for the first Donald Fagen solo CD, THE NIGHTFLY. (That CD ended up with seven Grammy award nominations, including album of the year.) I asked how he did, and he told me that "you never know with the Steely Dan guys until the CD comes out," but the producer, Gary Katz, really liked his playing and got him some tracks on the upcoming Joe Cocker and Diana Ross CDs. When THE NIGHTFLY CD came out, I believe it had Larry Carlton playing lead on all the tracks but one. Donnie told me there were a bunch of guitarists coming in to lay down their interpretations of the various songs requiring guitar. Unfortunately, it seems it's pretty difficult to beat out Larry Carlton for a Donald Fagen production!
- Craig Webb, fan; email to Frank Troiano, August 22, 2020

Gary Katz asked Dom to play on the Eye to Eye LP, SHAKESPEARE STOLE MY BABY. The band had had a lot of hype, and it appeared that they were going places. In addition to the LP, Dom performed with them for five nights, March 23–28, 1982, in New York City, Connecticut, and Pennsylvania. A March 27, 1982, New York Times review was positive.

In one of the year's most impressive pop album debuts, the British-American duo Eye to Eye, backed by top-flight studio musicians, has blended the pointillistic pop-jazz style of Steely Dan with the sophisticated pop-funk of Chic into a high-gloss sound of immaculate polish. But until the duo appeared at the Bottom Line on Thursday, with the five other musicians, it was difficult to imagine that anyone could recapture the intricate syncopation and moody inflections of the album in a concert setting. Surprisingly, however, the group—with the help of a sturdy reggae rhythm section and the guitarist Domenic Troiano—proved not only that this could be done, but also that it could give an extra punch to the duo's angst-ridden songs."

- "Pop: British American Duo," Stephen Holden,
    New York Times, March 27, 1982

Additional playing assignments in the 1980s involved some memorable artists such as the Partland Brothers (1986), Glen Johansen (1988), Murray McLauchlan (1981), Strange Advance (1982), and Canadian new wavers, Rough Trade (with whom Domenic played a sitar on the track *Paisley Generation* and is listed on the album cover as "Don 'Ravi' Troiano"!) Domenic also recorded with Veronique Beliveau, Canadian bands Dr. Music, The Front, and also made time to record again with his old friend Ronnie Hawkins.

In 1983, the group Ebony, featuring Wayne St. John (who was part of Domenic's band in 1976) recorded an up-tempo eighties-dance version of *We All Need Love* that Domenic produced for Quality Records, giving rise to the enduring qualities of the song as well as Dom's increasingly impressive production chops.

One of the most influential people in Canadian radio, Rosalie Trombley, was the music director at CKLW in Windsor. Rosalie's playlist selections could make or break it for certain records, and many artists, such as Bob Seger and The Guess Who were quick to attribute their success to Rosalie's influence. Her son, Tim Trombley, also went into the music business, and encountered Domenic early on.

In early 1981, I moved to Toronto to begin working with legendary Canadian record producer Bob Ezrin. Bob was in the middle of producing Murray McLauchlan. I'll never forget meeting Domenic for the first time at Manta Sound. Bob had booked Domenic to play on a couple of Murray's songs. We immediately had a connection, and of course I knew who Domenic was, as my mom and CKLW were a catalyst in breaking *We All Need Love*. I was a big Mandala fan as a teenager too. I was a very young man, new to the big city. Dom took me under his wing and provided guidance and big-brotherly friendship. We worked together on a Moe Koffman record that Dom was producing for Bob's production company. Dom had belief and faith in me and made me the production coordinator. I learned so much during this formative period in my career.

- Tim Trombley, A & R with Capitol/EMI, Dallcorte Records; email to Frank Troiano, June 2020

Domenic produced and played on an album for the great Canadian jazz artist Moe Koffman (saxophone & flute). Drummer Mike Sloski, who had played with Etta James, Bruce Cockburn, Dusty Springfield and Long John Baldry was enlisted by Domenic to play on the album.

It was interesting working with Donnie on the album he produced for Moe Koffman. His capability as a producer was indisputable. At one point during the three or four days we recorded the bed tracks, Moe came in and met with Donnie in the control room. They were together for maybe twenty minutes, after which Moe left. Donnie came out and announced that we wouldn't be needing any mo' of Moe! Moe was so pleased with the direction Donnie was going in that he didn't need to return until the overdubs.

- Mike Sloski, drummer; email to Frank Troiano, June, 2020

Released in 1983, the album IF YOU DON'T KNOW ME BY NOW was an attempt at "crossover" (mixing jazz and pop) and includes three Troiano originals: *Lonely Girl, Zingaro*, and *I Still Love You*. Guitarist Joey Miquelon was also on the album.

When Donnie got off the road, we started hanging out again and going to the Jazz clubs in Toronto. About this time, he started the first Domenic Troiano band, which I would often go and see. Also, some-where in the '70s I worked with Shawne again, and Donnie would often show up at the gigs to sit in, or at the rehearsals to work on arrange-ments either from her album or just tunes he thought we should do. In the early '80s he produced an album for Moe Koffman, and I played on most of the cuts.

- Joey Miquelon, guitarist; email to Frank Troiano, April 2020

Domenic continued to write, perform with, and produce records with Roy Kenner. In 1980, he co-wrote and recorded Kenner's single *Transparent Love*, and in 1983, Domenic produced a six-song EP entitled ROY KENNER/THE ROYALS, on which George Olliver also made a guest appearance.

***The Way to Paradise** and **Heads Up** were tunes that I had pretty well written in L.A., and I brought them back and then Donnie refined them enough that, as far as I was concerned, it was a co-written deal. **Transparent Love** was something that he and I put together. He had the title and I ran off with the words. We put that together, and it was like, "Well, what are we going to do with these?" **Transparent Love** came out as a single.*

- Roy Kenner, lead vocalist; interview with Jeremy Frey,
  troianomusic.com, August 2005

Transparent Love is a slick, eighties-style rocker. Kenner delivers one of his finest performances with a vocal line that soars with crystal clear pre-cision and expressive grace. Domenic's guitar work and production fore-shadowed the sensational *Night Heat* single that Domenic and Roy would create in another few years.

In 1983, Domenic co-produced a live album for George Olliver and Gangbuster, LIVE AT THE BLUENOTE, also featuring Shawne Jackson and Roy Kenner. It's a sensational disc. Olliver is not inaccurate when he refers to his band Gangbuster as being the "best players." Shawne Jackson steps up to the microphone with a confident and effortless delivery of *Heat Wave*, backed by the Gangbuster's horn section. George joins her for an evocative duet of the ballad, *Let it be Me*, and then the Gangbuster horns carry her off as she wraps up her set with her '70s hit, *Just as Bad as You*. Roy Kenner renders a masterful up-tempo version of *Midnight Hour* that segues right into the old Mandala hit *Love-itis*. Wayne St. John (Ebony) follows with the classic R & B *Good Lovin'*, and then a terrific and potent performance of Domenic Troiano's *The Outer Limits of My Soul*. The CD closes with Jayson King singing the rollicking *Fannie Mae*, followed by the plaintive anthem, *Stand by Me*. LIVE AT THE BLUENOTE is a celebration, and Domenic's production faithfully conjures up and reminds us of the glorious Toronto Sound that came out of those wonderful nights so many years before.

I was the major investor in the LIVE AT THE BLUENOTE album, and it was very successful. Domenic was very interested and impressed with my band, George Olliver and Gangbuster. We had all the best players and he was very receptive. I was happy to have him produce. If you look at the CD, you will see that Domenic and I were co-producers. Domenic came in and recorded it live at the club and it came out very well.
- George Olliver, lead vocalist; interview with Mark Doble, July 1, 2020

A chance meeting in 1981 led to Domenic reuniting with former Guess Who bandmate Bill Wallace, when a group led by fellow Guess Who alumnus Winnipeg guitarist/singer/songwriter Greg Leskiw happened to be playing at the same club (the Osbourne Village Hotel) as Black Market in Winnipeg one evening.

It was my last Black Market tour, and they were playing in a club downstairs from us, and that's where I got to see them. They were really terrific!

- Domenic Troiano; interview with Howard Mandshein, 92 CITI-FM, January 2005

In 1970, Greg Leskiw replaced Randy Bachman in The Guess Who, where he was a member of the group until early 1972, after which he remained in Winnipeg, performing and recording with a number of local ensembles. That particular evening in Winnipeg, Domenic liked what he heard from Greg and Bill and offered to produce their band.

Between sets, Troiano stuck his head in downstairs, liked what he heard, and offered his assistance in promoting Leskiw's material. The offer came at the right time; Leskiw had been unsuccessfully shopping an album around for a couple of years before releasing it on his own label. "The coincidence was quite amazing," enthused Leskiw of his meeting with Troiano. "If we hadn't been booked in the same hotel as Domenic, he may never have heard of us and the recording deal may never have happened."

- Greg Leskiw, vocalist, guitarist, composer; "Kilowatt's Energy Surge," Keith Sharp, *Music Express*, October–November 1982

Kilowatt released a self-titled LP in 1982, and a follow-up album, CURRENTS, in 1983. In addition to producing both albums, Domenic co-wrote *Loneliness* on the first album and is also credited on *Its so Easy* and *I'm Not a Kid Anymore*. Domenic also performed on several tunes.

Donnie got us our deal but I didn't like the recording situation. I think Donnie really over-produced the records and sucked the "oomph" out of the band. He tried to commercialize the records too much. He sort of watered the band down to the point where we got back from the second album and Greg wanted to quit.

- Bill Wallace, singer, songwriter, bassist; interview with Mark Doble, May 1, 2021

The slick rock sound was not everything Greg and Bill were hoping for, and Kilowatt disbanded in 1984.

World-renowned and Toronto-born record producer Bob Ezrin grew up admiring Domenic's playing in Toronto bands from Robbie Lane to the Mandala. Ezrin got his start working with producer Jack Richardson at Nimbus 9 recording studios, and would go on to produce some of the most important artists in rock and roll including Alice Cooper, Lou Reed, and Pink Floyd. He maintained a profound appreciation of Domenic as both a player and producer.

Donnie had played with all of my favourite Toronto musicians, from Joey Chirowski to Whitey Glan to Dave Tyson to Prakash John to Shawne Jackson and many more. And everyone said, "You've got to work with this guy! He's the best guitar player in the country and he's the nicest person you'll ever meet." Big words, those; and truer than I could have imagined back then.

Thankfully, we did work together. Donnie guested on Dick Wagner's solo album and Murray McLauchlan's STORM WARNING, and he pro-duced Moe Koffman's solo album for my production company. He was as brilliant at that as he was as a player, writer, and composer of music for TV and film. He could do it all, and truthfully, I was a bit jealous of him having figured out how to make a good living without leaving town! And all the work he did throughout all the years was of the highest calibre. All of that just added to the deep affection and admira-tion that I grew to have for him. I really enjoyed his company. We were two Toronto boys who'd joined the circus and seen the world, and who knew many of the same people, though in different ways. We had a lot of experiences in common and a good deal of respect for each other.
-   Bob Ezrin, Producer; email to Frank Troiano, May 2020

Domenic's influence continued well past his years in live performance. Matt Touchard, guitarist and author of an upcoming book about BC Rich guitars, was exposed to Domenic in the mid-1970s. Matt was always on the lookout for guitarists who possessed a unique sound. He eloquently imparts as to Domenic's influence on himself, as well as other great players.

A friend loaned me some albums to check out by the James Gang and The Guess Who. The guitar style on these records was fresh and exciting. I discovered that this remarkable guitarist was an Italian-Canadian named Domenic Troiano. I also noticed he played a very unique guitar. I concluded that the sound he got out of that guitar was what I needed. After years of searching, I found a guitar like Domenic's; an early 1970s, BC Rich Seagull in a blue-green sunburst, that was very close to his.

In the 1980s, I was in New York City on a guitar shop jaunt and I ran into Domenic Troiano at Manny's. I introduced myself, explaining how I put him in my top tier of guitarists. We had a nice chat about guitars (and my BC Rich that matched his guitar) and music styles from Toronto to New Orleans. I recall how gracious he was to me. As I was leaving, he said, "Let me see your left hand, hold it up." I held my left hand up, outstretched. "Yeah, you play a lot; I can see it. Keep rocking that BC Rich, Matt." We shook hands and he flashed a big smile that's impossible to forget.

- Matt Touchard, guitarist, author; email to Frank Troiano, May 2020

By this time, Domenic had accumulated enough production and session credits that his career was now fully focused on writing, recording, and music production, which seemed to lead naturally toward the next stage of his career as a professional musician.

Troiano Family—Raffaele, Gina, Shawne, Frank, Pasqua, Domenic, Rita, 1983
(*Troiano Family Archives*)

CHAPTER 10

ALL I NEED IS MUSIC

"I've been scuffling and shuffling throughout the land
Just existing from day to day
It's getting so hard for a man to do things
In his own special way
So people categorize you, they dehumanize you
Then put you up on a shelf
That you can be anything that's already been
Just don't try to be yourself!"
(*Is There No Rest for the Weary*, lyrics by Domenic Troiano)

Sonny Grosso, Domenic Troiano, 1990 (Troiano Family Archives)

I still like recording, although there isn't much session work to be had in Toronto. *Night Heat*, however, has definitely opened whole new vistas for me.

- Domenic Troiano; "They Shoot: He Scores," Jonathan Gross, *Starweek Magazine*, January 17, 1987

He loved television scoring and he also made really good money—probably more money from doing television than going out six days on the road. That paid very well for Donnie. He enjoyed creating music, because he would have to look at the screen, see these things, and being the creative genius he really was, he would sit there and he would "feel" these scenes, and the next thing you knew, he was creating music for it. He talked to me about how different it was, coming out of like a "garage-band" type of thing, and there he is, leading all these people and writing scores for television. And it was very different for him, but he wasn't intimidated by it whatsoever. He was able to jump into it and do it! It was an interesting time for him, and he loved it!

- John Donabie, radio host; interview with Mark Doble, August 3, 2020

People were in awe of Domenic's talent as a guitar player and artist; I was in awe of his kindness as a human being. He genuinely never had a bad word to say about anyone.

- Lisa Parasyn, casting director—*Night Heat*; email to Frank Troiano, February 2021

In the 1980s, with increased Canadian-made television programming, opportunities emerged to write and produce soundtracks. In addition to being musically talented, the job required knowledge and skill in the studio, and the discipline to meet tight deadlines. Domenic's skill set was perfectly suited.

With music for film and television, you can get a lot more adventurous. It has given me more of an opportunity to experiment. It has also afforded me the chance to get more involved with synthesizers and the computerized aspects of music. It has opened up many creative doors for me.

- "Domenic Troiano The Man behind the Music," Martin/Kierans, Toronto, 1987

In the 1996 Canadian Music Hall of Fame induction, American movie and television producer Sonny Grosso described his first meeting (eleven years earlier) with Domenic, and the opportunity to compose for a new series, *Night Heat.*

We were just getting into our series *Night Heat,* and I had been asked by Lee Segal from CTV to meet this guy, Domenic Troiano, before I settled on a music composer. I asked Domenic what TV shows he had done. He looked me right in the eye and said, "None." I thought for a second and said, "Movies?" He said, "No, no movies." Well there was an awkward silence and then I said, "If you've never done any of this stuff, why the hell are we meeting?" Domenic took a second, looked at me, and said, "I'm a damned good musician. Tell me what you want, and I'll give it to you." I stared at him for about a second; I reached over for the rough cut of *Night Heat* and handed it to him and said, "Here. Take a peek at this, and let me know what you think." He took it, smiled, shook my hand, and left. I thought, "Well, I'll never see this guy again." But the next morning, a tired Domenic came to my hotel with a cassette—he and Roy had just worked on it all night long—and it was that terrific theme from *Night Heat.*

- Sonny Grosso, television producer; Canadian Music Hall of Fame Induction Ceremony, Toronto, 1996

Domenic also remembered the meeting well.

We met. I liked what he was trying to do. On my way home that evening, I put together in my head the chorus for the theme song. I visited B. J. Cook for some lyrical help, and then the next day I went into the studio with Bob and cut a demo. I had no real experience with scoring, but Sonny went with his gut instinct, and asked me to do the show. The

theme song you hear now, and which A & M released as a single, is that demo we did way back then.
- Domenic Troiano; "MIDI Madness Reigns for Domenic Troiano," Ashley Collie, *Canadian Musician*, June 1987

The tune Domenic took back to Sonny is classic "killer" Troiano rock/R & B, perfectly suited to the program Sonny was producing.

An image of a cityscape flashes on the screen. The shot suggests the underbelly of big-city life, the dark side of streets ruled by office workers each day, but the territory of the lawless at night. There is tension, the kind that is created with crowds close in and tempers flaring. The streets offer seductive glimpses of late-night temptations. Two policemen move through fast-paced clips, rolling over cars, chasing criminals of all descriptions. Their movements are choreographed to a relentless beat, part jazz, part rock and roll—all sexy. Then a singer caps the mood … "I feel the night heat. I feel your heart beat…"
- "Troiano on Television" Lynda Ashley, *Broadcaster*, March 1987

Domenic's reputation as a "musician's musician," his demonstrated skill in the studio, and his musical versatility as a musician and producer (in 1980, Domenic was nominated for a Canadian Juno Award for producer of the year), had earned the respect and admiration of his peers. Domenic would not hesitate to call on these friends (a veritable "who's who" of Canadian music) for guidance and support.

Dom branched out into composing music for television and films. He loved movies, and had a great knack for writing music for the screen. In 1985, he submitted a music demo for *Night Heat*, a television series produced by Sonny Grosso, the New York cop whose real-life experiences were the basis for the movie *The French Connection*. Dom's music was chosen from more than fifty composers who submitted, and when he was interviewed by Grosso, they connected well and he ended up scoring several years of the series. I had focused on writing film scores in the 1970s and '80s and was active in the Guild of Canadian Film Composers, so Dom called me when he was negotiating with Grosso

and asked me about how film composers got paid, the upfront and back-end royalty fees etc.

- Paul Hoffert, keyboard, composer, band leader—Lighthouse; email to Frank Troiano, April 2020

Domenic co-wrote the theme song for *Night Heat* (his first television series) with B. J. Cook (with whom he had originally worked while she was in Skylark with David Foster in the early '70s in L.A.), assigned the lead vocals to Roy Kenner, and released the single *Night Heat* in 1986 on A & M Records, with an instrumental mix of the song on the flipside.

Donnie always stayed in touch, and when I moved to Toronto, it was he who took a chance on me as a writer, and I made a living thanks to the TV shows we collaborated on. It still brings a tear to my eye when I think of him, he was my confidant, my counsel, my conscience, and my dear, kind, and loyal friend.

- B. J. Cook, singer, writer, former member of Skylark; email to Frank Troiano, April 2020

Donnie called me up and said, "I'm going to be scoring a TV show. B. J. and I have written the theme song and we'd like you to sing it." Once again, I felt blessed to be asked, and it also happens to be another vocal performance I am proud of.

- Roy Kenner, lead vocalist; interview with Mark Doble, July 4, 2020

Although *Night Heat* was produced and released as a single, it failed to chart or achieve any kind of radio play.

It was recently released as a single by A & M Records. But Troiano readily admits it has yet to be a big success on radio. "The attitude seems to be, 'this is a TV theme, so why should we play it?' But we wanted to put it out, so we're going to keep working it."

- "Troiano on Television," Lynda Ashley, *Broadcaster*, March 1987

Up until 1986, Domenic's sister, Gina Troiano, worked for Revenue Canada. But the opportunity to work with Domenic represented a dream come true for her.

I remember thinking how wonderful it would be if one day he became so successful that he would hire me to work for him. That dream became reality when he became extremely busy with music scoring for television and film for producer Sonny Grosso. *Night Heat* led to *Diamonds, Hot Shots, Secret Service, True Blue, Top Cops, Counterstrike,* and the list goes on. I started working for Donnie in 1986 as his personal assistant.

- Gina Troiano; interview with Mark Doble, June 30, 2020

Recording engineer Bob Federer co-owned Round Sound Studios before Domenic purchased the studio. Bob stayed around to work with him for the next ten years.

I first met Donnie while he was working with Dan Hill and Moe Koffman on some tracks. He invited me in to do some synthesizer programming for those projects. After I, along with three partners, opened Round Sound Studios, Donnie began working on some projects there. He worked there so often that eventually, he bought out the partners and took over ownership of the studio. During the work day Donnie called the shots, and it all got done. I think everyone respected each other; we worked well together, and we accomplished a lot. He kept me on as his engineer. I worked with Donnie in that capacity from the early mid-80s until around 1995. We worked on Sonny Grosso's productions, which included shows like *Night Heat, Hot Shots, Diamonds, Top Cops, Counterstrike, Secret Service, True Blue,* and the movie *Gunfighters,* starring George Kennedy.

- Bob Federer, recording engineer; email to Frank Troiano, December 2020

Fresh out of school, Danny Sustar got his chance to work as a recording engineer with Domenic, thus beginning an association that would last almost twenty years.

I met Domenic four months after graduating from Trebas Recording School in 1985. I made an appointment to drop off a resume at Round Sound Studios and Domenic was making a coffee and he opened the door for me … physically and literally. He asked who I was, and I told him I'm looking for an audio position at Round Sound. He invited

214

me into the control room and allowed me to watch him work on the music for a new CBS show called *Night Heat*. At the end of the session, Domenic invited me back for the next day. By the end of this day I was already helping Bob (the engineer) with some of the recording of the tracks for *Night Heat*. That was the beginning of a twenty-year friendship. I became the assistant engineer at Round Sound and worked up the ranks. Eventually, Domenic became the sole owner of Round Sound and built his dream studio up in Concord. I was able to work at that studio and Domenic allowed a lot of input from me. We made lots of great music in that time.

- Danny Sustar, recording engineer; email to Frank Troiano, October 2020

Former touring musician George Rondina owned Number 9 Sound Studios and routinely supplied equipment for Round Sound.

We ran a pro audio rental company out of Number 9 and we were lucky enough to have Domenic and his studio (Round Sound) as clients. I would deliver the gear to the studio and Domenic would greet me like a family member visiting his home. He would ask me about the business and family and we would talk about the industry in general. I have to say in all my years I don't think anyone with so many incredible accomplishments treated me with such a kind heart. Such an amazing guitar player and human being! (We also had a lot of fun joking about food and the love of the Italian heritage we both shared.)

- George Rondina, Number 9 Sound Studios Inc.; Email to Frank Troiano, March, 2021

In 1986, Vancouver hosted the World Expo. The Ontario Pavilion featured a 3D Cinema production called "Dark Exhibit," a five-thousand-year history of Ontario, with a soundtrack by Domenic Troiano, described as "a mixture of rich special effects." The dramatic score included sound samples generated through the use of a Synclavier.

With the Synclavier, we had the flexibility of sampling any sound we wanted to use. We could alter it any way we wished. The Synclavier is really quite an amazing machine—it's also fast and easy to use. There's so much processing you can do with the Synclavier, so many parameters you can change a sound within. You can sample a natural sound and combine it with a garbage can, or a gorilla sound, or whatever you want—it's limitless.

- "Domenic Troiano—A Conversation with Canada's Foremost Musical Renaissance Man," Gerr Audio Promotional Material, 1986

Domenic's willingness to grow, to experiment, and try new things served well his transition from the fret board to the keyboard and facilitated the process and purposes of music scoring.

You can try a lot of different things, for example, you can get way out harmonically, as long as the mood is right. I really enjoy the whole challenge of putting music to film or television. It's opened up a whole new world for me in the last couple of years.

- "Domenic Troiano Hot on *Night Heat*," Paul Benedetti, *Hamilton Spectator*, March 5, 1987

Domenic scored music for hundreds of episodes for seventeen different network television series as well as twelve made-for-TV movies. *Night Heat* lasted four seasons. Domenic was nominated for a Gemini (Canadian Television) award in 1986 for Best Music Composition for a Series (*Night Heat*). He was nominated again in 1988 for his scoring for the series *Hot Shots*, and again in 1989 for *Diamonds*. (A comprehensive list of Domenic Troiano's scoring credits is included as an appendix to this volume.)

Songwriter Dean McTaggart reflected on working with Domenic on music for episodes of *Night Heat.*

As much as I was in awe of his playing, I was drawn to the quality of the tunes he was writing. Songs like *Don't Make Me Cry* (the Mandala), *Get Her Back Again* (James Gang), *All Night Radio Show, My Old Toronto Home* (TRICKY) inspired me to try to write better songs, and I still listen to my vinyl copies of all his records on a regular basis and they still stand the test of time. Donnie went on to produce the music for *Night Heat,* a TV show on CTV in Canada. What a thrill for me that he thought enough of *The Heart of the City* and *I Can't Let Go,* songs that I had co-written, to use them on the show.

- Dean McTaggart, songwriter; email to Frank Troiano, April 2020

The ability to score, write/compose/create and produce music was a new lease on life. It was a role that he embraced, and Domenic was determined to produce music of the highest standard.

The process is fairly simple. He sits down and watches a final cut of the episode with the director. They kick around a few ideas for certain sections of the show, and then Troiano heads home or to the studio and begins doodling around. Though he often writes music for certain sections, Troiano will also just doodle on the synthesizers until he's created a mood to match the action. "It's a bit like finger painting when you were in school. It's not as much music as mood," he said. "You want it feeling scary here, tense here, and you want to create the feeling." He may spend as much as thirty hours in the studio over a couple of days scoring the episode, using a blend of synthesizers and studio musicians, to achieve the final effect.

- "Domenic Troiano Hot on *Night Heat,*" Paul Benedetti, *Hamilton Spectator*, March 5, 1987

He would continue to seek out the best musicians to work with, such as the great Graham Lear, percussionist, who worked with Canadian rock vocalist Gino Vannelli, as well as Carlos Santana, one of the greatest guitarists in the world.

During those years in the '70s and '80s, he and I still worked together on other projects when time permitted and I remember well one of the sessions at his studio in Richmond Hill for the TV show *Night Heat.* He needed a military-style rudimental drum part for a cue so I set up my favourite snare and improvised quite a long, convoluted part from my early marching days. Finished, I looked to him in the control room to see if they were impressed. He asked casually if I had some more time because he wanted me to play the whole thing over again to double on to another track. My heart sank because I never wrote it down and couldn't remember exactly what I had played. I can still see

his wry smile through the glass as if to say, "That'll teach ya for leaving me hanging." That was Dom, and I truly miss his friendship.

- Graham Lear, percussionist; email to Frank Troiano, April 2020

Scoring for television provided income stability, and Domenic took advantage of this to help other musicians develop and promote their talent. Domenic was always ready and willing to help and encourage others. Myles Goodwyn of April Wine once recorded a song, *Rock and Roll is a Vicious Game*. That song title is a true statement.

"In the TV and film business, if they like what you do, they pay you on the spot," grins Troiano mischievously. "It's not like the music business where, if you sell a bunch of records, you might see some money in about nine years' time."

- Domenic Troiano; interview with Keith Sharp,
  Canadian Musician, 1992

Music executive Gary Hubbard recalls how the money from scoring became somewhat of a financial windfall for Domenic.

When I joined Alliance after a career at A & M Records, I discovered a drawer full of what appeared to be royalty publishing statements for a company called Propinquity. It seemed these statements had accumulated over several years, as no one in the company seemed to know what to do with them. One set of statements was for a company called Pasqua and included the titles *Night Heat* and *Diamonds*. I immediately associated these with Domenic. Without delay, we opened a bank account for Propinquity and cheques were cut and distributed, making many people, including Dom, very happy.

- Gary Hubbard, executive at A & M Records, Alliance Entertainment,
  Harris Institute; email to Frank Troiano, November 2020

Over the previous two decades, Roy Kenner and Domenic had become a formidable songwriting team, writing several albums of songs, including many things that never saw the light of day on record. Domenic was not averse to reaching back into that vault of musical materials to bolster his TV scores.

218

Over the years, there were a lot of things that we wrote that we never did anything with. But Donnie would take sections from these tunes and put them into the tracks of the TV shows as little bits of background music—I think Donnie got a kick out of telling me some airplay dollars would be coming my way! (That was Donnie!)

- Roy Kenner, lead vocalist, songwriter; interview with Mark Doble, July 4, 2020

From Day One, Domenic was always encouraging to others; willing to give of his time (and money) to ensure that a young musician was given a chance. And in the process of Domenic simply being Domenic, he became a lasting influence on almost everyone. Early on in his own career in the late 1960s, Domenic provided guidance and encouragement to singer-songwriter/recording artist/Juno award winner, Cathy Young.

It was the late '60s when I bought my Martin guitar. I was still a fledgling when it came to my guitar playing. I could sing and write lyrics, but the chords were another thing entirely. I needed help. I called the best guitarist I could think of, even though we were not close friends, Domenic Troiano, guitarist for the Mandala, who'd been the hottest group in town. We were acquainted through the Yorkville music circuit. I didn't know him well, but I was a huge fan of his talent. I told him my situation and asked if he would help me break in my guitar, as I didn't know many chords. What separated Domenic from other people is what transpired next. He offered to come to my house and help me. He showed up and played my guitar for over three hours straight. I thanked him profusely. He said, "Nice guitar!" Then he smiled his shy smile and left … Genius … I'm still shakin' his chords out of my guitar.

- Cathy Young, singer-songwriter; email to Frank Troiano, April 2020

Canadian singer-songwriter Dan Hill had a monster hit single in the late 1970s: *Sometimes When We Touch*. The song is a modern-day masterpiece, winning Juno awards for best song in both 1978 and 1979, and also helping Hill receive awards as a songwriter and vocalist. In the early 1980s, Dan worked with Domenic Troiano.

I worked quite extensively with Domenic in the early 1980s. He was immensely musical and when we were writing songs together, I was always amazed at his efficiency and sense of having a strong hook, or title. He demoed a few songs for me and the recording was quite extensive, and yet, when the project was completed, he waived his fee. That was Dom in a nutshell; extremely giving, generous, and considerate. He was also very warm and engaging, and a terrific storyteller.

- Dan Hill, singer-songwriter; email to Frank Troiano, April 2020

Hill also went on to win multiple Juno Awards and also Grammy Awards for song-writing. But the theme of Domenic's willingness to give of his time to help others was not just one or two isolated instances.

He played on a couple of tracks and wasn't in any hurry; he just wanted to make sure that we got what we needed. What he laid down was flawless and his rhythm was dead in the pocket. I would meet Domenic occasionally through the next five years, and one time he said, "Lance, if you ever need more tracks on a session, let me know. I just want to play." When I mentioned I was mainly producing blues records on my own label and the budgets were not very large, he said without hesitation, "Don't worry about the dough, I'll do it for whatever you can afford. I'd just like to play."

- Lance Anderson, keyboard; email to Frank Troiano, April 2020

John Harris, CEO and founder of the Harris Institute, (one of the top postsecondary music schools in Toronto, specializing in audio music production), fondly recounts Domenic's typical kindness and desire to "pay it forward."

When I started the school, Domenic was a regular guest lecturer. There were many terms where he would be a guest in two or three courses. I always looked forward to his visits and the short times we could spend together. He was the school's most regular guest lecturer for many years, and always declined to accept remuneration.

- John Harris, CEO—Harris Institute; email to Frank Troiano, April 2020

Well aware of his musical legacy, Domenic took care to provide input regarding the manner in which his back catalogue was released and reissued. In 1985, a vinyl album, CLASSICS, was released, containing songs from the Mandala's SOUL CRUSADE, along with the single *Opportunity/ Lost Love.*

"The biggest challenge putting this piece of vinyl together? Trying to trace the Chess Masters," says Troiano. "We finally found Marshall Chess and went to the warehouse, but there were ten thousand boxes to go through. … Instead they had to hunt up mint condition records to remaster." Does Troiano think there's a revived interest in the Mandala? "No, not really … although I've heard SOUL CRUSADE goes for about thirty dollars at record collector's conventions," he laughs, "I think the old fans just need a new copy of the record."
-   Domenic Troiano; "Mandala—CLASSICS," *Canadian Musician*, February 1986

(The original SOUL CRUSADE album was released on CD in 2010 on the "Pacemaker" label.)

In 1988, Jack Richardson produced TRACK RECORD, a two-CD compilation of music by The Guess Who, and as a bonus included the 1974 studio recording of *Sona Sona* (from the aborted movie soundtrack). As the piano ballad had no guitars on the original recording, Domenic was recruited to come into the studio on June 13, 1988, to record both acoustic and electric guitar tracks.

In 1981, Freedom Records repackaged and reissued BUSH on vinyl. And in 1995, Domenic supervised the remastering of BUSH for CD release, along with four bonus tracks from the band's last live performance at Los Angeles' Bitter End in 1971.

However, the plans to rerelease BUSH were not without complications, when suddenly, Domenic was contacted by lawyers for a band out of the UK with the same name, asking that he cease and desist with the use of the name "Bush." Led by Gavin Rossdale, Bush had a world-wide following—including Canada, where their albums SIXTEEN STONE and

RAZORBLADE SUITCASE sold over one million units. A Canadian group by the same name reissuing a twenty-five-year-old album was problematic, especially when Domenic responded to their concerns with his Canadian copyright in hand, forcing the British group to add the letter X to all materials advertising the band's name; slapping stickers on millions of CDs, posters, and promotional material.

"I thought it was kind of funny, and that was it as far as I was concerned," says Troiano when he heard about the new Bush. Things changed when it came down the pipeline that the new Bush, or at least their lawyers, might try to stop Troiano's Bush from putting out its old record. "When they started telling us that maybe we couldn't use the name, I got a little upset," said the Music Hall of Famer.
- "X Marks the Sore Spot for Mega-popular BushX," Betsy Powell, *Hamilton Spectator*, January 10, 1997

Thankfully, Rossdale and Troiano convened (without the lawyers!) to sort it out. In exchange for dropping the "X" from their promotional materials, the UK Bush agreed to donate $40,000; $20,000 each to the Starlight Foundation and the Canadian Music Therapy Trust Fund. A press conference attended by Rossdale and Troiano was arranged to announce the settlement.

Universal staffers looked relieved, especially since they don't have to have special artwork for Canadian releases anymore. The charities' spokespeople smiled. One veteran observer, looking on, said: "That Domenic's a class act. He could have stuck them for a hundred grand and walked away with it. Instead, two charities—both heavily supported by the music industries both in Britain and here—got a nice donation, and everyone comes away looking good."
- "British Bush Gets Name Back, Charities Get Cash," Richard Flohil, *The Record*, April 28, 1997

With his new career (and steady income) in television soundtracks, Domenic could afford to be generous. It was win-win for both bands and two deserving charities, through which Domenic never lost his sense of perspective.

In the meantime, the original BUSH got rereleased to modest sales, while BushX's SIXTEEN STONE went on to become one of the year's best-selling CDs in Canada. "What did they sell—five million? We probably sold about five," Troiano said with a laugh, adding, "maybe five hundred. I tell you what though—it's a good record. I dare say it's better than theirs."

- "X Marks the Sore Spot For Mega-popular BushX,"
  Betsy Powell, *Hamilton Spectator*, January 10, 1997

Continuing to produce records on his Black Market label, one of the more notable artists was singer David Gibson, with whom Domenic recorded several singles, as well as a self-titled album in 1989.

Donnie was the man who taught me that "music" and the "music business" had literally nothing to do with each other. I respected Donnie so much for his work ethic. It's something that stuck with me. He was confident, organized, and had vision, and he was smart enough to let musicians hired to play on sessions explore and bring their take to a track before offering direction, if he felt inclined. Musically, he was fearless and would try anything—just look at the way he successfully broke into TV and film scoring—having never done it before. He was a natural.

- David Gibson, singer-songwriter; email to Frank Troiano, April 2020

Johnny Rutledge was singing top-forty hits in Toronto clubs. In the mid-1980s, Rutledge got to meet Domenic and work with Shawne Jackson, Roy Kenner, and George Olliver, recording commercial jingles. Johnny even did some vocals on a number of television themes Domenic wrote. Finally, Domenic convinced Johnny to record his own album.

When Donnie finally sat me down and said that I needed to record my own album and that he would produce it, I immediately jumped at the chance. He provided everything I needed to complete it and see it through. That included the use of his own recording studio, the engineer and assistant, his own original compositions (although I could write my own if I wanted), marketing, promotion, and promotional materials, basically everything. The one thing that stands out in my memory is how he would greet me every time I arrived at his house or studio to work. His eyes would light up, he'd break into that famous smile, and give me an excited, "Heeeeey Johnny R!" Donnie had the ability to genuinely lift you up and make you feel so important. ... Domenic had such a natural, relaxed, and supportive demeanor as a producer. He not only knew exactly what he wanted and needed, he knew how to get it. He immediately made me feel like I was the perfect choice for this track.

- Johnny Rutledge, singer-songwriter; email to Frank Troiano, August 2020

Domenic also continued to be involved in the process of reissuing his back catalogue on CD.

In 1994, when I went to Mercury/Polydor, Dom came in to see me. He wondered if we could get his records back into the market. I thought it was a good idea and we came out with a compilation of the two Mercury solo LPs.

- Doug Chappell; email to Frank Troiano, April 2020

The list of CD reissues included BUSH (1994) with four live bonus tracks; TROIANO'S TRIPLE PLAY (1996), a compilation of his three Capitol Records albums; THE TORONTO SOUND (1998), a single CD containing both of Domenic's early 70s Mercury Records' solo albums; and in 2003, Universal Music issued THE BEST OF DOMENIC TROIANO—THE MILLENIUM COLLECTION, featuring selections from his solo repertoire as well as the Mandala, Bush, Black Market, and the James Gang. Domenic was very pleased when FLAVOURS and POWER IN THE MUSIC finally became available on CD in the late 1990s.

In 1996, Domenic recorded, produced, and played guitar on David Gibson's second album, RHYTHM METHOD. David recently reflected on Domenic's production values.

Donnie didn't have that temperamental side that so many artists seem to have. Donnie taught me to take the blinders off where my own songs were concerned. That wasn't always an easy ride for me and I'm damn sure I didn't make it easy for him. He was patient and again, that sense of fairness—he'd hear me out, and there were times he took my suggestions to heart and then I'd find myself—yes, me—offering playing suggestions to this world-class guitarist! I have to admit that more often than not, his vision was the one we ultimately went with.

- David Gibson, singer-songwriter; email to Frank Troiano, April 2020

It seems odd to note that Domenic never won a Juno award. (He was nominated for Producer of the Year in 1979 for the album FRET FEVER.) And so, in 1996, it was gratifying when it was announced that Domenic Troiano was to be recognized and inducted into the Canadian Music Hall of Fame during that year's Juno Award ceremonies.

"It's a nice honour," Troiano says modestly from his home in Toronto. "It's nice for my family; my parents are really pleased. It's going to be a fun night, but I was a little surprised."
- Domenic Troiano; "Domenico of Modugno,"
  Angela Baldassarre, *Tandem Magazine*, March 9, 1996

The ceremony took place on March 9 at the Metro Toronto Convention Centre, with Domenic's family in attendance. Burton Cummings, the master of ceremonies that evening, recognized Domenic and referenced the music they had done together in The Guess Who. Lifelong musical friend Roy Kenner then paid tribute, citing Domenic's Toronto beginnings. A video montage included tributes from former bandmates Prakash John and Whitey Glan, as well as jazz pianist Doug Riley. Lastly, film producer Sonny Grosso spoke of introducing Domenic to the world of television-film scoring. Finally, Domenic came to the podium to accept the award in perhaps the most understated manner of all of the inductees that evening.

Thank you very much. This is a great honour. It's an honour to be inducted with all the great people who are being inducted tonight, and all the people who are already there. I'd like to thank all the great musicians I've had the honour of playing with, who have helped me along the way; a great many friends, cousins, relatives, family, and especially my mother and father who are here tonight and have been behind me one hundred percent; always gave me the support I needed; always made me feel I was important and special; my brother and sister, Frank and Gina,

who have been there with me all along, and Frank's wife Rita who has brought two of the biggest joys into my life, Marcus and Julian, their sons. And last but not least, my wife, who's been with me through this whole ride, and I appreciate all her support, and all her understanding. Thank you very much.

- Domenic Troiano; "Acceptance Speech," Canadian Music Hall of Fame Induction Ceremonies, 1996

For the performances at the conclusion, Domenic enlisted the Dexters, a local R & B outfit that Domenic had occasionally been playing with at The Orbit Room in Toronto, to be the supporting band for the ceremonies. Dexters' drummer Mike Sloski was thrilled to be part the band that evening as well, and recalled playing for all of the new inductees.

One show I was fortunate enough to play under his directorship was the ceremony where he was inducted into the Canadian Rock and Roll Hall of Fame. Donnie put together a band featuring the Dexters, the horn section from the Men From Uncle, and the soulful Doug Riley on piano. We backed up all the people receiving the Rock and Roll Hall of Fame award that year—John Kay, Denny Doherty, Zal Yanovsky, David Clayton-Thomas, and Ronnie Hawkins. It was a fantastic gig, and a treat seeing Donnie receive his well-deserved award.

- Mike Sloski, drummer; email to Frank Troiano, June 2020

They performed the Mandala classics *Love-itis* and *Opportunity*. Video from the evening shows him completely at ease, smiling, and playing with elegance, and to perfection. The long-awaited recognition of his career and musical craft had arrived, and his family was there to celebrate with him. Domenic was at peace and happy. And Domenic Troiano was completely at home!

Canadian Music Hall of Fame Awards—John Sebastian, Zal Yanovsky,
Ronnie Hawkins, Bernie Labarge, Domenic Troiano, David Clayton-Thomas,
Peter Cardinali, Michelle Phillips, 1996 (Photo: Tom Sandler)

CHAPTER 11

WE ALL
NEED LOVE

"I was just a lonely man with a suitcase in my hand
Part of a travelling band—On the road—girl I was always away
from you
I never needed anyone—and my music was my fun
But I woke up late in life to regret it
We all need love I swear it's true—all God's children, me and you."
(*We All Need Love*, lyrics by Domenic Troiano)

Canadian Music Hall of Fame Awards—Lee Silversides, Denny Doherty,
John Kay, Domenic Troiano, Zal Yanovsky, David Clayton-Thomas, 1996
(Photo: Tom Sandler)

The term is "musician's musician." It speaks of admiration for a person's dedication, devotion, and commitment to excellence. Don Troiano was untouchable when we were kids, the crown prince of the Telecaster in the home of the Toronto Sound. The early hits were epic, as were his later singles and Shawne Jackson's *Just as Bad as You*. His soundtrack rock and fusion recordings speak of a diversity and a hunger. The reverence held for Donnie was of the highest order and even if at times he seemed overwhelmed by it, he was gracious; and in his later years had come to terms peacefully with his legacy; a highly evolved being.

- Danny Marks, guitarist; email to Frank Troiano April 2020

May 25, 2004—that final public performance of *Eleanora Fagan*. Domenic's eyes are closed. The elegiac instrumental melody advances slowly, beautifully, as Doug Riley's B-3 reverently distils church-like organ chords underneath. Domenic's single-line lead soars, octave after octave, straight from his heart and soul, and then mid-way through, that brooding bass riff starts repeating four quarter notes, each one on the beat over and over. Domenic's guitar stealthily tiptoes through a melodic phrase accompaniment; Riley goes wondrous and wild for about forty-eight bars until Domenic's guitar pronounces the benediction—and then it is over. We think about the man who created this music; that it's Domenic's final public performance—the heartache is profound—there are no words.

The cancer was no secret, but Domenic, like others who have endured similar circumstances, did not wish to dwell on his illness. One was welcome to call or to visit, but there were three topics of much greater interest to Domenic: music, family, and you. There was still life to live, and music, always more music to make.

During a 1995 medical checkup, Domenic's PSA was found to be well above normal and it was determined that he had inoperable prostate cancer. It had spread to the lymphatic system.

Very naturally, Domenic turned to his family for support. Sister-in-law Rita Troiano served as a family confidante. And through his illness, Domenic would later credit Rita's guidance and encouragement for extending his quality of life for more years than expected.

First of all, I connected him with my naturopath, who was a brilliant practitioner. Donnie was seeing his oncologist as well, but he also wanted to investigate alternative therapies and treatments. He started on a lifestyle change that was a complete turnaround. Donnie was asking questions all the time and even his mother had to change the way she cooked because he had stopped all dairy and everything had to be whole-grain and organic.
- Rita Troiano, sister-in-law; interview with Mark Doble, July 7, 2020

Rita also recalled Domenic's dining room table stacked with books and reading material, everything that Domenic could get his hands on regarding his illness and potential cancer treatments.

Now Donnie was enjoying a more holistic diet and everything new that he tried. He had a daily regimen of supplements and remedies. He travelled to Switzerland for specialized treatment at an integrative cancer clinic and had his fiftieth birthday while he was there. He came back and continued to see his naturopath as well as his oncologist. He then also learned of a natural supplement from California that helped him maintain stability for many years.
- Rita Troiano, sister-in-law; interview with Mark Doble, July 7, 2020

Within twelve months of his diagnosis, Domenic had lost over fifty pounds through sheer determination and willpower. Throughout this period he researched, consulting a myriad of doctors, health practitioners, and cancer survivors. For the next seven years Domenic was pain free, in relatively good shape, and very productive.

Singer-composer and Troiano protégé Patria related how Domenic dealt with his illness.

When he talked about his cancer in the late '90s and early 2000s, he said something very strange. He said that he was "blessed to have cancer." He said that it made him stop and look at his life, look at all the people in his life, look at what he had accomplished and what was left to be

done, and he knew it was time to reset his priorities. He never felt sorry for himself and he was never a victim.

- Patria, singer-songwriter; interview with Frank Troiano, June 12, 2020

Regardless of the treatment regimen required, Domenic was still determined to be musically active. Domenic owned his own studio in Vaughan (a suburb north of Toronto) that he used for creating soundtracks and records.

He bought Round Sound Studios, he bought some industrial units in Vaughan, and he built a first-class studio. I joined him full-time as an assistant doing overflow work. He then wanted me to take over the second season of *Counterstrike* and I said I didn't have enough experience. He said, "Why not give it a try?" The show was a success, and I had found a new level of confidence. By this time I had left Rough Trade, and I loved going into the new studio, as the atmosphere was relaxed and we had a lot of fun, but we also worked very long hours as Sonny had given us four series to do. I don't know how Donnie managed all the pressure. Needless to say, he was very well organized and always met the deadlines. The scoring of TV shows and movies went full tilt until the mid to late '90s, and during that time Donnie slowly turned his attention to founding Black Market Records and recording two LPs with David Gibson, one LP with John Rutledge, and one LP with Patria, and he allowed the studio to be used for other musical projects.

- Howard Ayee, assistant; interview with Frank Troiano, April 28, 2020

Guitarist Terry Blersh was recording with the Garth Hudson (The Band) at one point, and Domenic joined them in the studio.

Garth Hudson had been in town and I had managed to get him to play on my CD. When Domenic and Garth got together to do some recording at the same studio, I was able to witness those sessions. In fact, I was thrilled to lend Domenic my Princeton Reverb amp. It's a treasured memory.

- Terry Blersh, guitarist; email to Frank Troiano, April 2020

Domenic invested a great deal of energy and resources into one of his last projects as a producer and promoter, which involved a young singer named Patria. In an interview fifteen years after Domenic's passing, Patria attributed her professional success to his caring and competent guidance.

In 1996, Domenic invited me to record three of his songs at his studio, Round Sound. I told him that I also wrote lyrics and poetry and I gave him a number of lyrical ideas that I had. A few weeks later, he had added his music to some of my lyrics and we recorded those songs. About a month later he signed me to his record label, Black Market Records, and he signed me to his publishing company, Pasqua Music.

Over the next couple of years, I released an LP called MY RULES and a promotional EP. Two singles were released from the LP: *My Rules* and *Baby Feel My.*

Domenic had two videos shot for the singles, one on location in Mexico and the other in Toronto. We did a lot of promo for the LP, including a Canada-wide tour opening for Eiffel 64, and several radio, newspaper, magazine, and TV interviews.

We also travelled to Japan, London, England, Los Angeles, and NYC in order to move my career forward. Several of my songs found their way onto Domenic's TV and movie scoring productions, providing me with steady income in the late '90s and early 2000s.

Domenic was a musical mentor, a father figure, a shoulder to lean on and to cry on. He was generous, humble, sweet, well-organized, very knowledgeable, resourceful, headstrong, opinionated, intelligent, very caring, and driven, and he always maintained a positive attitude.

- Patria, singer-songwriter, protégé; interview with
  Frank Troiano, June 12, 2020

In 1999, Canadian musician Rick Worrall teamed up with producer Lance Anderson to release a blues album entitled WHEN LOVE IS RIGHT, which included Domenic Troiano playing a bluesy guitar solo on the title track.

In 2000, Domenic went into the studio again to lay down guitar parts for an independent release by well-known and respected Toronto R

& B bass player Chris Vickery. Vickery's extensive resume stretched back four decades and included gigs with names such as the Majestics, David Clayton-Thomas, and Lenny Breau. For the album TEMPORARY MEASURES, Vickery called in some of Canada's finest session musicians, including Domenic Troiano, who can be heard playing guitar on *Tatem*, *Maybe*, and *Tuff Stuff*.

Last time I saw him we got together to visit about a CD I had just recorded in '98. I will always remember Donnie not only as a wonderful musician and guiding light in that department, but as a very good and solid friend I could count on, always. He was indeed a legend, even in his own time! Donnie was indeed the salt of the earth, proud of his family and his heritage, and one hell of a guitar player!
- Bob Burrows (aka Bobby Kris), vocalist, teacher; email to
  Frank Troiano, April 2020

Family reasons were at the forefront in my decision to come back to Toronto. Business-wise, I knew that I was narrowing my possibilities by moving back to Canada, but business cannot be the only consideration in one's life. I'm glad I came back.
- "Domenic Troiano the Man Behind the Music,"
  Martin/Kierans, Toronto, 1987

Frank and Gina helped Domenic manage his various interests, and Frank and Rita's two sons (Julian and Marcus) were also a source of immense pride.

Donnie's nephews went to the Toronto Waldorf School in Thornhill. Music is big at the school, and nephew Julian became one of the high school's star musicians. Over the years, it was surprising to see the great guitarist standing on the stairs, waiting to pick up his nephews. That old stairwell held many interesting musical conversations. The school often used musical coffee houses for classroom fundraisers, and I played a few with Julian. I recall helping out accompanying vocalist Siobhan Duffy at one, when in Donnie's way of seemingly always giving of himself for his nephews, he appeared at the back of the room with great bassist Howard Ayee to listen and contribute his musical talent.

As family involvement is also big at the school, at these occasions I also got to see and meet Donnie's extended family, cheering performers on.

- John Ebata, Cosmo Music; email to Frank Troiano, April 2020

Imagine attending one of these school concerts and having Domenic Troiano cheering you on as you played your clarinet! Nephew Julian Troiano remembers visiting his uncle's large home.

Growing up, we would see my Uncle Domenic often. For lunch at my grandparents' house, family time with him and Auntie Shawne, and most notably, my and my brother's annual birthday parties. We would play hide and seek in his house, swim in the indoor pool, or play in the big toy room he had created for us. He treated us like we were his own children.

I was mesmerized by his studio as a kid, though I didn't really have an idea of what it was, or what it was for. It had so many buttons, keys, screens, and strings, which I loved to play with.

When I started playing clarinet, he would come over and jam on the guitar with me. He came to my recitals, and I still remember him telling me, "If you make a mistake, pretend nothing happened. The only way the audience will know is if you react to it." (This was after I stuck my tongue out and grimaced when screwing up a passage of music.)

I understood he was a guitarist and that he wrote music for film and television, but I had no idea how respected he was until I started working in the industry myself. I've met people all over the place—at music stores, performances, award shows, and schools, and they all say the same thing, more or less. His skill, work ethic, and talent as a musician were equally matched by his kindness, humility, and generosity as a person.

- Julian Troiano, nephew, singer; email to Ashley Collie, 2019

He was more than an uncle. He was very humble. As long as I can remember, he was a big part of our family. He was always there, picking us up for baseball, taking us to Wonderland, or the CNE. He wasn't pretentious; he always drove an older car, but he was generous. He took us shopping and took us out for meals. Julian and I were just kids. I saw him playing in the studio, but I was too young at the time to realize how big of a deal he was in the Canadian music industry. One night a few months before he died, I was with him at the hospital and I remember him asking me to take care of my brother, and to try hard and do well, and above all, to be there for our family. I was young, but even then I sensed that it was a special moment, that it was important for Uncle Donnie to say these words to me.

- Marcus Troiano, nephew; interview with Mark Doble,
  June 29, 2020

Domenic would routinely recount recent student recitals he had attended for Julian. He was genuinely proud. His considerate and generous nature was certainly not restricted to family.

In the early '90s, I went to work for Quality Records. Two of their European artists, KWS and Double-You, had huge dance hits: KWS with a song Donnie wrote entitled *Please Don't Go,* and Double-You with Donnie's *We All Need Love.* He had been calling Quality to collect his royalties, but had no luck. After a while, they wouldn't even take his calls. So, Donnie called me and asked if I could help him. I was so angry and embarrassed at Quality that they could do this to Domenic Troiano! I marched into the accountant's office and demanded Donnie's cheque right then and there or I would report him to all applicable authorities. I was prepared to get fired. He reluctantly handed me Donnie's cheque, which I personally delivered to him. He was so grateful he invited me to stay, and he played me all the new music he was working on.

In 1996, I got married to a studio owner in Calgary. I invited some of my recording artist clients, and of course I invited Donnie. He must have been diagnosed with prostate cancer by then, because he said he wasn't feeling well and wasn't going to be able to make the wedding. When he returned the RSVP, he included a cheque made out to me for a wedding present. The cheque was so large I couldn't accept it. It was the most anyone gave, more than even my very close relatives! I immediately called him and told him I couldn't accept it and that I was going to

rip up the cheque. His answer? "If you do, I'll never speak to you again." His friendship meant so much to me, I didn't defy him.
- Linda Nash, record executive; email to Frank Troiano, April 2020

Yet another example of Domenic paying it forward:

In 1997/98, I remember being excited about a young sixteen-year-old talent from Niagara Falls named Joel Zimmerman. He was working with a guy named The Funky Dread, who brought me some of his early music. I loved it, but cash at the time was scarce and I just didn't have the extra money to pay for the vinyl pressings. Donnie saw my excitement and cut me a cheque to pay for the first pressings and we released Joel Zimmerman's record. Had it not been for Domenic, maybe I wouldn't have been able to sign the record and release it. Joel Zimmerman many years later went on to become deadmau5, sold millions of albums, and toured the world, being the first Canadian artist to sell out the Rogers Centre.
- Asim Awesome Awan, founder—Awesome Productions & Management Inc.; email to Frank Troiano, April 2020

Domenic finally reached a point where he could be generous financially, and also with his time, even as the cancer progressed.

One afternoon, Paul and I met Donnie by chance and decided to go out for dim sum together. We nibbled and talked for hours, delighting in common memories and interests. We were stuffed and happy when we parted, and as we hugged goodbye, we vowed to have many more lunches and dinners together. However, shortly after that day, Donnie found out that his cancer had returned. We only had begun to explore our friendship, so I felt shy and reluctant to intrude on precious family and long-term friend time.
- Brenda Hoffert, manager—Lighthouse; email to Frank Troiano, April 2020

The outpouring of respect and love manifested itself in so many ways. But through it all, the diet, the exercise, the treatment, the hospitalizations, and even through the pain, there was always music.

I remember when he played at the Capitol Theatre on Yonge Street. I knew he was in a lot of pain and was having spasms. I never heard him play the way he played that night. I was so blown away by his performance. It was incredible and so moving. Whether the pain was transferred into his music or whatever—it's hard to explain.

- Rita Troiano, sister-in-law; interview with Mark Doble, July 7, 2020

I never knew him well but talent made him larger than life..to say the least. At a Rock and Roll Revival sponsored by CHUM Radio in 1999 Donny and I sat together in the dressing room before our respective performances. He with Bush and me with Mainline. Drummer Whitey Glan was nowhere to be found and Donny said to me...don't go anywhere Tony...you may be playing drums with us. Whitey did show up.. darn..lol...and all was well. But have to say...it would have been a treat. Many will strive to reach his level but...no one will surpass him! A true genius!

- Tony Nolasco, drummer, vocalist, McKenna Mendelsohn Mainline; email to Frank Troiano, March, 2021

Toronto-born jazz crooner Matt Dusk has had a hugely successful career recording and performing with some of the best musicians in the world. In 2004, Domenic was enlisted for Matt's debut album entitled TWO SHOTS, playing on two tracks: *Two Shots of Happy, One Shot of Sad* (Written by Bono and The Edge) and *Miracle*.

The White Ribbon Campaign is a global movement of men working to end violence against women and girls. It was formed by a group of pro-feminist men in London, Ontario, in November 1991 as a response to the École Polytechnique massacre of female students by Marc Lépine in 1989. It was a cause Domenic was committed to, performing a number of times in support. Former founder of the Canadian power trio Triumph, Rik Emmett performed with Domenic at one such occasion.

Domenic was a living legend to me. The evening of the 2004 White Ribbon gig, between the sound check, rehearsal, and the show, we went out for dinner to a local Thai restaurant. Although we knew Dom was battling cancer, he ate heartily, and chatted up the guys from the house band, the Dexters, as if they were all old friends. (They were.) There was no attitude, nothing awkward in the air. He made it easy for us to be hanging with him: he was just one of the guys in the band. That night, we jammed on George Harrison's *While My Guitar Gently Weeps*. And Domenic played his Strat like a house on fire. It is one of the treasured musical moments of my life.

- Rik Emmett, lead guitarist—Triumph; email to Frank Troiano, April 2020

Another internationally successful Canadian rock trio, The Tea Party, was founded and led by guitarist Jeff Martin. Martin recalls playing in a White Ribbon Campaign event with one of his musical heroes.

So, picture this. There's a very young boy in Windsor, Ontario. He's all of nine years old and the lead guitarist of his father's band, Brand X, gifts the boy a vinyl of an artist named Domenic Troiano, BURNIN' AT THE STAKE. Little did he know that a couple decades later, he would be sharing the same stage with Domenic. Toronto, the Phoenix Concert Hall, a benefit for the White Ribbon Campaign; this kid, lost for words concerning meeting one of his childhood inspirations. I recall the moment of sharing the stage with such a giant, simply exciting and mesmerising at the same time. I was aware he was still battling his sickness; the man was stoic, inspiring, and truly loving.

- Jeff Martin, singer, lead guitarist—The Tea Party; email to Frank Troiano, April 2020

Attending with Martin that same evening was Windsor guitarist Ken Koekstat, along with his son Grant.

Domenic was always so considerate about asking about Grant's progress in his battle with leukemia. I took Grant to meet Domenic at the Orbit Reunion and introduced him backstage. I was with the father of Jeff Martin from The Tea Party who had played bass in my band, Brand X. When Jeff was nine years old or so, I gave him a couple of Dom's LPs and told him, "When you can play these songs, you can call yourself a guitar player." I told Dom the story backstage and he asked Martin, "Well, did you get them down?" Jeff said, "Still working on them," and a big wide smile came over Domenic's face. Dom gave Grant a CD and signed it, along with his guitar pick. Grant and I attended all the Tribute shows.

- Ken Koekstat, guitarist, fan; email to Frank Troiano, April 2020

Jeremy Frey, a young man from Ann Arbor, Michigan, who took a great interest in Domenic's music, constructed a website (troianomusic.com), which is unquestionably the best online resource today on Domenic Troiano and his music. Jeremy maintained contact with him up until the end, even travelling to Canada on a number of occasions.

The Soul in the City performance (2003) was the one time I got to see Domenic perform, and he was in fine form. His guitar playing was still captivating live, and I'm grateful I got a taste of it that night. Domenic was a beautiful soul. He always had a kind word and was happy to share information I was hungry for. After his passing, many of his musical colleagues spoke about his warmth and class, and I'm thankful I got to spend a little time with Domenic and experience it for myself.

- Jeremy Frey, fan, musicologist; email to Frank Troiano, April 2020

In 1994, Tim Notter and Canadian rock superstar Alex Lifeson (Rush) opened a new club called "The Orbit Room" at 580A College Street in Toronto. Notter's friend and Capitol Records promotional rep Peter Taylor recalled encountering Domenic at The Orbit Room.

Tim Notter is my best friend and has been since we were seven. If you love good R & B music, you probably know Tim, the owner/operator/ musical director of Toronto's iconic Orbit Room, and my best friend. Tim opened The Orbit Room with our other guitar genius buddy Alex Lifeson, building it into the coolest club in Toronto. Donnie played The Orbit Room all the time. (Hey, if you can't play guitar yourself, the next best thing is hanging out with people who do!) Donnie was one of the nicest, most mellow cats I ever met in my life. A gentle man. Like Godfather 101, he didn't need to raise his voice. His Telecaster did that for him. Part of the thrill of getting to know your heroes is getting a "peek behind the curtain" at the real individual.

- Peter Taylor, promotional rep; email to Frank Troiano, June 2020

Movie executive Dan Frisch spent an evening in Toronto with Domenic, where they visited The Orbit Room. That evening Dan witnessed an amazing and memorable spontaneous expression of affection and regard for Domenic from none other than Alex Lifeson.

We walked into a club where upstairs a rock band was finishing a song. By the time we made it up the stairs, the band was about to start their next song. Suddenly, the lead guitarist interrupts the band and informs the audience a legend just walked into the room. He steps down from the stage and walks over to Dom, giving him a huge bear hug. After exchanging pleasantries, the guitarist returned to the stage and informed the audience that the legend was Domenic Troiano. Everyone turned to Dom and erupted into applause; he needed no more introduction than that. The two other band members bowed their respects as well. Confused, I asked Dom, "Who was that?" The band then started in with *Limelight*. The guitarist was Alex Lifeson, Geddy Lee was on bass and Neil Peart, drums. What a Rush!
-   Dan Frisch, movie executive; email to Frank Troiano, April 2020

Lou Pomanti was asked to start a house band at The Orbit Room, firmly rooted in the Toronto Sound made popular in the 1960s in clubs like the Club Bluenote. On November 11, 1994, the Dexters, with Lou (Pomanti) Dexter on keyboard, Bernie (LaBarge) Dexter on guitar, Pete (Cardinali) Dexter on Bass, and Mike (Sloski) Dexter on drums, made their debut. Domenic quickly became an *ex-officio* member, with a standing invitation to sit in with the group whenever he wanted. Domenic loved this informal arrangement and was very much at home with the Dexters.

In the '90s, Donnie would occasionally sit in with us (the Dexters) at The Orbit Room. Dexters' guitarist Bernie LaBarge was also a huge fan of everything Donnie, as was our good friend Alex Lifeson, who sat in with the Dexters almost every weekend. Donnie and Alex actually sat in together with Bernie and the band at one of The Orbit Room's anniversary parties, which coincided with owner Tim Notter's birthday bash. Sparks were flying! We ended up doing a lot of gigs together, like the White Ribbon Campaign, Soul in the City, and the Yorkville reunion

at The Guvernment where I actually got to be IN the Mandala for a night, with Roy Kenner on vocals and of course Domenic, playing all those great Mandala and Bush hits that had a big impact on my musical upbringing. I couldn't wipe the grin off my face for days.

- Peter Cardinali, bass guitarist—the Dexters; email to Frank Troiano, April 2020

The Lincolns are a fabulous Toronto based R & B outfit, founded by Bush alumnus Prakash John. Steve Ambrose was the original lead singer of the Lincolns, and paid tribute to Domenic's influence and encouragement.

As far as Dom and I go, I was a fan of his in Mandala, Bush, and his solo career. I only came on his radar August of '79, when I was chosen as the singer for Prakash John's band the Lincolns. That was a very exciting time for me, to play with world-class musicians, and be recognized by the artist community in Canada. Somehow, I got Dom's phone number and called him. I needed some advice about the music business. He was very communicative and never made me feel like a pain in the ass.

- Steve Ambrose, singer; email to Frank Troiano, June 2020

Danny Weis (Lou Reed, Alice Cooper, Rhinoceros) was playing guitar in the Lincolns and had known Domenic from his time in L.A. in the early 1970s.

I was invited by Prakash John to come up to Canada to join the Lincolns in 1980, and Dom would sit in with us at a few gigs around town. Dom was a highly respected guitarist, a gentle spirit, always had a smile, and he had a very unique style, especially when he used the Leslie speaker to get those amazing and soulful sounds.

- Danny Weis, guitarist; interview with Frank Troiano, May 2020

Dave Bingham is the former lead singer of the Ugly Ducklings, one of the more popular Toronto bands from the 1960s, who would often share bills with the Rogues or the Mandala. In his 2015 memoir *Noise from the North End: The Amazing Story of the Ugly Ducklings*, he recalled a conversation with Domenic in 1997 when the two of them were performing at a party to honour Pete Traynor for his contribution to Canadian music.

I mentioned to him how intimidated I had been, back in the day when we were playing on the same bills all the time. He grinned and told me how much he had enjoyed the Ducks and how he appreciated our energy and confidence and especially how much he had dug *Nothin'* when it had come out and that, in his opinion *Gaslight* was a Canadian classic. He told me that originality and imagination were the most important qualities in music and that, as far as he was concerned, we had what it took. And then he told me, quite seriously, that he had always admired Roger Mayne's guitar playing in the Ducks! I was floored and thanked him immensely.

- Dave Bingham, *Noise from the North End: The Amazing Story of the Ugly Ducklings*, FriesenPress, 2015

In 1999, Domenic and the Dexters performed at a rock and roll revival show at the Warehouse in Toronto.

He wasn't touring at this time and I really hadn't seen him perform live until a club I was working with, The Guvernment/The Warehouse, had a night of music from the '60s and '70s bands, and Dom performed. I forget the name of the evening. Wow, my eyes popped out, crystal guitar sounds exploded in my head. Such a clean player—he was in control of his guitar.

- Joanne Smale, publicist; email to Frank Troiano, May 2020

Rob Bowman was the emcee at the "Soul in the City" shows in Toronto in November 2000 and 2003.

It was at the second show where Domenic came out with the Mandala and Bush alumnus Roy Kenner and played a searing version of Sam Cooke's *A Change is Gonna Come* that left people gasping for air. Of course, his guitar playing was phenomenal, but beyond the exigencies of his awe-inspiring technique, it was his radiant humanity that came bursting out of the speakers that night. I remember standing at the side of the stage, shaking my head, thinking how lucky I was to know this man.

- Rob Bowman, writer, professor; email to Frank Troiano, May 2020

Another of Domenic's friends, Marvyn Williams, recalls the joy of seeing Domenic at The Orbit Room.

At the gig at a College Street lounge in 2004, Domenic was jamming with his band. Between sets, Domenic shared about his cancer. At the time, I was drinking heavily. I shared with him that I had the feeling that my life was going to be involved in a new journey. Domenic said to me, "Marv, whatever that journey is, just remember three things: live it with passion, do not be afraid, and stay the course." Domenic was a *good* friend, a role model, and someone you could just sit down and have a one-on-one intimate conversation with. Domenic's legacy in the music industry, that relationship, taught me that anything I want to accomplish is right there in front of me. I can still hear his voice. "Just relax, have patience, follow the course, and remember: *We all Need Love.*"

- Marvyn Williams, friend; email to Frank Troiano, April 2020

Near the end of Donnie's life, the Dexters were doing a gig at The Phoenix, which was around the corner from the hospital where Donnie was. All four of us walked over. When we got there, he was slumped over in a chair, barely showing any sign of life. But I swear to God, by the time we were there for ten minutes talking about music and the old days, the old Donnie came back. He perked right up and was so animated. He started to look tired again after awhile, and we all gave him a kiss and left. That was the last time I saw Domenic Troiano.

- Lou Pomanti, producer, arranger, composer, keyboard—
  the Dexters; email to Frank Troiano, April 2020

Guitarist and close friend Bernie LaBarge has many heartfelt recollections of his times with Domenic, but in particular made note of the fact that Domenic only joined in to play when he was invited. While he loved to play, he no longer needed the spotlight and was more eager that his friends would have their chance to shine.

I have a pet peeve about musicians who hound you to get up and play with the band, (especially when they yell it into your ear in the middle of a song). I find it obtrusive. Never in a million years would Donnie have asked to get up and play. He came to see the band. Donnie was a

class act through and through. He came to see me in the studio when I was recording my first album in 1983. When I asked if he'd like to play on a track he said to me, "You've been waiting for a long time to do this, Bernie. You don't need me to play."

I've never told anyone this, but just a few months before Donnie's final trip to the hospital, he called me one morning after a benefit we had played together the previous night. After telling me how generous I was to let him play (as if), he said to me, "Bernie, sometimes I don't think you realize how good a guitar player you really are." The memories of the years I spent as a pupil of this man flooded through my mind. As soon as I hung up the phone with Donnie, I called my mom and told her what he had said to me. She cried.

- Bernie LaBarge, guitarist; interview with Mark Doble, November 2020

By mid 2003 the cancer returned, becoming more burdensome by year's end. Additional treatment in Ireland was ineffective. Domenic and his family understood by now that his time was short. This made the May 25, 2004, live performance at The Orbit Room that much more precious.

After years of bugging him to headline at The Orbit Room, he finally gave in and on Tuesday, May 25, 2004, with Doug Riley at the B-3, Ben Riley on the tubs, and Howard Ayee on the electric bass guitar, he played the songs that he wanted to play. It was the last performance of his tremendous career. It was full circle for him. Right back to where he started. A little live music room with a Hammond organ on the second floor of a busy street in Toronto. At least this time he didn't have to lug his Tele and amp on the streetcar to get home. It was a dream come true for me to have him play at my club. I'll never forget that evening!

- Tim Notter, co-owner—The Orbit Room; email to Frank Troiano, May 2020

Thankfully, we have a beautiful limited edition CD, DOMENIC TROIANO'S LAST PERFORMANCE MAY 25, 2004, with the proceeds dedicated to Toronto East General Hospital. The band that evening featured Doug Riley on Hammond B-3, Howard Ayee on bass, Ben Riley on drums, and Domenic Troiano on guitar and lead vocals. The CD contains seven songs, four of which are Troiano originals: *Lonely Girl, Turn Down, Burnin' at the Stake*, and *Eleanora Fagan*. Also included were *Mercy Mercy Mercy, Melting Pot*, and *The Stumble*. Finally, and surprisingly, Domenic's first "live" album! Perhaps Domenic sensed that this was his last performance. Because that night he truly was phenomenal!

I also attended Dom's last performance at The Orbit Room on May 25, 2004. It is hard to put into words what I witnessed that night—one of the finest performances that I had ever seen in a club setting.
- Scotty Brown, roadie; interview with Frank Troiano, May 16, 2020

Donnie asked me to join in on bass. It was an amazing night of unbelievable solos and great performances all around. I knew that Donnie was in great pain from his tumour, and he could barely get up the stairs at the club. He was incredibly brave and gave the performance of a lifetime.
- Howard Ayee, bass guitarist; email to Frank Troiano, April 2020

Domenic seemed hesitant and slightly tentative. Our hearts went out to him. My immediate reaction was: "I hope they take it easy on him, and that he doesn't overexert himself." Doug was having none of that. He ripped into his first solo like it would be his last. You could see Dom straightening up, as if to say, "So, that's how it's going to be, eh?" Doug was taking no prisoners and the circle of keyboard players in the middle of the room by the bar would double over and slap each other, as Doug took the tune continually one level higher and higher. You could see the swagger come back into Dom. By the time his solo came around, he answered in kind. It gives me goosebumps thinking about it. For the remainder of that set, his cancer was vanquished, he was the master once again. Doug had done a beautiful thing for Dom and us. He stirred up the passion in Dom and gave us a night we will never forget.
- Lance Anderson, producer; email to Frank Troiano, April 2020

It must have been amazing, how music could bring Domenic back to life, even for one more special evening among friends, familiar tunes, and

246

that guitar, fingers flying across the frets—dancing to their own rhythm, straight from his heart and soul.

Despite their divorce, Domenic and Shawne Jackson remained close, and there was a tremendous bond of love that endured to the very end.

During his last hospital stay of nine weeks, I stayed with him every night. I think Frankie joined me once or twice—otherwise the overnights were handled by me. We had a twenty-four-hour family vigil with Donnie. A family member was with him twenty-four/seven while he was hospitalized. No one will ever love me like Donnie. There will never be another one like that for me, and I will never love anyone like I loved Donnie.
  -   Shawne Jackson; interview with Mark Doble, June 19, 2020

We will not conduct an in-depth analysis of Domenic Troiano's religious beliefs. However, the words of his long-time friend Sal Consiglio provide an indication of a spiritual dimension to Domenic's life.

One last thing in May of 2004, when Donnie realized that his cancer might be coming back he asked me to be his sponsor for his confirmation, which took place at St. Norbert's Catholic Church, as he had not been confirmed when he was a teenager. Dom knew that his mom Pasqua had always felt sad and guilty that he had not been confirmed, so he basically got confirmed in order to make his mom happy, and perhaps he was also thinking about his mortality. This process meant that I had become his godfather/sponsor even though he was much older than me.

The day after Dom died, I went to the house to give my condolences, and his mom said, "Parlava sempre di voi" (He spoke always of you). This meant so much to me. Donnie was my hero, my friend, a brother I never had, a godson, and a musician's musician. I miss him so much! Love you Donnie.
  -   Sal Consiglio, close friend; interview with Frank Troiano, April 2020

Any reader raised in the Church will understand the significance of making things right through the act of confirmation. Domenic was born into an

Italian Roman Catholic family. And while one could view references in the lyrics to *We All Need Love*, *Peace of Mind*, and *Look Up* as "Christian," or at least "spiritual" in their acknowledgment of a higher power, Domenic would never presume to preach.

Like everyone, Domenic had his flaws. And although he was disciplined and had limits, he lived the rock and roll lifestyle for decades. However, when one views the testimony of virtually everyone he knew, Domenic Troiano's actions spoke louder than the words to any song or belief system. The measure of grace, patience, love, and acceptance that he consistently administered to others is profound and entirely consistent with Christ's teaching in Mark 12:31 to *"love your neighbour as yourself."* At the end of his life, Domenic Troiano was grateful, not bitter, and he was at peace with God.

John Harris relates his last visit with Domenic:

When I visited his house after the family informed me that the end was near, medical staff informed me that he could no longer speak. But when I entered his room and told him that a scholarship was being created in his name to support education for new guitarists, he turned his head with the biggest smile he could muster and whispered, "John, that's fantastic." He passed away weeks later knowing his memory would endure. He was the best.
- John Harris, Harris Institute; email to Frank Troiano, April 2020

The level of affection and consideration extended to colleagues who were willing to travel across Canada in order to say goodbye.

The last time I saw Domenic was several weeks before his death. I got a call from my dear pal Joanne Smale, the publicist. She said, "I wanted to tell you that Donnie is now partially paralyzed, and he's at home in hospice. He won't be coming out to Vancouver anymore, so if you want to see him before he passes, get on a plane." I took her advice and did. I spoke with Robert Charles-Dunne, and he agreed that he wanted to join me. He came in from London and we both went to see him together. Donnie said, "So, who are you in town with, Paulie?" I said, "Nobody,

man. I heard from Smale that you wouldn't be coming to see me, so I came to see you, buddy!" Then Donnie said, "You mean to tell me that nobody's paying you and you got off your couch in Kits and flew on your dime to Toronto in the winter to just see me?" I said, "Yep, I'd heard that you weren't going to come see me anymore, and I love ya, buddy—and I wanted to see you and thank you for being my friend."

- Paul Gruenwald, promo rep—El Mocambo Records;
  email to Frank Troiano, April 2020

Domenic did not want family and friends feeling sorry for him. He was at peace, but still determined to pass on something positive—music, encouragement, a special kindness—a love for friends and family that was true and pure.

Several years later while visiting Toronto, I was staying at Doc's (Doug Riley's) house downtown and he told me that Donnie had been very ill and didn't have much time left. We drove up to Richmond Hill to say goodbye. He was very weak, but awake and alert. I got to hold his hand for a moment and tell him how much I had always admired him. Doc spent a little time with him, they were very close … two kindred spirits and two of the most gifted musicians I'd ever known. Doc and I left the Troiano house and drove back downtown to Doc's place. A few hours later we got a phone call from Bernie LaBarge, telling us Dom had passed … we both cried.

- David Clayton-Thomas, lead vocalist; email to Frank Troiano,
  April 2020

It is hard to write about these things. Visiting a loved one who is suffering is intensely personal and private. And the visiting, especially at the very end, is usually and understandably restricted to immediate family. But for the Troianos it was different. So intent on having a positive impact, friends were welcomed into his home right up until the last possible moment.

This writer has a personal recollection: May 24, 2005, the day before Domenic passed, Frank and Rita insisting that a visit would *not* be an intrusion. Standing by Domenic's bed that Monday afternoon, three words came to mind—courage, grace, and love.

After the visit, heading home that afternoon, alone in the car for at least an hour, putting on some music for the drive. And suddenly out of the speakers, Domenic was playing *Eleanora Fagan*, the slow and sweet instrumental—to the listener the emotions are profound. There are no words.

Final Concert at Orbit Room—Ben Riley, Domenic Troiano, Doug Riley, Howard Ayee, 2004 (Photo: Gary Taylor)

CHAPTER 12

YOUR PAST IS A PART OF YOU

"Everybody has a story—Everybody has the right
To find their own place between the darkness and the light
And everybody needs an answer to a question in their mind
Everybody needs a purpose—They'll spend a lifetime trying to find."
(*Your Past Is a Part of You,* lyrics by Domenic Troiano)

Domenic Troiano, BJ Cook, David Clayton-Thomas, Brenda Russell, Doug Riley,
Shawne Jackson-Troiano, David Foster, 1997 (Troiano Family Archive)

We lose people. It's a fact of life and an essential part of the human condition. And I've lived long enough to have lost quite a few, including very close family and dear friends. Each of them leaves a small imprint in their own shape on the walls of your heart, like an internal monument. And you can go there and visit with them forever. Some fade over time, but some remain deep and comforting forever. I often think of Donnie when I walk through that gallery and think of the privilege and honour I was given in knowing him.

- Bob Ezrin, producer; email to Frank Troiano, June 2020

There have been numerous posthumous tributes, benefits, scholarships, and awards that keep Domenic's memory alive at least in the hearts of his many admirers, not to mention the thousands of dollars that have been raised for worthy charities in Domenic's name. Marcus Troiano shared that it wasn't until after he passed that he fully understood the impact of his Uncle Donnie's legacy.

Even fifteen years after Domenic's passing, the ever-articulate Roy Kenner reflected:

I realize now what an interesting bond we had. It didn't matter how long we had been away from each other, because we were always in touch. We were on the same page on so many things. Donnie liked having someone he trusted, with whom he could share things, and sometimes deep personal thoughts other than music. So many of our conversations seemed to commence with one of us asking rhetorically, "Do you believe this shit?" or, "What do you think about...?" The fact we had that kind of relationship for so long is special to me. Over those forty-one years, I can think of three issues that I had with him. But none of these ever resulted in our breaking that bond with each other. And when you think of it, forty-one years and only three issues of disagreement—that's pretty damn good! We were truly brothers.

- Roy Kenner, lead vocalist; interview with Mark Doble, July 4, 2020

Jim Norris, publisher of *Canadian Music Magazine*, served with Domenic as a member of Metronome and was instrumental in the establishment of the scholarship in his honour.

In 1999, I became a board member of Metronome, the proposed Music City on Toronto's waterfront. Domenic was a board member emeritus, and I saw him regularly at meetings at Harris Institute. He was a constant and enthusiastic crusader for the Metronome cause. John Harris and I came up with the idea of establishing a tribute to Domenic's accomplishments, which became the Domenic Troiano Guitar Scholarship. John and I visited Domenic at his house shortly before his passing and in a very emotional visit, we showed Domenic the logo and told him about our plans for the Scholarship. I will never forget the smile on his face.

- Jim Norris, publisher—*Canadian Music Magazine*; email to
  Frank Troiano, June 2020

Through the scholarship program, one $10,000 scholarship or two $5,000 scholarships were to be presented annually to a Canadian guitarist or guitarists who were pursuing postsecondary guitar education. As soon as friends, fans, musicians, relatives, and music industry personnel found out about the Troiano Fund, dozens of contributions were sent in. Over a nine-year period, just under $100,000 was raised and twelve awards were given out to aspiring guitarists.

John and Jim formed a scholarship selection committee of trustees composed of Kevin Breit, Rik Emmett, Jim Norris, Bernie LaBarge, Shawne Jackson-Troiano, Frank Troiano, John Harris, and Alex Lifeson.

To this day, I have a deep love and admiration for a man who truly knew the meaning of soul. I am proud to be a humble part of his enduring influence.

- Alex Lifeson, lead guitarist—Rush; media release—
  Troiano Awards, May 2015

The Troiano Awards ran until 2015. It was decided at that time to wind down the fund and the remaining money ($7,700) was sent to the Unison

Benevolent Fund, a charity providing counselling and relief to professional music-makers in times of hardship, illness, or economic difficulties.

In the late '90s, Domenic became a patron of Toronto East General Hospital. He wanted to give back to the community of East York where he was raised, and the hospital had provided medical care for his family and friends over the years.

He donated substantial monies and his time to help the hospital in their fundraising initiatives. While attending the various meetings, he befriended Michael MacMillan, CEO of Alliance Atlantis, Mark Dailey, Saul Korman, Eugene Levy, Pinball Clemons, and many other volunteers/patrons. His involvement culminated in the seventy-fifth anniversary of the Hospital Major Fundraiser in 2004. Domenic was honoured as a "Citizen of Distinction" later that year by the hospital.

After Domenic's death in 2005, the Toronto East General Hospital (TEGH) reached out to Shawne Jackson-Troiano and the Troiano family and suggested that an annual event be established as a tribute to Domenic Troiano.

Domenic felt strongly about his involvement in supporting the fundraising efforts of the TEGH Foundation and he gave freely of his time over the past several years. The Troiano family is very proud and honoured to be presenting this very special event, and we know that Domenic would be very touched by this celebration of his musical legacy. The night of April 20 will be an evening of music, dancing, food, family, friends, and sharing of "Donnie" stories and memories.
-   Frank Troiano; Toronto East General Hospital—Tribute to
    Domenic Troiano, 2006

The first tribute was held on April 20, 2006, at Joe Badali's Ristorante on Front Street in Toronto, and hosted by John Donabie. The house band was comprised of Bernie LaBarge, Howard Ayee, Whitey Glan, Michael Sloski, and Doug Riley. Featured performers were Haydain Neale (Jacksoul), Justin Abedin, Daniel Mical, Sharon Lee Williams, Joan Besen, David Celia, David McMorrow, Jay Jackson, Shawne Jackson-Troiano, Bill

King, Michael Burgess, Roy Kenner, George Olliver, Gregory Vitale, Eric Mercury, Adrien Breda, Grant Smith, and David Clayton-Thomas.

The first winners of the Domenic Troiano Scholarship (Lucas Haneman and Aimée Piché) were presented with their awards. The event raised over $60,000, and the Troiano family designated the proceeds to the new Child and Adolescent Mental Health Service at TEGH.

A second tribute was held on May 29, 2007, at the newly opened and fully renovated "Palais Royale Ballroom" on the Toronto lakeshore. Jay Jackson emceed, and the house band was comprised of Bernie LaBarge, Howard Ayee, Paul DeLong, Grant Slater, and Doug Riley. Featured performers were Roy Kenner, Julian Troiano, Colina Phillips, Gregory Vitale, Sharon Lee Williams, Cal Dodd, Prakash John, John Finley and the Checkmates, Wayne St. John, Ali Slaight, Shawne and Jay Jackson, Bill King, and David Clayton-Thomas. About $50,000 was raised, and the Troiano family designated the proceeds to the Minimally Invasive Surgery Program at TEGH.

The third and final tribute took place on May 15, 2008, at the Palais Royale. The occasion was emceed by Mark Dailey and the house band was comprised of Bernie LaBarge, Howard Ayee, Paul DeLong, Rob Gusevs, and Grant Slater. Featured performers were Debbie Fleming, Danny Marks, Roy Kenner, Gregory Vitale, Julian Troiano, Sharon Lee Williams, Shawne and Jay Jackson, Colina Phillips, Doug Mallory, Steve Kennedy, Bill King, Shakura S'Aida, the Dexters, Motherlode, Neil Donnell, Prakash and Jordan John and the Lincolns, the Jay Douglas Band, and the Nite Gang. Slaight Communications (Gary Slaight) promoted the evening and coordinated the production of a commemorative CD of the evening's performances.

The limited edition commemorative CD, WE ALL NEED LOVE (Tribute to Domenic Troiano) was produced by Shawne Jackson-Troiano, and featured the live performances from the May 15, 2008, tribute evening. Like any Troiano performance, the musicianship and renditions are masterful—the supporting band represented a "who's who" of the Toronto Sound—Bernie LaBarge, Howard Ayee, Paul DeLong, Rob Gusevs, and Grant Slater. Notable performances that evening included Julian Troiano's *Wildflower*, Roy Kenner's rendition of Gershwin's *Summertime*, Prakash's son Jordan John on the country classic *I Fall to Pieces*, and Shawne Jackson's original *Open Up Your Heart*.

Julian Troiano is a professional singer in Toronto—justifiably proud of his uncle, and a successful artist in his own right. Music historian and owner of the indie label Other People's Music, Jan Haust tells of a chance meeting with Julian.

August 2018: Got on the St. Clair streetcar heading west from Yonge, sitting across from this young man. After a couple blocks of looking out the window, I hear "Excuse me, are you in the music business?" from the fellow. Surprised, I say "Well, no, not really; more a music archivist these days. Why do you believe I'm in the music business?" "That sticker on your shirt pocket" he politely laughed. I look down and ... shit, I've forgotten to remove the "Universal Music Canada VISITOR" security sticker from my meeting at their offices an hour earlier. I'd been up to chat with the UMG execs about distribution for the Roman Records Presents: "The Toronto Sound of The Sixties" vinyl series, including a rare Mandala/Five Rogues record project. The research that Dom and I had begun together back at that Yorkville chicken shack so many years ago was finally coming to light. So, the kid and I chatted a bit ... he was a musician, and it turned out his uncle had been a guitarist and had even known Jackie Shane in the '60s on Yonge Street! His uncle's name? Domenic Troiano! His name: Julian Troiano, one of Frank's sons. And there for a brief second was that same powerful, brooding gaze with the lightning humour, self assured and understated all at the same time. His quick smile lit up that streetcar just like Dom's would've as I said goodbye. Got off at my Winona stop full of goosebumps and in a daze.

- Jan Haust, music historian; email to Frank Troiano, June 2020

Musician, US booking agent, and manager Randy Schwoerer enjoyed a long relationship working with Domenic.

I was in Los Angeles, working as an agent, artist manager, record producer, and USO show producer. I was meeting with Bernie Solomon on a record deal when I noticed a picture of Domenic on his table. I explained that Domenic was one of my guitar heroes. After we shared

stories, he commented that he thought Domenic and I would like each other. Several weeks later, Domenic called and a warm voice on the phone said, "Randy, Bernie thinks you and I would get along, can we talk business?"

Our first meeting was in Calgary, where Domenic was performing. As I watched him, the spotlight hit the stage, he started to play—we knew we were in way over our heads! I think I remember saying something like: "Damn, he is from another planet and I have no idea how to help him. HE'S THE REAL DEAL!"

After the show, Domenic and his brother Frank took us out to an all-night Chinese restaurant. He and Frank immediately made me feel comfortable and at home. It is a special memory because our topics ranged from his life on the road with major artists, our experience with bands in the Midwest building regional success, but most of all our shared love of family and what we valued in life.

Within a year, Domenic became part of our family, staying at our home numerous times. The first night in our home, Donnie stayed up playing guitar after we all called it a day. The next morning, I found my four-year-old son, Aaron, strumming on one of Donnie's BC Rich guitars, each made specifically for Domenic. I immediately yelled, "Aaron, no!" Donnie walked out of his room and said, "That's OK, he's digging it. Let him jam on that one." Eight years later, when our family visited Donnie, he spent an hour or two each night teaching guitar technique that Aaron has used his entire career. The week ended with us all at the studio as Donnie finished an episode of *Night Heat*. All of his guitars were on the floor and Aaron was told to enjoy them and tell Donnie which one he liked best. Donnie was patient and always willing to encourage others.

Years later, I was in Toronto and called Donnie to have lunch. We got together and talked about the road we shared. Prior to that, I had not known about his medical issues but he explained it was under control and he was enjoying life. He reached into his bag and pulled out two CDs. I knew the songs very well, for they were from the time period I had worked with Donnie. He said, "Read the credits." My name was listed as a "special thanks", and I cried.

My wife and I spent two days at the hospital with Donnie on his final stay there. We laughed, cried, and shared the love that was rooted in our relationship. We were and still are family.

- Randy Schwoerer, musician, manager, booking agent; email to
  Frank Troiano, June 2020

The National Jazz Awards were held at the Phoenix Theatre in Toronto on June 21, 2005. The executive director, Bill King, arranged for a celebration and tribute to Domenic Troiano. An all-star band comprised of Roy Kenner, Prakash John, Whitey Glan, Bernie LaBarge, Rik Emmett, Jeff Healey, Rob Gusevs, and Steve Kennedy performed three Troiano originals. Frank Troiano accepted the tribute on behalf of Domenic's family and related that Domenic would have been particularly touched by this recognition from the world of jazz.

A Tribute to Domenic Troiano
Reception and Plaque Dedication

In late July of 2013, the Toronto East General Hospital held a plaque unveiling and reception in memory of Domenic Troiano. Guests included members of the Domenic Troiano Tribute organizing committee, TEGH patrons, and hospital staff. Speeches were followed by a ribbon cutting and unveiling of the Domenic Troiano Plaque celebrating his contributions to patient care in the East York community.

Domenic was a long-time supporter of Metronome Canada. The foundation was founded by John Harris and a number of supporters in the 1990s. Its mission statement read:

To integrate, educate, celebrate, and promote Canada's music, and to transform a heritage landmark on Toronto's waterfront into an international symbol of Canada's cultural self-determination.

John Harris remembers:

Domenic was a strong supporter and contributor to Harris Institute since its beginning in 1989. He did more guest lectures than anyone in

the school's history. Some terms he was a guest in two or three courses, due to his breadth of experience and knowledge. His Leslie speaker cabinet is now used regularly in our studios. On each visit, he would ask me about the progress of Metronome.

He became a major contributor and an inspiration to me. At a fundraiser we did at the Molson Amphitheatre, Domenic arrived with a guitar to be donated for the silent auction. He was in significant discomfort and pain. When I suggested that he go home, he insisted on staying to the end of the event four hours later to sign the guitar. His dedication was second to none. That was his last public appearance before he passed away at home months later. After his death, his board status was changed to: Board Member—Emeritus.

- John Harris, Harris Institute; email to Frank Troiano, June 2020

SOCAN Awards

The Society of Composers, Authors, and Music Publishers of Canada (SOCAN) is a Canadian performance rights organization that represents the performing rights of more than 135,000 songwriters, composers, and music publishers.

In 2010, a SOCAN award was presented posthumously to Domenic Troiano, Pasqua Music, for *Dancin' Fool* co-written with Burton Cummings (performed by the Guess Who), commemorating more than 100,000 radio performances in Canada.

This was Domenic's second SOCAN award. In 2000, his single *Just as Bad as You* (performed by Shawne Jackson) was also recognized for receiving more than 100,000 radio performances in Canada.

Induction of *Opportunity* by the Mandala into the Canadian Songwriters Hall of Fame

In September 2019, the Canadian Songwriters Hall of Fame notified the Troiano family that *Opportunity*, written by Domenic Troiano and performed by the Mandala, was being inducted into the Hall of Fame along with five other classic Canadian songs. The special event was to take place at the Phoenix Concert Theatre on November 21, 2019. The press release was as follows:

CELEBRATING TORONTO'S MUSIC SCENE THROUGH THE DECADES:

Toronto, ON (October 22, 2019)—The Canadian Songwriters Hall of Fame (CSHF) today announced the induction of six influential songs from the Toronto music scenes of the 1960s, '70s, and '80s, that will be celebrated at a special concert event taking place on Thursday, November 21 at Toronto's Phoenix Concert Theatre. Songs included are *Let Your Backbone Slide* (Maestro Fresh-Wes), *Rise Up* (Parachute Club), *(Make Me Do) Anything You Want* (A Foot in Coldwater), *Calling Occupants of Interplanetary Craft* (Klaatu), *Opportunity* (the Mandala), and *I Would Be the One* (Kensington Market). The newest song inductions will be celebrated at an industry and public event titled DECADES: Toronto Sound of the '60s, '70s, and '80s.

"We're very excited to honour some of the amazing songs that were inspired and reflect the unique city of Toronto from a group of talented songwriters who bring different perspectives from three distinct decades," said Vanessa Thomas, Executive Director of the Canadian Songwriters Hall of Fame.

The first song inducted was *Opportunity*, and was introduced by the Hall as follows:

A fine example of the late 1960s Canadian soul music nicknamed "the Toronto Sound," the Mandala's high-octane 1967 single *Opportunity* was penned by and featured the celebrated late Italian-Canadian guitarist, Domenic Troiano. *Opportunity* was the debut single for the Mandala, the five-piece house band at the Club Bluenote in Toronto, where they backed US soul and R & B performers. The Mandala also performed at Ronnie Hawkins' talent-rich the Hawk's Nest, before landing gigs to capacity crowds in late 1966 at wildly popular Hollywood clubs such as Whiskey-a-Go-Go and the Hullabaloo. The 45-rpm single of *Opportunity*, with *Lost Love* on the B side, was released in late January 1967. It immediately entered Toronto's CHUM chart at number forty, and rose quickly to number three by February 20.

That evening, *Opportunity* was performed by the song's original singer, George Olliver, and backed by a house band led by David Gray, which also included Shawne Jackson-Troiano and Cathy Young on background vocals. Before the performance of the song, Frank Troiano and his sister Gina Troiano appeared onstage to accept the Hall of Fame Award.

Blaine Pritchett was close to Domenic for many decades. We have referenced many of his memories throughout this volume; however, at the conclusion of his interview for this book, his recollections were particularly heartfelt, and representative of the manner in which Domenic's legacy and memory continue to live on in the hearts of others.

If it wasn't for Domenic Troiano, I either would have been in prison or ended up dead. I was a Cabbagetown kid and it was easy for us to get into trouble in those days. Donnie kept me on the straight and narrow. He legitimately cared about people. It was just a natural thing for him to do. He cared about their welfare. When he talked to people, it was with respect, whether you were a little kid starting out to play or whether you were Joe Pass. He never looked down his nose at any musician. He had no ego. Donnie always found the good side of everybody. He listened to a guy play and went, "Wow, that guy can play."

He's the best friend I've ever had—he made my life better than it could ever possibly be. I loved the man. There was nobody better than Donnie for me. I'm not talking about how great a guitar player he was; there are a lot of great guitar players; I'm talking about him as a human being. He saved my life. He did. I was headed down a real bad path, and Donnie turned me around. He always looked out for me. He made sure that I was OK. Not a day goes by when I don't think about Donnie.

- Blaine Pritchett, sound technician; interview with Mark Doble, July 21, 2020

Domenic Troiano Legacy—Nicholas Jennings

Toronto author and Canadian rock music historian Nicholas Jennings has written extensively on Canadian music from the '60s and '70s and is possibly the foremost expert on the origins of the Toronto Sound. Nick kindly agreed to document the various tributes that have been placed in various historic locations in downtown Toronto to commemorate the Toronto Sound as well as Domenic's significant contribution to this great music.

Domenic Troiano at the Friar's Music Museum

The Friar's Music Museum opened in June 2018 on the second floor of the Shoppers Drug Mart flagship store at 279 Yonge Street (the site of Friar's Tavern, one of Toronto's most important live music venues). The museum, the first of its kind in Toronto, is the brainchild of Mark Garner, executive director of the Downtown Yonge BIA, and curators Jan Haust and Nicholas Jennings decided that the museum's first exhibit be devoted to Yonge Street's most influential musicians of the 1960s—chief among them is Domenic Troiano, who performed with such popular bands as the Disciples, the Rogues, and the Mandala. Visitors to the museum are greeted by three display cabinets full of rare Troiano memorabilia. The prized items, all generously loaned by the Troiano family, are the guitarist's Lou Myles-designed striped Mandala suit jacket, his Basque navy beret, his Fender Deluxe amplifier, and, most significantly, his 1963 Fender Telecaster electric guitar. The latter, whose bluesy wail helped define the Toronto Sound, remained Troiano's instrument of choice through his years of international stardom with Bush, the James Gang, and The Guess Who. Enriched by these Troiano artefacts, the Friar's Music Museum earned a Public History award nomination at the 2019 Heritage Toronto Awards.

Domenic Troiano in the Yonge Street Music Mural

In 2018, the Downtown Yonge BIA unveiled a massive mural featuring the music legends of Yonge Street. Painted on the south side of the Toronto Community Housing building at 423 Yonge by artist Adrian Hayles, the mural depicts over a dozen performers, including the Band, David Clayton-Thomas, Rush, Carole Pope, and Salome Bey, as well as such key venues as the Gasworks, Brown Derby, and Piccadilly Tube. The painting of Domenic Troiano and his group the Mandala has a place of pride in the twenty-two-storey-tall mural, showing the band of brothers in their striped suits reaching heavenward ecstatically. This is entirely fitting, as the Mandala were fixtures at Yonge Street's Hawk's Nest, while the group's predecessor, the Rogues, was the house band at the nearby Bluenote club. This was the second music mural the BIA sponsored featuring Hayles' depictions of famous Yonge Street musicians. The first, on the north side of the same building, features venues like Le Coq D'Or and such artists as Gordon Lightfoot, Dianne Brooks, Glenn Gould, Jackie Shane, and Ronnie Hawkins. There's also a Troiano connection to that initial mural, which received a Public History award nomination at the 2017 Heritage Toronto Awards: it was with Hawkins that the revered guitarist got his start playing on Yonge Street.

Domenic Troiano and the Yonge Street Heritage Plaques

The names of Domenic Troiano and two of his bands are enshrined in a pair of historical Toronto plaques. In December 2016, Heritage Toronto and the Downtown Yonge BIA unveiled a plaque for the Bluenote, the after-hours club that was the city's home to rhythm & blues. The plaque includes an image of the Mandala's album SOUL CRUSADE, and mentions the Troiano-penned hit song *Opportunity*, while stating that Troiano, George Olliver, and their bandmates, then known as the Rogues, were one of the Bluenote's house bands. Olliver performed *Opportunity* at the plaque's unveiling ceremony. Also performing that special night were such other Bluenote regulars as Shawne and Jay Jackson, John Finley, and Joanne Brooks. Two years later, Heritage Toronto and the Downtown Yonge BIA unveiled a plaque for Le Coq D'Or, the popular bar that featured some of the biggest names in blues, rock, and pop, including rockabilly legend Ronnie Hawkins. The plaque lists Troiano's the Mandala as one of the local bands featured upstairs in the Hawk's Nest. During his time on Yonge Street, Troiano also performed many times downstairs in Le Coq D'Or with Hawkins as a member of Robbie Lane's Disciples. The installed plaques for these Troiano-related sites can be found at each of the venue's original locations: 333 Yonge (Le Coq D'Or) and 372 Yonge (the Bluenote).

- Nicholas Jennings, author, music historian; submission to Frank Troiano, July 2020

The Tele

Prior to its installation at the Friar's Music Museum in 2018, guitarist Bernie LaBarge was granted custody of Domenic's legendary 1963 Fender Telecaster guitar.

In 2006, during one of several Troiano tribute shows, I got to play Donnie's legendary 1963 Fender Telecaster. After the concert, Frank Troiano asked me to keep the guitar. In my heart I know that the guitar will always belong to Donnie. No one will ever make it sing like he did, but I'm thrilled to be its caretaker. Thank you, Frank. That guitar looks like a prototype of every guitar that came after. It was a living, breathing workbench! It oozes the Toronto Sound, although only Donnie's fingers could massage it to perfection. At some point, I think the guitar should be in a music museum. Whenever I play, I always have in the back of my mind "WWDD?" (What Would Donnie Do?) Donnie was my hero and my friend. I'm so incredibly lucky. I will honour his memory to my last breath.

- Bernie LaBarge, guitarist; interview with Mark Doble, November 2020

Terry David Mulligan

Terry David Mulligan, actor, radio host, and television personality, worked closely with Canadian musicians in the 1970s and knew Domenic very well. His recent remembrance is reflective of that of so many others.

Domenic Troiano was as fine a human being as I've met. The music business has always been infested with movers and shakers, cons and shysters, egos and golden-tongued liars. Dreamers and schemers. Domenic Troiano was none of those. Imagine my astonishment to not only find a real live human being at the end of my microphone, but a true artist. He could write memorable songs, sing his face off (even if he didn't think he was that great), and best of all could play a guitar like few others. And he knew the history of music. Not just rock and blues, but classical and jazz. He knew where his roots came from and had no problem schooling me along the way. What I remember most was the guy. What a guy. He basically made me realize that you didn't have to be a dick to be in the music business. That there was another way to meet it, feel it, and deal with it—with kindness and humour. Loved the man. Miss him still today.

- Terry David Mulligan, actor, radio host, television personality; email to Frank Troiano, July 2020

In Closing

The manifestation of love and admiration that has endured is striking. In the course of compiling this biography, interviews and submissions from over 180 friends, fans, family, and former colleagues were received. So many were willing to talk or put pen to paper (or fingers to keyboard) fifteen years after Domenic's passing and share fond memories that are consistently and profoundly heartfelt. The exercise of editing and assembling these submissions has been rich and humbling. One wants so badly to honour these memories appropriately.

Domenic Troiano may have been born in Modugno, Italy, but he was a Toronto kid through and through, who rose to great heights professionally and publicly. But Donnie never forgot where he came from or the people who helped and encouraged him on his journey. Nor did he neglect to "pay it forward" (so to speak), always on the lookout for the *opportunity* to share his success, to acknowledge and encourage others—friends, family, and even fans—to help them out, even to the point of meeting their basic needs if necessary.

One would like to believe that he would have been pleased with the way in which his legacy has lived on, that he would have been honoured by the tributes, and grateful for the way in which his name and legacy have been a vehicle to help others. Because truly, his memory and his legacy does endure, not just in the old LPs, or the CDs, or even the commemorative murals and plaques found around downtown Toronto, or the scholarships and awards. Certainly, his music carries on through these avenues, but his memory, that of a generous, thoughtful, remarkable, musical, talented, and caring human being lives on in so many hearts of the people he loved.

It's been about fifteen years and there isn't a day where Donnie doesn't cross my mind. I keep a button with Donnie's picture on the visor in my car. I watch this button colour with age, but I talk to that button all the time. In my mind, I'm still talking to Donnie. I look up at the button and say, "Do you believe this shit … What do you think about …?" He's still my sounding board! I miss him dearly.
-   Roy Kenner, lead vocalist; interview with Mark Doble, July 4, 2020

Pentti (Whitey) Glan, Roy Kenner, Domenic Troiano, Blaine Pritchett, Bernie LaBarge, 1996 (Photo: Tom Sandler)

DISCOGRAPHY: SINGLES

Robbie Lane and the Disciples

Fannie Mae/	Hawk Records HR001	Canada
The One for Me		1964

Ronnie Hawkins and the Hawks

Got My Mojo Working/	Hawk Records HR002	Canada
Let the Good Times Roll		1964

The Five Rogues

I Can't Hold Out No Longer/	Unreleased	Canada
I'll Make it Up to You		1965

The Mandala

Opportunity/	KR Records KR-109	Canada
Lost Love		1966
Give and Take/	KR Records KR-0121	Canada
From Toronto 1967		1967
Love-itis/	Atlantic Records 45-2512	Canada/USA
Mellow Carmello Palumbo		1968
Love-itis/	Atlantic Records	Belgium/France
World of Love	BE 650130	1968
You Got Me/	Atlantic Records 45-2567	Canada
Help Me		1968

Bush

I Can Hear You Calling/	ABC Dunhill D 4245	USA (1970)
The Grand Commander	RCA D-4252	Canada (1970)

The James Gang

Looking for My Lady (stereo)/	ABC-11325	Canada/USA
Looking for My Lady (mono)		1972
Looking for My Lady/	ABC-11325	Canada/USA
Hairy Hypochondriac		1972
Madness/	Probe Records IPR 10139	Canada/USA
I'll Tell You Why		1972
Had Enough (stereo)/	ABC-11336	USA
Had Enough (mono)		1972
Kickback Man/	ABC-11336	Canada
Had Enough		1972

Domenic Troiano

The Writings on the Wall/The	Mercury Records 73312	Canada/USA
Wear and the Tear on My Mind		1972
Try/	Mercury Records 73342	Canada/USA
I Just Lost a Friend		1972
All Night Radio Show/	Mercury Records 73379	Canada/USA
The Greaser		1973

The Guess Who

Dancin' Fool/Seems like I Can't	Nimbus 9 PB-10075	Canada/USA
Live with You but I Can't Live		1974
Without You		
Loves Me Like a Brother/	Nimbus 9 PB-10216	Canada/USA
Hoedown Time		1975
Rosanne/	Nimbus 9 PB-10360	Canada/USA
Dreams		1975

When the Band Was Singin'	Nimbus 9 PB-10410	Canada/USA
Shakin' All Over/		1975
Women		

Domenic Troiano Band

Master of Concealment/	Capitol Records 72789	Canada/USA
Lonely Girl		1977
Savour the Flavour/	Capitol Records 72792	Canada/USA
Savour the Flavour		1977
Here Before My Time/	Capitol Records 72795	Canada/USA
Spud		1978
Maybe the Next Time/	Capitol Records 72800	Canada/USA
Road to Hell		1978
We All Need Love/	Capitol Records 75017	Canada/USA
Ambush		1979
Your Past Is a Part of You/	Capitol Records 72810	Canada/USA
Achilles		1979
It's You/	Capitol Records 72816	Canada/USA
Achilles		1979

Black Market

Turn Back/	El Mocambo	Canada
The Shooter	Records ELMO-762	1981
Dr. Dee Jay's Band/	El Mocambo	Canada
Girls	Records ELMO-517	1981

Domenic Troiano with Roy Kenner

| Night Heat/ | A & M Records 716 | Canada |
| Night Heat (TV Mix) | | 1986 |

DISCOGRAPHY: ALBUMS

The Mandala

SOUL CRUSADE	Atlantic Records SD 8184	CAN/USA 1968

*World of Love/One Short Year/Love-itis/Come on Home/Every Single Day/
Mellow Carmello Palumbo/Can't Hold Out/Don't Make Me Cry/Stop Cryin' on
My Shoulder/Faith*

SOUL CRUSADE
(CD reissue)	Pacemaker PACE 084	CAN 1998

Track list identical to original LP

CLASSICS (compila-
tion reissue)	Wea Music 25 23291	CAN 1985

*Love-itis/Opportunity/Give and Take/Faith/Lost Love/Mellow Carmello
Palumbo/World of Love/Every Single Day/Don't Make Me Cry/Can't Hold Out/
One Short Year/From Toronto-67*

Bush

BUSH	ABC Dunhill D5 50086	CAN 1970
	Probe Records SPB 1012	USA 1970

*Back Stage Girl/Yonge St. Patty/Got to Leave the City/I Miss You/The Grand
Commander/Cross Country Man/I Can Hear You Calling/Messin' around with
Boxes/Livin'Life/Turn Down/Drink Your Wine*

| BUSH (CD reissue) | Magada Records | CAN 1994 |
| | MAGHDCD 22 | |

Track list identical to original LP with 4 live bonus tracks: *Try/Lookin'/Wicked Woman/Cross Country Man*

The James Gang

| STRAIGHT SHOOTER | Dunhill | CAN/USA 1972 |
| | Records ABCX-741 | |

Madness/Kick Back Man/Get Her Back Again/Looking for My Lady/Getting Old/I'll Tell You Why/Hairy Hypochondriac/Let Me Come Home/My Door is Open

| STRAIGHT SHOOTER (CD reissue) | MCA MCAD-22051 | CAN/USA 1991 |

Track list identical to original LP

| PASSIN' THRU | Dunhill | CAN/USA 1972 |
| | Records ABCX-760 | |

Ain't Seen Nothing Yet/One-Way Street/Had Enough/Up to Yourself/Everybody Needs a Hero/Run, Run, Run/Things I Want to Say to You/Out of Control/ Drifting Girl

| PASSIN' THRU (CD reissue) | MCA MCAD-22066 | CAN/USA 1992 |

Track list identical to original LP

Domenic Troiano

DOMENIC TROIANO   Mercury Records SRM   CAN/USA 1972
                         1 639

*The Writings on the Wall/The Answer/Let Me Go Back/I Just Lost a Friend/
Try/The Wear and the Tear on My Mind/Is There No Rest for The Weary/Hi
Again/356 Sammon Ave./Repossession Blues*

TRICKY   Mercury Records SRM   CAN/USA 1973
                         1 670

*All Night Radio Show/If You See Me/My Old Toronto Home/All I Need Is Music/
Tricky (Fannie Mae/Blues for Ollie/I'll Get My Own/The Greaser)*

THE TORONTO SOUND   Polygram Records 453856   CAN 1999
(CD compilation)

*The Writings on the Wall/The Answer/Let Me Go Back/I Just Lost a Friend/
Try/The Wear and the Tear on My Mind/Is There No Rest For the Weary/Hi
Again/356 Sammon Ave./Repossession Blues/ All Night Radio Show/If You See
Me/My Old Toronto Home/All I Need Is Music/Tricky (Fannie Mae/Blues for
Ollie/I'll Get My Own/The Greaser)*

The Guess Who

FLAVOURS   Nimbus 9 CPL1-0636   CAN/USA 1974

*Dancin' Fool/Hoedown Time/Nobody Knows His Name/Diggin' Yourself/Seems
like I Can't Live with You but I Can't Live Without You/Dirty/Eye/Loves Me Like
a Brother/Long Gone*

FLAVOURS (CD reissue)   Iconoclassic ICON 1022   USA 2011

Track list identical to original LP with 4 bonus tracks: *A Fool a Fool I Met a
Fool/Save a Smile/Roll with the Punches/Your Backyard*

POWER IN THE MUSIC   Nimbus 9 APL1-0995   CAN/USA 1975

*Down and Out Woman/Women/When the Band Was Singin' Shakin' All Over/
Dreams/Rich World-Poor World/Rosanne/Coors for Sunday/Shopping Bag Lady/
Power in the Music*

POWER IN THE MUSIC   Iconoclassic ICON 1038   CAN/USA 2014
(CD reissue)

Tracklist identical to original LP with 2 bonus tracks: *When the Band Was
Singin' Shakin' All Over (rehearsal)/Coors for Sunday (rehearsal)*

TRACK RECORD—   BMG Music KCD2-7115   CAN 1988
THE GUESS WHO
COLLECTION
(CD Compilation)

Double CD set includes 30 previously released Guess Who songs as well as the
bonus: *Sona Sona*, a 1974 outtake to which Domenic added guitar parts in 1988
specifically for this reissue

LIVE IN '75 (live)   Orbit   Europe 2018
     Record ORB2CD106

Remastered broadcast recording from April 15, 1975, Winnipeg Playhouse
Theatre, Winnipeg, Manitoba, Canada: *Down and Out Woman/Dirty/Hand
Me Down World/Albert Flasher/Diggin' Yourself/Star Baby/Those Show Biz
Shoes/Straighten Out/Seems like I Can't Live With You/Clap for the Wolfman/
Medley(The Way We Were/Laughing/These Eyes/Undun/Hang on to Your Life/
American Woman)/Rosanne/When the Band Was Singin'/Long Gone/No Time/
Dancin' Fool/Instrumental Interlude/Orly*

Domenic Troiano Band/Troiano

BURNIN' AT THE STAKE   Capitol Records ST-11665   CAN/USA 1977

*Burnin' at the Stake/Peace of Mind/Savour the Flavour/Lonely Girl/Willpower/
Master of Concealment/I'd Rather Be Your Lover/Rock and Roll Madness/The
Outer Limits of My Soul*

LIVE AT   Capitol Records SPRO-11   Unreleased 1977
THUNDER SOUND

(Recorded for FM Radio Broadcast) *Burnin' at the Stake/Peace of Mind/Savour
the Flavour/War Zone/The Outer Limits of My Soul/Lonely Girl/Willpower*

THE JOKE'S ON ME   Capitol   CAN/USA 1978
                         Records SW-11772

*The Joke's on Me/Maybe the Next Time/Spud/Here Before My Time/Eleanora
Fagan/Road to Hell/War Zone/Look Up*

FRET FEVER   Capitol Records ST 11932   CAN/USA 1979

*South American Run/Ambush/We All Need Love/It's You/It's Raining, It's
Pouring/Give Me a Chance/Your Past (is a Part of You)/Fret Fever/Brains On The
Floor/Victim of Circumstance/Achilles/The End*

TROIANO TRIPLE PLAY   EMI Music   CAN 1996
(CD compilation)   Canada E2724383735921

*We All Need Love (extended mix)/Savour the Flavour/Burnin' at the Stake/Peace
of Mind/Maybe the Next Time/It's You/Brains on the Floor/Gypsy (previously
unreleased)/Intermission (previously unreleased)/South American Run/Ambush/
Fret Fever/The Joke's on Me/Here Before My Time/War Zone/Draw Your Own
Conclusions (previously unreleased)/The End*

Black Market

CHANGING OF THE GUARD El Mocambo Records ELMO-762 CAN 1981

Changing of the Guard/Turn Back/Oh Carol/Doctor Love/Girls/I'm Bored/Dr. Dee Jay's Band/Hell's Got No Fury/Lolita/Independence/The Shooter

Domenic Troiano

THE BEST OF DOMENIC TROIANO—THE MILLENIUM COLLECTION (CD compilation) Universal Music Group 0249811687 CAN/USA 2003

Opportunity/I Can Hear You Calling/Turn Down/Kickback Man/The Writings on the Wall/Try/Let Me Go Back/The Answer/Lonely Girl/Eleanora Fagan/ Ambush/Fret Fever/Turn Back

DOMENIC TROIANO'S LAST PERFORMANCE MAY 25, 2004 (Recorded live at The Orbit Room) Limited Edition (2006) Proceeds of CD go to Toronto East General Hospital
Domenic Troiano (guitar), Doug Riley (B3), Howard Ayee (bass), Ben Riley (drums)

Mercy, Mercy, Mercy/Lonely Girl/Turn Down/Melting Pot/Burnin' at the Stake/ Eleanora Fagan/The Stumble

A comprehensive discography including all official releases, various artist compilation releases, unreleased demos, outtakes, selected live performance recordings, Domenic Troiano's recordings with other artists, including performance and production, has been professionally archived at the University of Toronto Archives under the direction of Brock Silversides. The authors are indebted to Mr. Silversides, Director of Media Commons/University of Toronto for providing the resource material for the compilation of this discography.

UNRELEASED DEMOS AND LIVE RECORDINGS

(Domenic Troiano Archive, Media Commons/University of Toronto)

The Mandala—studio demo session: September 1966, RCA Studio, Toronto

Opportunity (v 1, voice mix—
D. Troiano)

Opportunity (v 2, voice mix—
D. Troiano)

Opportunity (v 3, backing track—
D. Troiano)

Opportunity (v 4, backing track—
D. Troiano)

Time Will Make Them Pay

The Mandala—performance for television CTV Studio, Agincourt ON, October 1966

Five Steps to Soul (D. Troiano-
G. Olliver)

produced by Peter Reilly

The Mandala—studio demo session: Fall 1966, RCA Studios, Toronto

Opportunity (D. Troiano)

Bring Your Love (D. Troiano)

The One for Me (D. Troiano)

I'll Make It up to You (D. Troiano)

To Be With You

Forget Your Pride Girl

Time Will Make Them Pay

The Mandala—studio demo session 1967

Gonna Make a Comeback (D. Troiano)   *One Short Year* (D. Troiano)

The Mandala—live performance May 28, 1967, Cheetah Club, Los Angeles (1st set)

Long Intro by Humble Harv   *Let Out* (D. Troiano)

Fingertips (S. Wonder)   *Respect* (O. Redding)

Gimme Some Lovin' (S. Winwood)   *Think* (L. Pauling)

Knock on Wood (E. Floyd-S. Cropper)   *Five Steps to Soul*—with sermon by

churchy organ instrumental (J. Chiroski) D. Troiano

If Somebody Told You (J. Brown)   *Lost Love* (G. Olliver)

Crusade sermon by D. Troiano   *Give and Take* (V. Chambers)

The Mandala—live performance May 28, 1967, Cheetah Club, Los Angeles (2nd set)

Long Intro by Humble Harv   *Lost Love* (G. Olliver)

Jazzy instrumental   Crusade sermon by D. Troiano, then

Think (L. Pauling)   G. Olliver, then guitar soloing

Respect (O. Redding)   *Give and Take* (V. Chambers)

The Mandala—live performance July 18, 1967, The Scene, New York City

World of Love (D. Troiano)   *Come on Home* (D. Troiano)

I'll Make It Up To You (D. Troiano)   *Instrumental*

Ain't No Mountain High Enough   *Try a Little Tenderness* (J. Campbell/

(N. Ashford-V. Simpson)   R. Connelly/H. Woods) *Knock on Wood*

One Short Year (D. Troiano)   (E. Floyd-S. Cropper)

Five Steps to Soul—sermon by   *Faith* (D. Troiano)

D. Troiano

The Mandala—studio demo session summer 1967

Faith (D. Troiano)

The Mandala—studio demo session February 1, 1968, Atlantic Studios, NYC

Help Me (D. Troiano-R. Kenner)

Love

Something Cooling

Forget Your Pride

The Answer (D. Troiano)

I'm Losing You

The Mandala—studio demo session Fall 1968

Listen to The Music

You Got Me (R. Kenner-D. Troiano)— 15 takes

Help Me (D. Troiano-R. Kenner)— 2 takes

The Mandala – studio demo session fall 1968

Help Me (D. Troiano-R. Kenner)

Forget Your Pride

The Answer (D. Troiano)

Somethin' Comin'

Let Out (D. Troiano)

If I Needed You

Why Am I Cryin'

Don't Let Him Break Your Heart

Go Your Own Way (R. Kenner-D. Troiano)

The Mandala—studio demo session September 5, 1968, Atlantic Studios, New York

Listen to the Music—rough mix

The Mandala—studio demo session February 2, 1969, Tera Shirma Sound Studios, Detroit

I Can Hear You Calling—Version 1 (P. Glan/R. Kenner/H. Sullivan/D. Troiano)

I Can Hear You Calling—Version 2 (P. Glan/R. Kenner/H. Sullivan/D. Troiano)

Why Don't You Leave Me Alone

Lazy Day (D. Troiano-R. Kenner)

Instrumental Blues (D. Troiano)

Cross Country Man (D. Troiano)

The Mandala—compilation of early demo/recording sessions, Toronto, 1965–1968

contains 32 songs:

Bring Your Love—Version 1
(D. Troiano)

Betty Jo (F. Carter)—Robbie
Lane session

Can't Hold Out (D. Troiano)

I'll Make It Up To You—Version 1
(D. Troiano)

Out of My Mind

Givin' In

Get You

Bring Your Love—Version 2
(D. Troiano)

Opportunity (D. Troiano)

The One for Me (D. Troiano)—
Robbie Lane single

I'll Make It up to You—Version 2
(D. Troiano)

To Be with You

Forget Your Prize Girl

Time Will Make Them Pay

Help Me (D. Troiano-R. Kenner)

Call On Me?

Find the Answer (D. Troiano)

Something's Cookin

Let tt Out (D. Troiano)

If I Needed You

Why I'm Cryin'—Version 1

Don't Let Him Break Your Heart

Go Your Own Way (R. Kenner-
D. Troiano)

Can't Buy Me Love (J. Lennon-
P. McCartney)

Stop Cryin' on My Shoulder
(D. Troiano)

Wait No Longer

Sack of Woe (J. Adderly)

Don't Let Him Break Your Heart

Can't Hold Out (D. Troiano)

Watch Your Step

Stuck on You

Why I'm Crying—Version 2

Every Single Day (D. Troiano-K. McKie)

Bush—"Tape #2" live performance June 1971, Bitter End, Los Angeles

Try (R. Kenner-D. Troiano)

Is There No Rest for the Weary
(D. Troiano)

Looking for My Lady (D. Troiano-
R. Kenner)

Drink Your Wine (R.
Kenner-D. Troiano)

I Can Hear You Calling (P. Glan/
R. Kenner/H. Sullivan/D. Troiano)

Messing around with Boxes (R. Kenner-
D. Troiano)

Cissy Strut (A. Neville/Z. Modeliste/
L. Nocentelli/G. Porter Jr.)

Repossession Blues (D. Troiano)

Mama's Second Boy Child

The Writings on the Wall (D. Troiano)
Wicked Woman (R. Kenner-D. Troiano)
Turn Down (R. Kenner-D. Troiano)
I Just Lost a Friend (D. Troiano)
My Door Is Open (D. Troiano-
R. Kenner)

Got to Leave the City (R. Kenner-
D. Troiano)
I Do Love You
Stewin' Around

Bush—"Tape #3" live performance June 1971, Bitter End, Los Angeles

Try (R. Kenner-D. Troiano)
The Writings On the Wall (D. Troiano)
I Can Hear You Calling (P. Glan/
R. Kenner/H. Sullivan/D. Troiano)
Wicked Woman (R. Kenner-D. Troiano)
Drink Your Wine (R. Kenner-
D. Troiano)
I Just Lost a Friend (D. Troiano)
Mama's Second Boy Child
Looking for My Lady (R. Kenner-
D. Troiano)

Cross Country Man (D. Troiano)
Backstage Girl (R. Kenner-D. Troiano)
Is There No Rest for the Weary
Got to Leave the City (R. Kenner-
D. Troiano)
Messin' around with Boxes (R. Kenner-
D. Troiano)
Turn Down (R. Kenner-D. Troiano)
There's Got to Be a Change
Repossession Blues (D. Troiano)

Domenic Troiano—"Writer Demos 1971"

Screwing Around (D. Troiano)
Country Air (D. Troiano)
The Day Grows Longer (D. Troiano)
Blackbird (D. Troiano)
Getting Old (D. Troiano)
My Old Toronto Home (D. Troiano)

Watch Your Step (D. Troiano)
What You Can't See Won't Hurt You
(D. Troiano)
Find The Right Way (D. Troiano)
Madness (D. Troiano-R. Kenner)
Kickback Man (D. Troiano-R. Kenner)

James Gang live performance August 12, 1972, Festival of Hope, Roosevelt Raceway, Westbury NY

Funk #49 (D. Peters/J. Fox/J. Walsh)
I'll Tell You Why (D. Peters-D. Troiano)
Stop (J. Ragavoy-M. Schuman) into
You're Gonna Need Me (A. King)

My Door Is Open (D. Troiano-
R. Kenner)
Walk Away (J. Walsh)

Lost Sleep Blues/Lost Woman Blues
(C. Dreja/J. Beck/J. McCarty/
P. Samwell-Smith)

Roll Over Beethoven (C. Berry)

James Gang—Television performance broadcast February 5, 1973,
***Rollin' on the River,* CTV Studio, Agincourt ON**

Run, Run, Run (R. Kenner-D. Troiano)

The Wear and the Tear on My Mind
(D. Troiano)

**The Guess Who—performance for television broadcast January 3,
1975,** ***Midnight Special,* NBC**
NBC Studios, Burbank CA

Clap for the Wolfman (B. Cummings/
B. Wallace/K. Winter)

Dancin' Fool (B. Cummings-
D. Troiano)

Bus Rider (K. Winter)

Sour Suite (B. Cummings)

No Time (R. Bachman-B. Cummings)

Diggin' Yourself (B. Cummings-
D. Troiano)

Dirty (B. Cummings-D. Troiano)

**The Guess Who Live Performance for Television—broadcast
February 22, 1975,** ***Don Kirshner's Rock Concert*—Recorded 23
December 1974, Hofstra University, Hempstead NY**

No Time (R. Bachman-B. Cummings)

Dancin' Fool (B. Cummings-
D. Troiano)

Long Gone (B. Cummings-D. Troiano)

Straighten Out (B. Cummings-
B. Wallace)

Glamour Boy (B. Cummings)

**The Guess Who—Live at Bottom Line, NYC January 1975, Bottom
Line, New York City**
CD—Remasters Workshop RMW699

Dirty (B. Cummings-D. Troiano)

Albert Flasher (B. Cummings)

Hand Me Down World (K. Winter)

Star Baby (B. Cummings)

No Time (R. Bachman-B. Cummings)

Sour Suite (B. Cummings)

Those Show Biz Shoes (B. Cummings-
D. Troiano)

Straighten Out (B. Cummings-
B. Wallace)

Hoedown Time (B. Cummings-
D. Troiano)

Diggin' Yourself (B. Cummings-
D. Troiano)

Long Gone (B. Cummings-D. Troiano)

Guess Who—Live at Electric Ladyland 1975 January 1975, New York City

Dirty (B. Cummings-D. Troiano)

Diggin' Yourself (B. Cummings-
D. Troiano)

Hoedown Time (B. Cummings-
D. Troiano)

Dancin' Fool (B. Cummings-
D. Troiano)

Eye (B. Cummings-D. Troiano)

Straighten Out (B. Cummings-
B. Wallace)

Long Gone (B. Cummings-D. Troiano)

Sour Suite (B. Cummings)

Orly (B. Cummings)

Domenic Troiano Band Demo Tape—Recorded September 9, 1978

Ten

The Song

Working Man

World of Extremes (D. Troiano)

Melting Pot (D. Troiano)

Brains on the Floor (D. Troiano)

Your Past Is a Part of You (D. Troiano)

Victim of Circumstance (D. Tyson)

Achilles (D. Troiano)

When, Where or How

Surprise Surprise

Zingaro (D. Troiano)

Troiano performance for television/radio simulcast 1979 on City TV and CHUM Radio

It's You (D. Troiano)

War Zone (D. Troiano)

We All Need Love (D. Troiano)

recorded: Much Music Studios, Toronto

Troiano performance for radio September 18, 1979, Dollar Bill's, Kingston
engineered by Pat Jackman—broadcast 1979 on CFLY, Kingston
Produced by Doug McClement

Joke's on Me (D. Troiano)

Your Past Is a Part of You (D. Troiano)

South Amercian Run (R. Kenner-
D. Troiano)

Fret Fever (D. Troiano)

Savour the Flavour (D. Troiano)

It's You (D. Troiano)

Road to Hell (D. Troiano)

War Zone (D. Troiano)

Look Up (D. Troiano)

Rock 'n Roll Madness (D. Troiano)

Burning at the Stake (D. Troiano)

Peace of Mind (D. Troiano)

We All Need Love (D. Troiano)

Give Me a Chance (D. Troiano)

Outer Limits of My Soul (D. Troiano)

Melting Pot (D. Troiano)

Draw Your Own Conclusions
(D. Troiano)

Repossession Blues (D. Troiano)

Instrumental

Willpower (D. Troiano)

Domenic Troiano—"Sound Kitchen Demos" December 1979

Oh Carol

Changing of the Guard (D. Troiano)

Doctor DJ (D. Troiano)

I'm Bored (D. Troiano)

Highway Blues (D. Troiano)

Girls (D. Troiano)

Lolita (D. Troiano)

God Save the King (D. Troiano)

Hell's Got No Fury (D. Troiano)

Random Notes (D. Troiano)

Black Market—Live Set 1981

Changing of the Guard (D. Troiano)

I Can Hear You Calling (W. Glan/
R. Kenner/H. Sullivan/D. Troiano)

South American Run (R. Kenner-
D. Troiano)

Ambush (D. Troiano)

Oh Carol

Dr. Dee Jay's Band (D. Troiano)

Drink Your Wine (R. Kenner-
D. Troiano)

Hell's Got No Fury (D. Troiano)

Turn Back (D. Troiano)

Domenic Troiano—"1982 Demos"

Take Me Home (D. Troiano)

Denied (D. Troiano)

Amnesia (D. Troiano)

Bye Bye (D. Troiano)

Working Man

Drink Your Wine (R. Kenner-
D. Troiano)

Sincere thanks to Brock Silversides, Director of Media Commons/ University of Toronto (Music Archives) for his support and advice in compiling this inventory.

DOMENIC TROIANO

SCORING CREDITS

1984–2003

Production	Episodes	Network
Night Heat	96 episodes	CBS
Diamonds	44 episodes	CBS-USA Network
Hot Shots	13 episodes	CBS
Air Waves	13 episodes	CBC
Gunfighters	2-hour movie	Tribune Network
Cop Talk	13 episodes	Tribune Network
The Playground (Ray Bradbury)	2-hour movie	HBO
Lifetime	400 episodes	CTV
Scandals	2-hour program	HBO
True Blue	Movie of the Week	NBC
True Blue	13 episodes	NBC
Top Cops	105 episodes	CBS
Counterstrike	66 episodes	USA Network
Moment of Truth	Pilot	CBS
The Swordsman	Theatrical Movie	Republic Films
Secret Service	22 episodes	NBC

Police File	Pilot	ABC
Juvenile Justice	75 episodes	Genesis Ent.
Fahrenheit	Sega Interactive	CD ROM game
Remember Me	Movie of the Week	CBS
While My Pretty One Sleeps	Movie of the Week	Family Channel
Let Me Call You Sweetheart	Movie of the Week	Family Channel
Moonlight Becomes You	Movie of the Week	Family Channel
Mary K. Letourneau Story	Movie of the Week	USA Network
All American Girl		
Loves Music, Loves to Dance	Movie of the Week	PAX Network
Pretend You Don't See Her	Movie of the Week	PAX Network
Haven't We Met Before	Movie of the Week	PAX Network
You Belong to Me	Movie of the Week	PAX Network
Lucky Day	Movie of the Week	PAX Network
All Around the Town	Movie of the Week	PAX Network

ADDITIONAL TRIBUTES

"Domenic was a genius, and I for one, as an old Toronto 'soulman,' am extremely proud to have met him and followed his career from the early days. He will always be missed, and I thank God we have his body of work to keep his memory fresh and alive. I have had much admiration and love for Domenic for many decades through Robbie Lane, the Rogues, the Mandala, Bush, James Gang, The Guess Who, and his stellar solo works. Over the years there has not been a copy of any song or album done by Domenic that hasn't entered my collection and held in the highest regard. I have caught him play live on many occasions, with the last one being at the Capitol Theatre on Yonge Street where he accompanied the Dexters and George Olliver. My last conversation with Donnie was at a show which featured Jon Finley and the Checkmates at the Blue Goose in Mimico, and it was great seeing Domenic just relaxing while catching Finley do his magic. For Toronto music lovers raised on soul, I am proud to see Domenic Troiano's memory live on in our hearts and music. He will forever remain a guitar hero and a wonderful gentleman and I hold him in the highest esteem. Viva La Musica, Viva Troiano!"

- **Peter Vickery, friend and fan**

"I was a sixteen-year-old Los Angeles high school photography student when I first experienced Domenic Troiano and the Mandala, decked out in pinstripe gangster-style suits under strobe lights, in November 1966 at the Hullabaloo club in Hollywood, California. The high-energy theatrics of the Mandala's "Soul Crusade" was a golden opportunity for me, starting a photography career I never could have imagined. Domenic and I remained friends for thirty-plus years. I got a call every time he started a new gig, and

photographed record albums for Bush, James Gang, The Guess Who, and his solo albums."

- **Ed Caraeff, rock photographer to the stars**

"Donnie was interested in how we were doing, and was always offering guidance and advice when asked. Then something hit me. No matter who I met through Donnie, or who it was that talked about Donnie, the consensus was always the same. He was a special guy. He made you feel special. He genuinely took an interest in what it was that you were doing. And he was always available to you if you needed him."

- **Luke Vitale, cousin**

"I have many fond memories of Domenic regaling us with tales of the great musicians he knew, performed, or jammed with, and his music business dealings. He was always patient and kind and took the time to clearly explain what he wanted, understood the business side of the music business, and acted with integrity, which can be rare in the music industry. He valued the lawyer-client relationship and always paid his bills on time; not always a sure thing in a private music law practice. Over the ensuing years, I also got to know, value, and worked closely with his sister Gina as an assistant for his business endeavours. He loved his family immensely, and Toronto, which was his true home. I learned that it was his family members that helped make Domenic such a great person."

- **Paul Sanderson, entertainment lawyer—Sanderson Law**

"My company at the time, TMP (The Music Publisher), administered all of the music rights of the entertainment conglomerate Alliance Communications Corporation, whose main business was film and television production. It turned out Dom scored many of their productions, so we got involved in those together quite frequently. Domenic will always remain an important part of, and contributor to, the fabric that was Toronto and Canada's unique music scene in the latter half of the twentieth century."

- **Frank Davies, music publisher**

"He dealt with things so naturally, so calmly, effortlessly, and clearly. Just like his guitar playing, he was so good. You wouldn't have known that he was in the middle of a battle for his life. He never made it an issue. He never made anything about him. It was always about that moment and whatever we were discussing and sharing. I remember asking him if he was worried about what the future might hold. 'There's no use in worrying about the things we can't control. I can only do what I can do,' he said so calmly. 'That's life. You can't have the good without some bad.' He had created so much good in his life. He was one of the greatest people I have ever had the pleasure of knowing. Not because of the music. Not because of the fame. But because none of that got in the way of him just being such an incredible human being. Just being Donnie."

- **Basil Farano, cousin**

"Only four players from the Toronto Scene influenced me on a massive scale: William 'Smitty' Smith, Doug Riley, Michael Fonfara, and Domenic Troiano. (Not necessarily in that order.) Given that I am a keyboard player, Doug, Michael, and Smitty would be on the list. But oddly enough, Domenic was on there too. He had a style that made his guitar enter into the keyboard world. He had a command of voicings, like Bill Evans had on piano. He played guitar passionately, with total command, like Lenny Breau. These are people that are gifted with a talent and creativity that normal people can't learn from a book. The show that happened at The Orbit Room on May 25, 2004, was absolutely amazing! I am privileged to have been there that night. It was magical!"

- **Gabor Szepesi, keyboardist and owner of PA Plus**

"I met Dom one night when I was DJ-ing at the Chalet Discotheque in Toronto. We were both eighteen. I was simply blown away by his playing. He was a pro. We met many times at other places where I did the sound. Dom usually had a million questions about the songs I was playing and always requested Outrage *by Booker T. & the M.G.s. His friendly, easy-going manner made him a pleasure to spend time with. Although not a musician*

myself, he always treated me as an equal, inviting me to a recording session at his studio and for cappuccino at his home."

- **Merv Buchanan, DJ and friend**

"The name Domenic Troiano first came to my mind in 1972 as the new guitar player in the James Gang, having replaced Joe Walsh. I bought STRAIGHT SHOOTER, and was fascinated with the new and especially more funk-oriented sound. I was blown away by the excellent musicianship and mix of various styles. I followed Dom's musical career back to the earlier years (the Mandala, Bush) as well as with The Guess Who and further on as a session or solo artist until his untimely death in 2005. The love for his music also shaped my interest in the Canadian music scene in general, and especially the Toronto Sound."

- **Klaus Sander, friend and fan**

"A story that took place back in 1965 when The Rolling Stones came to play Maple Leaf Gardens: The band asked where they could see a decent local rock band and someone took them to the Bluenote Club where Domenic was playing guitar with The Five Rogues. They watched them play and one of the members in The Rolling Stones commented, 'Holy shit, here's a local bar band that is far better than what we will be playing in Maple Leaf Gardens tomorrow night!'"

- **Vito Ierullo, CEO of Entertainment One**

"In the fall of 1992, I had the privilege of working with Domenic Troiano on a short film and a pilot for a television series. I was amazed at how Domenic worked at his craft and I quickly realized that I was watching a true master at work. His passion, his dedication, and his commitment to perfection was something wonderful to experience."

- **Giacomo Moncada, director/executive producer—Star Media Entertainment**

"Domenic's career and musical influence has been largely overlooked. He was 'the guy.' He had a strong but subtle influence on the musical scenes not only in Canada, but also in New York and Los Angeles. I consider myself fortunate to have seen him in his heyday with the Mandala and with one of my favourite bands, The Guess Who. RIP Domenic."

-   **Harvey Kubernik, music journalist, Los Angeles**

"I was a kid watching The Midnight Special. Domenic was fronting the James Gang and they were lip-synching their latest release. I thought the guitar player was the epitome of cool and I couldn't take my eyes of his heavily customized Telecaster. It started a lifelong obsession with that guitar. A few years later I saw Domenic with The Guess Who, and absolutely loved his playing and the way he fit in to the rhythm section—deep-groove rhythm playing and cool melodic soloing with few effects. Just great tone. He always looked like he was having a blast. To me he was the definition of taste and groove."

-   **Howard Forman, professional guitarist**

"As my brother and I grew into our high school years, Donnie was by then a very much 'closer' cousin—he'd often check out my brother's hockey games at Henry Carr. He helped source our first stereo system for the house. He taught me the Day Tripper riff at Zia Pasqua's kitchen table, and would always drop by for a late Christmas eve visit—always there for us. Fortunately, I was one of the lucky ones who caught one of those shows at The Orbit Room. But it will always be his smile, humble presence, and kindness that I will truly cherish and remember."

-   **Gregory Vitale, cousin**

"So, it was decided that I would call up Domenic and ask him if we could hire him for a session. I was shaking and stammering on the phone. He was a world-famous musician, but because he knew Mike Tilka and Ray Daniels, he agreed to come down. Of course, he played some amazing guitar and did it in a few takes! When it came time to pay him for the session, I took out my checkbook and asked him how much and he just patted me on the back and *wished me luck. He wouldn't accept any money! He just complimented me on the songs, said my voice reminded him of Don Henley, and said he really liked the song, wished us luck and off he went. What an incredibly generous soul. We were all blown away."*

- **Gary Taylor, drummer—Sisters of Euclid**

"I met Domenic in August 1975, in Flint, Michigan, before one of The Guess Who's last concerts. He was uniquely cool, friendly, and humble. I was fourteen. He and drummer Garry Peterson treated my best friend and me—and my mother, who drove us to the show—with such respect and appreciation. We were swelling with joy for months afterward. And, wow, could he play! An experience I will never forget."

- **William Hanson, Guess Who fan**

"What I remember most about Domenic was not his talent on the guitar, but his kindness toward everyone he encountered. No airs about him when he walked into a room. He was humble, quiet, and supportive. Whatever Domenic wrote or created, it had to help make this world a better place. That is what was important to him. The sound made from his fingers on the guitar chords were like little gifts that capture our hearts. He was a wonderful man that many only knew though his music. I was honoured and fortunate to know him through his kindness. I will never forget how well he listened when one spoke to him. He was always interested in the other person."

- **Diane Dupuy, founder and president—
  Famous People Players**

"I first discovered Domenic when I first heard The Guess Who's FLAVOURS album. Having been a fan of the band for some time, I was determined to acquire the entire discography, and I had always heard such great things about Domenic. When I heard the album, I was immediately taken aback by his virtuoso skills on tracks such as Dancin' Fool *and* Long Gone. *Domenic's playing on this album was fluid, dynamic, and utterly fantastic, as his style of playing added flair and excitement to each track. Domenic's playing was*

different than that of previous guitarists Kurt Winter and Randy Bachman, as it retained a groove all its own."

- **Christian Bisciello, lead vocalist—The Gypsy Felons, teacher**

"At the beginning of each season, Donnie would ask for my baseball schedule and tell me that if he could make time he would get out to see me play whenever possible. And he did, more than you could imagine. That was Donnie to me; making time for me when he had so much on his plate. His devotion to family stays ingrained in my life to this day. For me, these moments meant the world."

- **Marlon Jackson, nephew**

"I grew up and spent the majority of my life on Linsmore Crescent, living next door to one of the most amazing families I have ever known. Every time I would be at the house visiting with the Troiano family, even as a child, and Donnie was over, when it was time for him to leave he would always kiss his mom's hands before he would kiss her goodbye. Domenic was an amazing musician, but he was also an amazing son, brother, and friend, even as it was coming to an end; asking his mom for his wallet and showing her the one-hundred-dollar bill she had given him as he was on his way to California to expand his music career; asking his sister constantly how she was feeling; and asking me about what was new in my life. I will never forget the last night I saw him, and I still can't believe that I was the last person that saw him before he left and joined all the angels in heaven. Before I even got the call from Gina that Donnie was gone I somehow knew midway through my drive home. I was lucky enough to have two families growing up and throughout my life, my family and my friends, the Troiano family became and will always be my family."

- **Anna Sourtzis, family friend**

"Domenic Troiano was one of the most talented guitarists I had the joy of experiencing back in the day. He was so soulfully gifted that when he played

you didn't just hear it, you felt the vibe he was bringing, because it hit you like a lighting bolt. Whew! One of the original greats of blue-eyed soul."

- **Charles "Spider" Jones, Canadian journalist, author, and former amateur boxer**

"I was working part-time at Stop 8 Music located at Danforth and Coxwell in Toronto. Domenic was rehearsing at the store and I used to sneak into the recording control room and listen to the rehearsals. I was lucky enough to be invited to the recording session of Fret Fever with a buddy at Sounds Interchange Studio. A few years later, I was invited to Domenic's brand new Round Sound Studio for a visit. Domenic had a profound influence on how I approach music as a jobbing musician."

- **Andy Fong, musician, Stop 8 Music Equipment**

"One of the best people I will ever know, Donnie helped everyone that he knew. His musical talents were absolutely amazing. The songs Donnie wrote were incredible, and his guitar abilities were second to none. He was definitely one of the very best musicians to come from Canada."

- **Mitchell Cohen, Troiano family friend**

"Sure, he'd built his style firmly on that Telecasting Toronto Sound ... but from there his finely sharp blister and razor bite brought his solos in particular to heights seldom even imagined by all his cohorts up and down the Yonge Strip. Yes, each and every note seemed to sit ideally in its perfect place, serving as opposed to competing with the song at hand. A musician's musician, always ready and available to play up and lay down his brand of magic in the studio, on the stage, and into the lives of all he indelibly touched. I listen to him often. As so should you."

- **Gary Pig Gold, singer, record producer, music journalist**

"My career as a guitar restoration and repair specialist was just beginning when Donnie entrusted his guitars to my care. Much of the work was mundane, wear-and-tear service: refrets and electronic repairs. Donnie's style

was aggressive, with a hard, right-hand attack. He used an unusual flat pick glued to a plastic banjo-style thumb pick, which allowed him more scope for a more complex right-hand technique. I learned that I had to make all setup and intonation adjustments with this in mind or he would not be happy with my work. So, no matter how cleanly my fret polishing and setup was done, it was no help to Donnie if it did not intonate properly with his aggressive touch.

Donnie often dropped by my shop. He always had yarns to tell about some adventure on the road. We became fast friends, had many lunches together, and I would get him going with incredible tales about the idiocy of record companies, wonderful people he had met in L.A. at parties, and various dodgy characters he had met during his lifetime. Throughout all his stories, his sense of humour and sympathy for others convinced me that he truly had no regrets. He thoroughly enjoyed every minute of his life, from lugging his Fender Super Reverb onto streetcars as a skinny kid, through to his later years in his lovely recording studio. And through all of this, his love of his family and memories of growing up in Toronto never left him; truly a shining example of a man who lived a life well-lived."

- **Grant MacNeill, owner and founder—The Twelfth Fret Guitar Shop**

"In 2012 I was hired to teach a music and cultures course at the Metalworks Institute in Mississauga. I looked over the class list and noticed a student named Julian Troiano. I instantly thought, could he be related to Domenic? No way, what are the chances? I was floored to find out yes, Domenic was his uncle. This re-ignited my interest in Domenic's catalogue and I turned my attention to tracking down all his records and session work. I was shocked to discover that the guitar I was hearing on late era Guess Who records was him, and that he also was responsible for the theme to Night Heat, the show I loved as a kid. I learned his session credits included the James Gang, Diana Ross, and The Partland Brothers. I realized Domenic's playing was always with me, it just took me a while to recognize that. His sound and legacy will live on as one of Canada's most naturally gifted guitarists who could play effortlessly in virtually any style and is deserving of wider recognition."

- **Josh Laing, guitarist, DJ, music educator**

"*Domenic was, and still is one of the most influential musicians in the history of Canadian rock music. He was a good man who always had time for the people around him and always gave one hundred percent to whatever he was doing. Still miss him as do many others. The good die young, and he was definitely one of the best! Never to be forgotten.*"

- **Tom Wilson, bass player—Little Caesar and the Consuls**

"*Many, maybe even the majority of guitar players, are like encyclopedias of every known guitar lick they've ever heard. There are few rare guitarists who solo with an original sense of artistry. Dom was a member of that latter group of gifted players. I not only admired his playing, but also his humility with regard to his own talent and status as a Canadian musical icon.*"

- **Ian Thomas, singer, songwriter, recording artist, actor and author**

PHOTO CREDITS

The images appearing in Domenic Troiano, His Life and Music are drawn primarily from the Troiano Family Archives. In some cases, the original copyright holder could not be found; in other cases, copyright has expired; and in still other cases, publicity photographs and LP/CD covers are considered fair use in illustrating a biographical or critical position.

Special mention to all the great photographers that worked with Domenic over the years: Ed Caraeff, John Rowlands, Tom Sandler, Bruce Cole, Gary Taylor, Patrick Harbron, David Street and many others.

Special thanks to Julian Troiano, Timothy Lam, Dimo Safari and Russ Horner for their technical assistance in the production of the photos for this book.

Front Cover: Troiano Family Archives; Back Cover: Gary Taylor

Every effort has been made to credit the source and photographer. Omissions will be corrected in subsequent reprints.

Cover Concept and Design: Julian Troiano and Timothy Lam

AUTHORS' ACKNOWLEDGMENTS

It has been a joy and a privilege to co-author this biography. We would like to acknowledge the more than 180 good folks—friends, fans, and fellow musicians—who either agreed to interviews or provided their written recollections of Domenic "Donnie" Troiano. They too, are all co-authors of this story along with us.

Consistently, these heartfelt recollections affirm that Domenic "Donnie" Troiano was a phenomenally talented musician and an exceptional person who was loved and admired. We are humbled and grateful for the effort that went into these thoughtful submissions. The challenge for us was to ensure these feelings were conveyed in a way that did not become too maudlin or repetitive. For that reason, some obvious editing was required, for which we ask forgiveness.

We are truly grateful for and acknowledge the support of the following Canadian rock writers:

- Martin Melhuish has written extensively on Canadian rock music. In the mid-1990s, Martin conducted several hours of one-on-one interviews with Donnie, and generously shared his interview tapes with us.

- Larry Leblanc is widely recognized as one of the leading music industry journalists in the world. Larry has been the Canadian editor of *Billboard*, *Record World*, and *Celebrity/Access*. Larry was publicist with The Guess Who when Domenic was part of the group. Larry gave of his time and resources, offering constructive criticism, advice, as well as making contact with some of the more notable names from the past.

- "The Old Professor," author/rock music historian John Einarson has written numerous books on the Winnipeg music scene in the 1960s and 1970s, as well as excellent volumes on Randy Bachman and The Guess Who. John's firsthand recollections of Domenic in Bush and The Guess Who, and his willingness to share resources and act as a sounding-board at times proved to be invaluable.

- Nicholas Jennings, author of *Heart of Gold*, has written extensively about Domenic Troiano, the Mandala, and the Toronto Sound. We are grateful for his submissions that are provided in the final chapter of this book.

- Robert Lawson has recently published his book *Wheatfield Empire*, a comprehensive examination of the music of The Guess Who. Robert provided very practical guidance, feedback, and encouragement.

- Ralph Chapman has written extensively on The Guess Who, having interviewed all of the surviving band members from 2009 through 2017 for the liner notes of the Iconoclassic Records CD reissues of THE GUESS WHO CATALOGUE. Ralph offered rare insight and good advice.

- Brock Silversides, director of Media Commons/University of Toronto has curated the Domenic Troiano Archive, and greatly assisted our efforts. Brock is currently engaged in a biographical project on the Mandala, and we are looking forward to its successful completion.

Almost twenty years ago, Jeremy Frey built a website in Domenic's honour at www.troianomusic.com containing a comprehensive inventory of all of Domenic's recordings, interviews with fellow musicians and producers, as well as news/magazine articles dating back to the days of The Five Rogues. We have consulted Jeremy throughout the writing process, and he has been enthusiastic and generous.

In 2008, Eric Ausman started a Facebook site, "Domenic Troiano Fans," currently boasting over 1,400 members and located at https://www.facebook.com/groups/35179022713/about.

These efforts go a long way in keeping Domenic's music alive, and also provide a place where like-minded fans of his music may connect.

Many thanks to the following individuals who offered additional advice, support, and encouragement during the writing process: Bob Ezrin, Jim Fox, Robbie Lane, B. J. Cook, Mitch Markowitz, Eric Mercury, Ken Koekstat, and Ashley Collie.

Sincere thanks to the following for their love and support: the Troiano family; Frank, Rita, Gina, Julian and Marcus Troiano, Shawne Jackson-Troiano, as well as "ex-officio" family members: Blaine Pritchett, Bernie LaBarge, and Roy Kenner.

Road Managers, Sound, Light & Guitar Techs, Roadies, Stage Hands

We know that Domenic would want us to acknowledge all the people that worked tirelessly on load ins, set ups, lights, sound, technical support, equipment repairs and load outs during his long touring career. They are:

Al Waugh, John Wood, Don Ogilvy, Carmelo Palumbo, Roland Paquin, Lenny Pasternak, Blaine Pritchett, Peter Traynor, Neal Moser, Bill "Toad" Becker, Mike Rellinger, Jim "Jumbo" Martin, Tim Hardacre, Dave Gardon, Drew Tennant, Frank Troiano, Gerry Duncan, Grant MacNeill, David "DR" Roberts, Paul Gruenwald, Scotty Brown, Jamie Dufton

Thank you for making it all possible!

This book is dedicated to the memory of Domenic Troiano, the man, and his music. "Donnie" Troiano was a distinctly humble person with standards for life and music that were high. It is our desire that he would have been both honoured and pleased with this volume.

Frank Troiano and Mark Doble

December, 2020

ABOUT THE AUTHORS

Mark Doble has a Bachelor of Music from McMaster University, and has written for fan magazines, websites and blogs about Canadian music, with a particular focus on the Guess Who. It was as a fan of the Guess Who that Mark first encountered Domenic in the mid-1970s, later meeting and befriending him in the mid-1990s. Mark lives with his wife Terry in Lindsay, Ontario.

Frank Troiano worked with his older brother Domenic as a road manager in the 1970s and '80s, and the two brothers remained close throughout their lives. Since Domenic's passing in 2005, Frank has promoted numerous tributes, scholarships, and memorials in his brother's honour. Frank lives with his wife Rita in Richmond Hill, Ontario.

Printed in Canada